ecpr PRESS

The Nordic Voter

Myths of Exceptionalism

Å. Bengtsson, K. M. Hansen,
Ó. Þ. Harðarson, H. M. Narud
and H. Oscarsson

ecpr PRESS

First published by the ECPR Press in 2014

The ECPR Press is the publishing imprint of the European Consortium for Political Research (ECPR), a scholarly association which supports and encourages the training, research and cross-national cooperation of political scientists in institutions throughout Europe and beyond.

ECPR Press
University of Essex
Wivenhoe Park
Colchester
CO4 3SQ
UK

Typeset by Anvi

Printed and bound by Lightning Source

British Library Cataloguing in Publication Data

A catalogue record for this book is available from the British Library

Paperback ISBN: 978-1-907301-25-4

www.ecpr.eu/ecprpress

ECPR – Monographs
Series Editors:
Dario Castiglione (University of Exeter)
Peter Kennealy (European University Institute)
Alexandra Segerberg (Stockholm University)
Peter Triantafillou (Roskilde University)

Other books available in this series

Political Conflict and Political Preferences: Communicative Interaction Between Facts, Norms and Interests (ISBN: 9780955820304) Claudia Landwehr

Political Parties and Interest Groups in Norway (ISBN: 9780955820366) Elin Haugsgjerd Allern

Regulation in Practice: The de facto Independence of Regulatory Agencies (ISBN: 9781907301285) Martino Maggetti

Representing Women?: Female Legislators in West European Parliaments (ISBN: 9780954796648) Mercedes Mateo Diaz

The Personalisation of Politics: A Study of Parliamentary Democracies (ISBN: 9781907301032) Lauri Karvonen

The Politics of Income Taxation: A Comparative Analysis (ISBN: 9780954796686) Steffen Ganghof

The Return of the State of War: A Theoretical Analysis of Operation Iraqi Freedom (ISBN: 9780955248856) Dario Battistella

Transnational Policy Innovation: The role of the OECD in the Diffusion of Regulatory Impact Analysis (ISBN:9781907301254) Fabrizio De Francesco

Urban Foreign Policy and Domestic Dilemmas: Insights from Swiss and EU City-regions (ISBN: 9781907301070) Nico van der Heiden

Why Aren't They There? The Political Representation of Women, Ethnic Groups and Issue Positions In Legislatures (ISBN: 9780955820397) Didier Ruedin

Widen the Market, Narrow the Competition: Banker Interests and the Making of a European Capital Market (ISBN: 9781907301087) Daniel Mügge

Please visit www.ecpr.eu/ecprpress for information about new publications

Contents

List of Figures and Tables

Tables

Authors

ÅSA BENGTSSON, PhD is professor of Political Science at Mid Sweden University and currently works as Academy Research Fellow at the Department of Political Science, Åbo Akademi University. She is a member of the steering group of the Finnish National Election Studies and a collaborator within several comparative research projects such as the Comparative Candidate Study and The True European Voter. Her research focuses on political opinion and behaviour with a specific interest in attitudes towards political processes, preferential voting patterns, roles of representation, economic voting and minority politics. Bengtsson has published books, edited volumes and articles, e.g. in *European Journal of Political Research, West European Politics, Journal of Elections, Public Opinion and Parties and Scandinavian Political Studies*.

KASPER M. HANSEN, PhD is professor of Political Science with special responsibilities within applied quantitative methodology at University of Copenhagen, Department of Political Science. His research focuses on applied research in democracy: political behavior particular voting behavior and public opinion. Hansen has published a number of articles in *European Journal of Political Research, Journal of Elections, Public Opinion and Parties, Public Choice, Electoral Studies, International Journal of Public Opinion Research, Scandinavian Political Studies, Public Administration, Politica, Økonomi and Politik*, and *Metode and Data*. Hansen is part of the team conducting the Danish National Election Studies. Furthermore, he is presently principal investigator in a large voter turnout research project and in an electoral campaign project. For more information *see* www.kaspermhansen.eu.

ÓLAFUR Þ HARÐARSON, PhD is professor of Political Science at the Faculty of Political Science, University of Iceland. His research focus is on electoral behavior, public opinion, and democracy. He has been the principal investigator of the Icelandic election study from its beginning in 1983, and takes part in international projects, including the Comparative Study of Electoral Systems (CSES), and the True European Voter. Harðarson has published books, book chapters and journal articles, e.g. in *Electoral Studies* and *European Journal of Political Research*. He is a member of the Excecutive Committee of the ECPR.

HANNE MARTHE NARUD, PhD (died 20 July 2012) was professor of Political Science at the University of Oslo. Her main research focus was on coalition behaviour, political recruiting, and voting behaviour. She published articles in *Comparative Sociology, European Journal of Political Research, Electoral Studies, West European Politics, Scandinavian Political Studies, Party Politics, Journal of Legislative Studies, Journal of Theoretical Politics* and *Acta Politica*, in addition to numerous contributions to books in Norwegian and English. She also wrote a book with Henry Valen on political representation in a multiparty system. She was frequently used as a commentator on Norwegian politics in the news media.

HENRIK OSCARSSON, PhD is professor of Political Science, electoral studies at the Department of Political Science, University of Gothenburg. His research focus is on representative democracy, opinion formation, voting behaviour and political methodology. Oscarsson is currently research director of the SOM Institute at UoG and also the head of the Swedish National Election Studies program (SNES). He has published numerous monographs, edited volumes, book chapters and articles (in *Scandinavian Political Studies* and *Party Politics*) on democracy, public opinion, political behaviour and social science methodology.

Foreword

A book-length comparative analysis of voting behaviour in the five Nordic countries has been in the making for decades. Already in the 1980s, the teams of the national election studies in Denmark, Norway, Finland, Sweden, and Iceland, came together at a number of meetings discussing chapter drafts for a volume on Nordic voters. Most of this research was eventually published in various fora but no book saw the light of day at that time. In the 1990s, the collaboration between the National Election Studies (NES)-teams resulted in comparative analyses of political behaviour in the three referendums on EU-membership (*To Join or Not to Join* 1998, edited by Anders Todal Jenssen, Pertti Pesonen and Mikael Gilljam) and a study of political representation (*Beyond Westminster and Congress* 2000, edited by Knut Heidar and Peter Esaiasson). Still, in spite of close cooperation between Nordic electoral researchers, a comparative analysis focusing on voting behaviour in all five Nordic countries has been missing. *The Nordic Voter: Myths of Exceptionalism* is our answer to this absence.

The unforeseen difficulties of performing comparative analyses are probably key explanations to why a book on Nordic voters has had such a long pre-history. We embarked on this journey with the perhaps naïve expectation that a study of Nordic voters would offer unusually good opportunities for comparison. The national election studies of the Nordic countries have a lot in common. We share the same intellectual history, as we are all inspired by the early studies from Columbia and Michigan, and heavily influenced by scholars as Stein Rokkan, Henry Valen, Jörgen Westerståhl, Bo Särlvik, Ole Borre, Pertti Pesonen, among many others who introduced the study of elections and voter behaviour in the Nordic countries in the period 1950–1970. As a consequence, there are numerous examples of diffusion of normative perspectives, theories, explanatory models and operationalisations between the Nordic NES-teams. A great deal of collaboration and cooperation has been accumulating over the years. Nevertheless, we soon came to realise that our insights from studying voter behaviour in our own political systems unexpectedly did not travel as easily to the other Nordic contexts. The objects of the study – the Nordic countries – were not as similar as we expected.

This book project was initiated at a meeting in Aalborg in 2005, where The Nordic Election and Democracy (NED) consortium was established. The purpose of this formalised cooperative structure has been to bring the Nordic election study teams closer together, identify joint research interests and to facilitate comparative research. As always, many colleagues have made important contributions to a comparative book project of this sort. From the very beginning in 2005, the self-proclaimed 'old dinosaurs' of the Nordic NES-teams – Sören Holmberg, Bernt Aardal, Lauri Karvonen, and Jørgen Goul Andersen – have been among our strongest supporters, partly due to the fact that, in the original plan, the dinosaurs would provide a follow-up book of their own. Colleagues and members of the NES-teams have had the opportunity to comment on our work in progress at several meetings. We wish to express our gratitude to Rune Stubager, Stefan Dahlberg, Maria Oskarson, Elin Naurin, Per Hedberg, Nicholas Aylott, Lars Bille, Karina Kosiara-Pedersen, Ole Søe Eriksen, Kimmo Grönlund, and Viktor Orri Valgarðsson. A special thanks goes to Wouter van der Brug who offered invaluable critique to the first draft of the entire manuscript in June 2009. Research assistants Jacob Severin, Per Oleskog Tryggvason and Karen Helmer-Hansen helped us immensely during the intense final stages of analyses, proof reading and editing.

Spending five years together on a common project, with a seemingly endless row of Skype meetings and book conferences, have made us all very good friends. In the process, we have learned a lot not only about Nordic voters, and the many obstacles of comparative research and scholarly collaboration, but also about the frailty of life itself. Our beloved friend, colleague and co-author of this book, Professor Hanne Marthe Narud, was diagnosed with cancer in the summer of 2011. She left us a year later, only 54 years old. We miss her immensely. Hanne Marthe possessed all the qualities you could hope for in a social scientist: engaged, intelligent, hardworking, thorough, productive, energetic, with a sharp wit and in touch with all the new on-going research in her field. At the same time she possessed a great sense of humour and had a very pleasant easy-going nature. She was always generous with ideas and comments and very supportive of younger scholars. Her early departure leaves the discipline bereft of many years of the highest quality political science research. We dedicate this book to her memory.

Åsa Bengtsson, Kasper M. Hansen,
Ólafur Þ. Harðarson, and Henrik Oscarsson
November 2013

To Hanne Marthe Narud

.

Chapter One

Introduction

The Nordic countries have been looked upon as unusually stable political systems. [...] Remarkable similarities in party systems and voter alignments between the Nordic countries have reflected corresponding similarities in terms of social structure and political institutions (Lane *et al.* 1993: 195).

Introduction

As Jan-Erik Lane and colleagues (1993: 195) in the quote above emphasise, the five Nordic welfare states – Denmark, Finland, Iceland, Norway and Sweden – are often regarded as 'remarkably similar'. In many contemporary comparative analyses of electoral behaviour, the Nordic countries are lumped together in a single category. We think this is a mistake. As will be clear throughout this book, we argue that the Nordic countries are distinctly dissimilar on a number of key aspects of voter alignment and elements of the political systems. In this first full length book on electoral behaviour in the five Nordic countries, we highlight the many differences and test the country comparative differences' explanatory power in our quest to understand the electoral behaviour of Nordic voters better.

This book challenges the idea of the five Nordic countries being exceptional as regards stability and similarity in terms of electoral behaviour. Our point of departure is the well-known 'decline of the party-in-the-electorate' thesis, that argues that party-based representative democracy is slowly eroding, examples being, the decline in the share of the electorate being members of a party, and the decline in turnout along with other modes of conventional political participation (e.g. Dalton and Wattenberg 2000; Dalton 2004; Mair 2006).

In this book, we set out to examine electoral democracy in a Northern European context. Our focus is on the 'party-in-the-electorate' (Key 1966) in the five Nordic countries – Denmark, Finland, Iceland, Norway and Sweden – mapping out the key features of these five electorates, their political attitudes and electoral behaviour in the twenty-first century. How well do the Nordic countries fit the more or less universal picture of party decline that exist in previous research? And to what extent is the performance of the five Nordic democracies challenged by a changing and more individualistic electorate?

The state of electoral democracy has increasingly been subject to scrutiny in Western political systems. Scholars have devoted particular interest to the challenges facing political parties, because in most established democracies the parties have functioned as the main vehicle for popular representation. As party membership and voters' party attachment have declined, and voter volatility has increased, a number of scholars have claimed that political parties are weaker today than a few decades ago (e.g. Dalton and Wattenberg 2000; Dalton 2004; Mair 2006). It is widely agreed that the organisation, position and role of political parties have changed significantly during the twentieth century. Many of these trends are due to changes in the electorates, others to institutional changes and developments in the international environment. The decline of traditional social identities and old cleavages, post-industrial work habits, new family structures, the emergence of non-partisan mass media, and the rise of the EU as a political system have challenged political parties in numerous ways (Bergman and Strøm 2011).

One dimension that is often questioned is the capacity of parties to connect the citizenry with government agencies, another is voters' declining confidence and trust in the political institutions in which parties operate as well as in parties and politicians themselves (*see* e.g. Strøm and Svåsand 1997; Dalton and Wattenberg 2000; Dalton 2004; Mair 2006; Rosema *et al.* 2011). Large-scale social changes, the 'educational revolution', affluence, and financial security are all developments that have entailed shifts in voters' value orientations and political preferences. Consequently, rather than leaning on the effectual, habitual partisan bonds from traditional politics, voters' motivation and behaviour are structured by the campaign context and new types of issues. This is also expressed by the fact that social demographics variables today explain much less than previously when it comes to party choice. The consequences are voters with more individualistic behaviour, who are more critical towards incumbent parties, and less willing to exchange their support for policy packages offered by the government. As stated by Bergman and Strøm (2011: 22): 'voters are more difficult to please than ever before'.

No doubt, there is ample evidence of electoral change in a Nordic context during the past decades. Some of these trends are well documented in country-specific analyses of voting behaviour from the election studies teams in each respective country (Oscarsson and Holmberg 2008b; Aardal 2011; Paloheimo 2005; Borg 2012, Stubager *et al.* 2013; Goul Andersen *et al.* 2007; Harðarson 1995). Electoral alignments are weakening, volatility has been increasing, more voters decide closer to Election Day, and political trust has been declining, hence, 'the old order is crumbling' to use the words of Dalton and Wattenberg (2000: 262). However, we argue that it is often overlooked in contemporary comparative analyses that there exist many interesting deviations too – and numerous differences between the Nordic countries – due to institutional, contextual, and political factors. In fact, on many key indicators, the trajectories of electoral behaviour in the Nordic countries are diverging. For instance, whereas there has been a clear and almost monotonic downward trend in party identification in four of the countries, the decline has been more modest in Denmark. Similarly, gross electoral volatility has increased steadily in all the Nordic countries since the 1960s, but since the mid-eighties it has been much higher in Norway than in the other four countries. Furthermore, class voting has slowly but steadily declined in Denmark and Norway, whereas it has been stable over last two decades in Sweden, even though at a much lower rate than in the 1960s and 1970s (Aylott 2011: 304–8). In other words, the Nordic countries share many of the common traits of party decline that have been demonstrated in a broader international context. Yet, the electoral changes are not equally affecting them; the general impression is that differences between the five countries have increased during the last 20 years. Given the many historical, cultural and political similarities between these countries, an obvious research question is why developments have not been uniform. Why are some changes evident in some Nordic countries – and not in others?

At our hand we have the five countries and five electorates that over the years have been presented as internally similar and deviating from other western democracies. The Nordic countries have, by many, been looked upon as unusually stable and well-functioning political systems (Lane *et al.* 1993; Esaiasson and Heidar 2000). Of course, the assessments of stability and exceptionalism depend on the perspective: no doubt, in a broader international context they are all 'working multiparty systems' (Rustow 1956) with a high degree of affluence, peace, and with highly developed welfare systems. The five countries also share many historical and cultural traits, they are linked by geography and by linguistic bonds, and they have many political similarities, such as interest group representation and an early dominance of class divisions (Arter 1999). Because of their many commonalities, in comparative politics literature the Nordic countries have often been treated as 'most similar systems' (e.g. Arter 1999; Damgaard 1992). Yet, as will become clear in this book, the five countries are less homogenous than many think. We need to revise the image of Nordic exceptionality and similarity.

This line of argumentation is far from new. In fact, in his seminal work Stein Rokkan (1967) placed the Nordic countries in four different spaces in his 'conceptual map' of state-building in Western Europe. The Nordic countries differ with regard to historic preconditions, economic resources, and their foreign policy orientations, the latter owing to variations in strategic location. Three of them (Denmark, Finland and Sweden) are members of the EU, two of them (Iceland and Norway) are not. Three were founding members of NATO (Denmark, Iceland, Norway), two were not (Finland and Sweden). They have adopted different arrangements for key institutions as the head of state, the election system, nomination systems, as well as parliamentary organisation (Grofman and Lijphart 2002; Narud, Pedersen and Valen 2002; Bergman and Strøm 2011). In recent years the development of their party systems have differed too, even though their systems still encompass the five 'old' parties from the classic Nordic five-party model (Berglund and Lindström 1978).

These trends of both similarities and differences make the Nordic countries a particularly intriguing case. In principle, it allows for an examination of electoral developments more generally, holding some variables constant, and uncovering the significant variations in key institutional and political variables. However, to be able to harvest the sweet fruits of comparative analyses of the Nordic countries, these dissimilarities and similarities need to be systematically mapped out in more detail. We consider this book a contribution to this endeavour.

The aim of this book is therefore twofold. The first is to provide the reader with a general outlook of how voters in the five Nordic countries, by way of their electoral behaviour and attitudes, can be positioned in a wider comparative perspective. Can they be considered as deviating or extreme cases, or can they be considered as voters in any other advanced democracy? The second, and more accentuated aim, is to present a more refined and nuanced picture of the political behaviour and opinions found among Nordic voters. Here we intend to highlight apparent differences as well as similarities by presenting an overarching development over time for a selection of key factors – and a more in-depth micro level comparative analysis of voter behaviour, using a unique comparative data set of recently available national election surveys. *See* Appendix for a detailed description of the national election surveys in the five Nordic countries.

While Chapter Two presents the main features of the Nordic countries, the next sections of this chapter deal with certain aspects of 'Nordic exceptionalism' as it has been previously presented in the international debate (Goul Andersen and Hoff 2001). The main aim of this discussion is to put the content of this book into a wider and, to some extent, a historical perspective. The remainder of the chapter provides the reader with the essential information about the data that is used throughout the book, as well as the main outline of each of the seven empirical chapters.

Nordic exceptionalism

In contemporary literature, the five countries, Denmark, Finland, Iceland, Norway and Sweden, named the Nordic sphere, are most commonly considered as a distinct group of states. The concepts, Nordic and Scandinavian countries, are often used as synonyms. However, strictly speaking, Scandinavia only comprises of Denmark, Norway and Sweden. To avoid misunderstandings we will use the concept 'Nordic' throughout the book. The most obvious similarities have to do with geography and history (*see* Chapter Two). The five countries, located in the Northern region of Europe, are all small states that during different stages of their development towards modern times have been involved with each other, with two states playing the role as dominating actors (Denmark and Sweden) and three states as successors (Finland, Iceland and Norway) (Arter 1999). They also share strong linguistic and cultural bonds, are dominated by protestant religious traditions, and have been considered as ethnically homogenous (Amnå *et al.* 2007).

Yet, it is not only an involved historical development that has created the image of the Nordic countries as a related, or even a distinct group of states. The advances in the political and economic sphere as modern representative democracies and, in particular, since the Second World War, when these countries took similar paths and developed many common traits, has been of even greater significance. In the 1960s Herbert Tingsten described the Nordic countries as 'happy democracies' (Tingsten 1966). The combination of stable party systems allowing for representation of a wide range of interests and extensive welfare states, made them at this stage appear capable of achieving a considerable amount of equality with powerful economic growth – a successful combination that made the Nordic countries remarkable in an international context. Later, these countries have been described as closer than most others in fulfilling the ideal of a strong party based representative democracy, well founded on popular support, and enjoying high levels of democratic legitimacy (Amnå *et al.* 2007).

Exceptional or not, there are two main aspects that have made the five Nordic countries well known during a large part of the post-war period. The first aspect is the Nordic model of decision making constituted by similar institutions, structures and cultures for decision making (Arter 1999). *The Nordic model of government* is distinguished by compromise politics, social consensus, corporatism and social engineering, to a large extent driven by strong Social Democratic parties (Lane 1991). Iceland has been a partial exception – the Social Democrats were, for instance, the smallest of the four major parties for most of the 20th century.

Stability and size have been key factors in the political development of the region. Stable five-party systems, strongly linked to social strata and reinforced organisational structures, a dominating class division as well as relatively small scaled societies, are all factors that have contributed to their stability and played an important role in forming the Nordic model of government (Arter 1999; Lane *et al.* 1993).

The second aspect that has made these countries known as a group of their own is the output side of democracy in terms of social policy. *The Nordic welfare model* was built by comprehensive social engineering and is well known for, among other things; social rights based on citizenship, active labour market policies, the public sector as the main provider of services financed by a relatively high taxation, and a strong element of income distribution with equality as an explicit goal (Marklund and Nordlund 1999; Esping-Andersen 1990). The Nordic countries could, at least until the end of the 1980s, be characterised as some of the world's most ambitious welfare states. Since the 1990s, the Nordic welfare model has been under pressure, although the actual extent of the welfare retrenchment is under debate (Greve 2007; Kvist and Greve 2011). Exogenous as well as endogenous factors have created a more limited space for welfare expansion (Nygård 2006).

Alongside with the Nordic model of government and the Nordic welfare model, a *Nordic or Social democratic model of citizenship* is claimed to have developed. This model of citizenship is described as pertaining to all areas of social life, and characterised by being activist, participatory, and egalitarian (Hernes 1988). And the Nordic countries have indeed been characterised by comparatively high levels of turnout, high levels of political inter-electoral activity, many voluntary organisations as well as high levels of social and political trust (Goul Andersen and Hoff 2001; Rothstein and Stolle 2003; Delhey and Newton 2005; Amnå *et al.* 2007). In general, voters in the Nordic countries have traditionally been considered as stable in terms of voting behaviour, politically active, willing to trust their fellow citizens as well as their political representatives, and to stand up for collective interests.

Seen from a perspective of societal modernisation, the Nordic countries have been regarded as forerunners, or at least countries that are moving in the front of development. This concerns objective measures such as technological developments, gender empowerment and equality, but also at subjective value dimensions such as self-expression values and secular-rational values (Inglehart and Welzel 2005). Some of the most collectivistic electorates in the world (at least when it comes to the historically strong social cleavage structure and levels of party loyalties) are, at the same time, the ones where individualisation trends are the most pronounced.

Not so exceptional anymore?

The general impression of the countries in the Nordic region is thus, that of stable and healthy democracies (Goul Andersen and Hoff 2001). However, the stable image stands in stark contrast to the observations made by the Danish political scientist Ole Borre (1980), who, 30 years ago, already wrote about 'the increasing instability of the Nordic countries'. We believe the developments that have taken place during the last two-three decades fundamentally challenge the so-called exceptionalism of the Nordic countries. Signs of cracks in the stable five-party systems became visible in the 1960s and 1970s when new parties entered the scene in Denmark, Finland and Norway (Arter 2008; Lane *et al.* 1993). In fact, in the Norwegian case, deviations from the model began as far back as in the 1930s when a religious faction of the Liberal Party broke out and formed the Christian People's Party (Valen and Katz 1964). In the previously stable four-party system in Iceland, new and short-lived fifth and sixth parties have obtained parliamentary representation in most elections since 1971 (a more detailed account of the development of Nordic party systems can be found in Chapter Three). Challenges of both exogenous and endogenous character have, since the end of the 1980s, altered the prerequisites of the political as well as the economic arena. The challenges are far from unique. Most Western European democracies have been pressured by globalisation and a higher degree of individualisation, caused by among other things developments in the financial market, growing influence of the European Union, and developments towards an information society. At the same time many countries have become less homogenous with higher rates of immigration (Karvonen 2004).

The above mentioned changes are but a few of the examples of developments that have altered the fundamentals for the political and economic sphere in the countries, most importantly by reducing the room for manoeuvre of national political actors. A general impression is that nation-states are less capable of conducting offensive social policy today and that the 'Nordic welfare model' is facing serious challenges (Pierson 2001; Taylor-Goodby 2004; Kautto *et al.* 2001). Based on the Swedish case, Lindvall and Rothstein (2006) describe it as the decline of the strong state, where the belief that society can be changed by means of offensive policies has withered. The functionality of the 'Nordic model of government', based on consensus has also been questioned. An international trend towards 'governance' rather than 'government' further complicates the picture (Pierre and Peters 2000). Moreover, the Social Democratic parties have, in most Nordic countries, lost their dominating or even hegemonic role and are faced with decreasing popular support. Surely, one important reason for these developments has been the changing social base of these parties, due to, among other things, the declining number of blue collar workers.

In line with social developments in the Nordic societies, in which the most distinct changes have been a decreased share of the population employed in the industrial sector and a rapid growth of the middle class, the social base of political parties has been altered. Consequently, the traditional model of stable cleavage-based voting has been weakened over the past generation (Oskarson 2005; Aardal 2003, 2007), even though the extent of the decline varies (Holmberg and Oscarsson 2004). As a natural response to the changes that have taken place in the Nordic societies and their surroundings, the political agenda has changed too. New political issues linked to such areas as the European Union, immigration, and the environment have emerged. In some cases the existing parties are divided on these issues, particularly the question of the EU – which has been a constraint on the policy-making of these parties. Short-term modes of political participation also appear to have become more popular, as the role of the strong and politically organised 'peoples movements' and as well as other types of long term associational engagement have become less prominent (Amnå *et al.* 2007; Togeby *et al.* 2003; Bengtsson 2007).

To sum up, we will in this book provide analyses that will show if, and in what ways, the Nordic electorates are slowly becoming less exceptional and more different from each other in terms of political attitudes and behaviour.

Data and analysis

Our overarching aim with this book is to compare electoral behaviour across the Nordic countries. Such a book has long been due. Not only because a comparative book-length analysis of electoral behaviour in a Nordic context has never been done before, but also because these five countries are well suited for comparative research. More importantly, we believe that the comparison of our five countries can generate valuable insights about the functioning of small democracies in general, and will also contribute to the study of electoral behaviour in particular. Although the Nordic countries share many common traits, and from a broad international perspective may appear as strikingly similar, we have found that important differences exist among them that help shed light on the underlying patterns of change that are to be found more generally. Hence the fact that these countries share several politically relevant characteristics facilitates the sorting out of potential explanatory factors.

Taking a more myopic view, despite their commonalities, a major conclusion of this research is that the five countries differ to a relatively large extent when it comes to electoral behaviour. Comparative analyses presented in this book will call into question the exceptionalist view of the Nordic electorates. Furthermore, the Nordic countries will sometimes share the same trends in the data, but the developments are lagged by time, and on other occasions, trends do not seems to follow each other at all but reveal diverging patterns. Our ultimate aim is to elucidate these differences, even though – given our broad study design – we cannot hope to explain all differences between the Nordic countries in all respects.

The book is a product of a newly awakened cooperation of the national programs of election studies in each of the Nordic countries, the NED-research consortium (Nordic Elections and Democracy). Consequently, our data are drawn from the national election studies programs in each country, based on interviews with large representative samples of the population. The Swedish and the Norwegian election study programs were founded already in the 1950s (Sweden in 1956 and Norway in 1957). The Danish Election Project was founded in 1971 and has since then conducted surveys in conjunction with all subsequent national elections. The first survey of the Icelandic Election Study Program was carried out after the 1983 election, and post-election telephone surveys have been conducted after all parliamentary elections since then. In Finland there is no long-standing tradition of electoral research. The first large-scale post-election study was performed in the aftermath of the parliamentary election in 1991. However, at the beginning of the new millennium, a group of Finnish scholars initiated a program of electoral research, and since then three studies have been completed, in 2003, 2007 and 2011. More detailed accounts of each of the national election programs are offered in Appendix.

Due to common intellectual roots (American in terms of election research) and intra-Nordic exchange of ideas within the research community, there are many similarities between the election studies in the five Nordic countries. The theoretical and methodological bases of the research programs have thus been more or less the same. Questions are often formulated in a similar manner or, at least, using a common model and cover more or less the same thematic areas. However, apart from the set of questions included in the CSES-modules (the Comparative Study of Electoral Systems), the national surveys have never been designed for genuine comparative purposes. Each country has used their own research design and their own set of questions (and coding), attempting to cover own time-series as well as salient issues in the national election campaigns. In this regard, the CSES data offer unique opportunities. All of the Nordic countries have, since the late 1990s, taken part in this collaborative program of research, which involves a common module with questions included in the post-election surveys in each of the participating countries. However CSES only covers a very limited part of the Nordic election surveys, three-quarters of the Nordic election surveys are still created independently by each national team of election researchers. We have carefully gone through the election surveys in each of the countries and created a unique common data file exclusively for this book project, covering many of the traditional time-series questions. In addition, we have been able to create joint scales on various issue dimensions. These efforts allow us to perform cross-national analyses which previously have been impossible due to data restrictions. The Appendix provides more information on the data set.

In our empirical chapters we provide time series data on most dependent variables and more detailed multivariate analysis of the latest survey available for each country. Although we include comparative data for other than the Nordic countries and time-series data for our five countries, the focal interest of the study is synchronic by observing within-case variation at a single point in time. This approach involves detailed analyses of the areas where changes have occurred. By analysing each of the countries' latest available national election survey by multivariate statistical tools, we have been able to provide in-depth knowledge about the electoral behaviour in small multiparty systems in general – and in our five countries in particular.

The outline of the book

Chapter Two provides an introduction to the Nordic political systems, using the book's general discussion of Nordic exceptionalism and similarity as a backdrop. This is an overarching presentation of the Nordic countries, accounting for the most relevant factors that have been shown to impact electoral behaviour in the Nordic countries in previous research (Paloheimo 2005; Borg and Paloheimo 2009; Aardal 2011; Borg 2012; Oscarsson and Holmberg 2013; Goul Andersen *et al.* 2007; Stubager *et al.* 2013; Goul Andersen and Borre 2003; Andersen *et al.* 1999; Harðarson 1995). These factors include the historical background of the Nordic communities, the development of the economy and welfare state expenditure, institutional variations (with particular importance given to the electoral systems), and government formation patterns. The emphasis is on the similarities and differences that form the framework for parties and voters in the five countries.

In Chapter Two we also discuss the prospects of designing explanatory comparative studies of electoral behaviour based on existing institutional variation. We discuss the design of our study and focus on the features of the institutional setting that are assumed to have an influence on the types of political behaviour that will be analysed in the empirical parts of the book; i.e. macro variables that are identified as potential explanations to why voting behaviour may differ between the Nordic countries. Towards the end of the chapter we present the common data set that was constructed exclusively for the current project. We also introduce the set of independent variables included in our explanatory models and we justify the choice of approach to the descriptive and regression analyses that we apply in subsequent analyses.

The empirical section of the book (Chapters Three – Nine) covers seven chapters organised in order to cover key aspects of voters' electoral behaviour and political attitudes. As often is the case (but perhaps seldom acknowledged) in comparative political analysis, our key aspects or 'list of dependents' have been selected by letting theory negotiate with data availability and data comparability. The main justification for the selection of key aspects of electoral behaviour is that we wanted the analyses to include the ties between voters and the democratic system, voters and the parties, and voters and the candidates respectively in the Nordic countries. In addition, we wanted to address the well documented development of the decreasing predictive power of social cleavages, and the voters' increasing sensitivity to short term factors (campaigns, issues, economic cycles) affecting party choice.

In Chapter Three, we map out the historic evolution of the Nordic party systems, the origins of the political parties and their contemporary locations along six issue dimensions. Here, we introduce the history and development of the Nordic party systems using the classic Lipset and Rokkan (1967a) cleavage model as a natural point of departure. The party systems of the Nordic countries are then systematically compared with party systems in other established democracies. We also present a new and exclusive spatial analysis of the Nordic party voters' placements along six different issue-dimensions (left-right, public-private, pro-con environment, pro-con the European Union, moral-conservative, and anti-immigration dimensions), which gives a detailed map of the Nordic party space of today. The ideological issue dimensions will later be used in our analyses as determinants of party choice.

Chapters Four – Nine deal with one key indicator of electoral behaviour (or dependent variable) at the time. The general idea behind the sequencing of chapters is well known to most students of electoral behaviour: the 'funnel of causality' (Campbell *et al.* 1960; Miller and Shanks 1996; Thomassen 2005). We begin with stable and long term features of electoral behaviour (democratic legitimacy and the emotional ties between voters and parties), then shift focus to the more short term determinants of political behaviour (candidates, campaigns, economic cycles and government performance), and finally, explaining party choice. More specifically, the chapters focus on the following indicators: satisfaction with democracy and turnout (Chapter Four), party identification (Chapter Five), preferential voting (Chapter Six), time of vote decision (Chapter Seven), government performance (Chapter Eight), and party choice (Chapter Nine).

The empirical analyses of Chapters Four – Nine are all essentially organised in the same fashion, presenting both diachronic and synchronic analyses alongside with a broader comparative outlook: a) In each chapter, we begin by placing the Nordic countries in an international comparative perspective in order to discuss if, how and why the Nordic countries deviate from other countries in the world; b) we move on with analysing the trends across time within the five Nordic countries and, finally, c) analyse the effects of micro level determinants. All chapters (Four – Nine) have a concluding section with a summary of results.

While this book is about the 'state of the art' of Nordic electoral democracy, it is also about the general political developments that have occurred in the region and how the Nordic democracies should be viewed from an international perspective. The main task is, however, to provide the reader with a more refined picture of the attitudes and behaviour of the voters in the five Nordic countries. Following the six chapters of analyses, Chapter Ten sums up the empirical evidence on the state of the Nordic democracies and their electorates. It brings together the most important developments in the five countries and discusses their 'exceptionalism' compared to other Western states.

Chapter Two

The Nordic Political Systems and our Research Design

If an instance in which the phenomenon under investigation occurs, and an instance in which it does not occur, have every circumstance in common save one, that one occurring only in the former; the circumstance in which alone the two instances differ, is the effect, or the cause, or an indispensable part of the cause, of the phenomenon (Mill 1843: 455).

A comparative case study of the Nordic countries

This book focuses on the political behaviour of the electorates in the five Nordic countries of Denmark, Finland, Iceland, Norway, and Sweden. At our hand we have five countries that often, in the literature, are presented as similar (Koch and Ross 1949; Allardt 1981; Arter 1984; Damgaard 1992) – an observation that from many respects can be considered as to the point. The purpose of this chapter is to examine the earlier accounts of what actually constitutes the similarities of the Nordic countries, and to make some introductory illustrations of how the Nordic countries group together on key features that may have a direct bearing on citizens' political behaviour at the polls.

As will become clear from the brief introduction of the Nordic countries in this chapter, the five countries share many historical and cultural traits, they are linked by geography and by linguistic bonds, and they have many political similarities, such as party system characteristics, interest group representation and dominance of the class division (Arter 1999). It has also been customary to talk about the more profound similarities of culture that constitutes a Nordic model of government (*see* page 5), characterised by compromise politics, social consensus, political stability and comprehensive social engineering (Lane 1991; Castles and Sainsbury 1986; Elder *et al.* 1988; Graubard 1986).

In the 1960s Herbert Tingsten presented the Nordic countries as 'happy democracies' (Tingsten 1966). The combination of stable party systems allowing for the representation of a wide range of interests, and extensive welfare states did, at this stage, appear capable of achieving a considerable amount of equality with a strong economic growth – a successful combination that made the Nordic countries exceptional from an international perspective. The exceptionalism of the Nordic countries has, however, been questioned since the late 1980s (Lane *et al.* 1993).

Even if the Nordic countries no longer are considered as exceptional, or even as 'happy democracies', in the terms of Tingsten, they can still be characterised as five of the world's most ambitious welfare states. The Nordic welfare model (*see* page 5) has, among other things, included social rights based on citizenship, the public sector as the main provider of services financed by taxation, and a strong element of income distribution with equality as an explicit goal. The Nordic countries may also be described as both stable and rather healthy democracies (Goul Andersen and Hoff 2001). From the perspective of societal modernisation, the Nordic are pioneers. This concerns objective measures such as income distribution, social security spending, technological developments, gender empowerment and equality, but also at the subjective value, dimensions such as self-expression values and secular-rational values (Inglehart and Welzel 2005).

In this chapter we will provide a brief introduction to some of the main features of political life and political institutions in the Nordic countries as well as the data and methodology used in throughout the book. A more detailed discussion on specific aspects of relevance is found in each of the seven analytical chapters to follow.

The Nordic community, a brief overview

The five Nordic countries which consist of Denmark, Finland, Iceland, Norway and Sweden cooperate through the Nordic Council, established in 1952 with a common labour market and free movement across borders without passports for the countries' citizens. The combined population is 25 million where Sweden alone counts for 9.4 million. In terms of international relations, the Nordic countries have, however, followed different routes. Denmark, Iceland and Norway are members of NATO while Finland and Sweden have remained neutral. Three of the countries – Denmark, Finland and Sweden – are members of the European Union, while Norway and Iceland have chosen not to join. Figure 2.2 lays out the geographical map of the Nordic countries along with its population density. The density especially highlights the differences between Denmark and other countries, which all have a very large part of their country with a low population density. Furthermore, Sweden is almost 4.5 times the size of Iceland and more than ten times the size of Denmark, Iceland being twice the size of Denmark. The size of Denmark is 43,094 km^2, Iceland 103,001 km^2, Finland 338,424 km^2, Norway 385,252 km^2, and Sweden 449,964 km^2.

The North Germanic languages (Danish, Norwegian and Swedish) are mandatory taught in school in all five nations and have many common characteristics. Icelandic is a North Germanic language – close to Old Norse – and has some similarities to West Norwegian dialects. Finnish, on the other hand, belongs to the Uralic family of languages and shares more similarities with, for example, Estonian than the other Nordic languages.

In the fourteenth century, Denmark, Norway (with Iceland) and Sweden (with Finland) were united under one regent, in the Kalmar Union which Denmark dominated. In the early sixteenth century Sweden reestablished itself as a sovereign kingdom. Denmark's rule over Norway lasted until 1814 when the king was forced to surrender Norway to the king of Sweden. The Union with

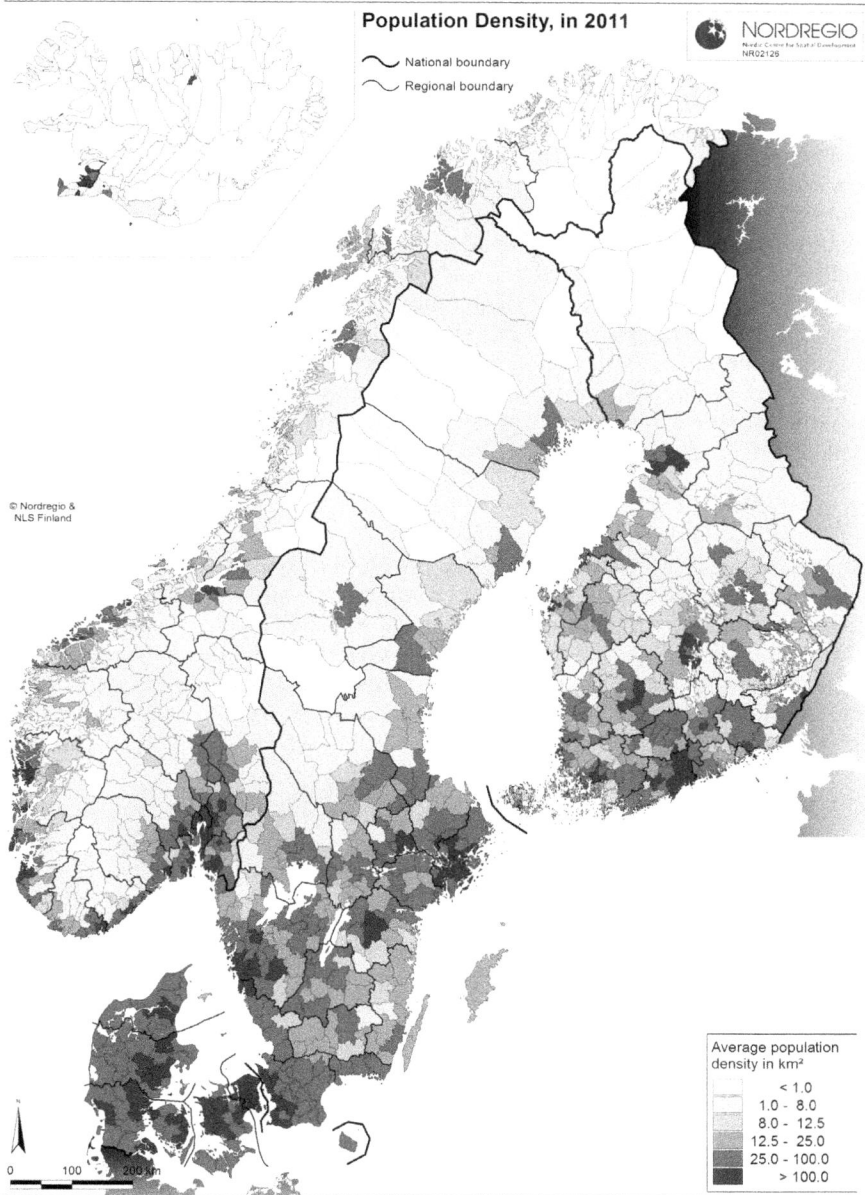

Figure 2.1: The Nordic countries (population density)

Sweden was dissolved in 1905 when Norway gained its full sovereignty. Iceland obtained home rule in 1904, became a sovereign state in a royal union with Denmark in 1918, and a republic in 1944. Finland was under Swedish rule until 1809 when it was occupied by Russian forces. The Russian Era lasted until 1917. During the Russian Revolution, Finland declared its independence from Russia and after the civil war in 1918, Finland became a presidential republic in 1919, gradually orienting towards the Nordic community. Throughout history, internal mobility within the Nordic sphere has been extensive. In modern times the main mobilisations have been from Finland to Sweden, when during the 1960s and 70s some 400,000 Finns emigrated to Sweden (Pesonen *et al.* 1998). During the last decade there has, in turn, been a larger movement from Sweden to its neighbour countries of Norway and Denmark. The overlapping and shifting domination of the region throughout history also helps in understanding why there is still a Nordic identity today. Sweden, Norway and Denmark are constitutional monarchies with a parliamentary system, whereas both Finland and Iceland are parliamentary republics.

Welfare states

One of the most well-known aspects of the Nordic countries has to do with the welfare systems, that are often labelled as *the Nordic model*. And indeed the five countries share similar traits in the policies implemented under the postwar period, especially in the socioeconomic area. All the Nordic countries have established large tax-funded, public welfare sectors. In most cases, this is due to the political ambitions of the Social Democratic governments that were in power during the interwar period in the Nordic countries (Esping-Andersen 1991). Figure 2.2

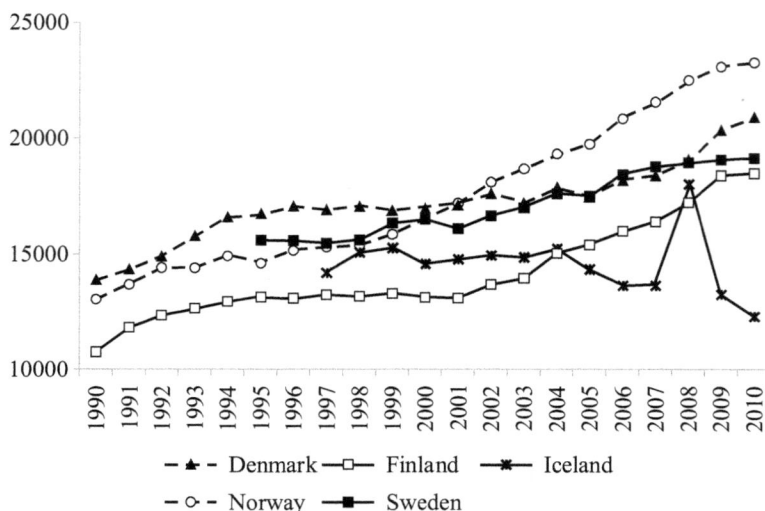

Figure 2.2: Total government expenditure per capita (1990–2010)

Based on OECD-data – Fixed prices (USD) 2005 level (http://stats.oecd.org/)

illustrates this point, showing the development of government expenditure per capita in the Nordic countries between 1990–2010.

Since 1990, as Figure 2.2 shows, there was a steady growth in government expenditure per capita in four of the five Nordic countries. Iceland was particularly hard hit by the global financial crises (Harðarson and Kristinsson 2009), and experienced a dramatic drop in expenditure from 2008 onward. In 1990 Denmark was the country with the highest level, today Norway is substantially ahead of all the other countries. Comparing 1990 and 2010, the Nordic countries are more different than ever before when it comes to government expenditure per capita. Yet another strong bond between the countries is trade. The Nordic countries are strongly interdependent when it comes to imports and exports. Economic development in the Nordic countries and its effect on electoral behavior will be discussed in more detail in Chapter Eight on voters and governments.

Much of the literature on the Nordic model was produced and based on the golden era of the 1980s, when all of the Nordic countries belonged to the most prosperous area in the western world. During that time much pointed to the success of the Nordic model, described as a combination of excellent economic performance and social justice (Kautto *et al.* 1999). Since then, the economic downturn, particularly in the 1990s and also since the economic crisis in 2008 has, to some extent, influenced not only the economic success of the Nordic countries, but also has led them onto diverging paths.

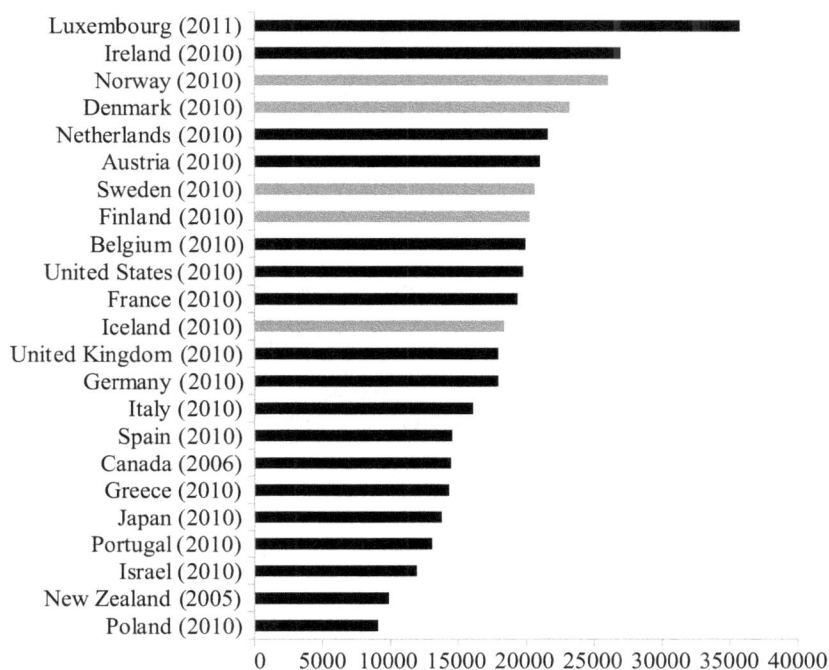

Figure 2.3: Total government expenditure per capita in $, current prices, (2010)

Figure 2.3 illustrates the total government expenditure per capita in current 2010 prices (USD) – a rough measure of the size of the welfare state. Norway and Denmark take third and fourth place, Sweden seventh, Finland eighth and Iceland twelfth. Clearly the Nordic countries are among the developed countries with the highest level of government expenditure per capita, but many other developed countries also have that feature in 2010. Furthermore the Nordic countries are not grouped together in Figure 2.3. Today the Nordic countries are, hence, not particularly exceptional nor similar when it comes to the size of government expenditure per capita.

Strong democracies

The Nordic countries are not only well-known for their large welfare states but also as strong democracies – or as 'happy democracies' (Tingsten 1966). Although this is a perception that will be further scrutinised throughout this book it seems fair to say that the level of political trust still stands high in all of the countries we have measures for (*see* Figures 2.4 and 2.5). Iceland is not part of the European Social Survey so we do not have a direct comparable measure for Iceland. However, surveys carried out by Capacent Gallup, show that the Icelandic parliament enjoyed great trust of 44 to 40 per cent from 2003 until 2008 which then, after the financial crises, decreased drastically to only 13 to 10 per cent of the voters. Hence, not only are these countries characterised by large welfare states, citizens also display high levels of trust in the actors and institutions that exercise control over the public sphere, with the exception of Iceland after the financial setback. More detailed analyses of how Nordic voters relate to the system of representative democracy will be accounted for in Chapter Four where, in particular, satisfaction with democracy and turnout in the five countries are analysed in more detail.

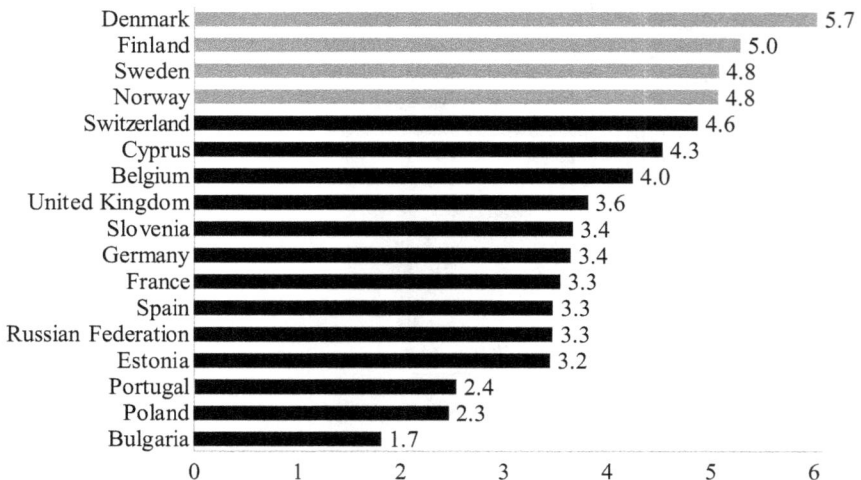

Country	Value
Denmark	5.7
Finland	5.0
Sweden	4.8
Norway	4.8
Switzerland	4.6
Cyprus	4.3
Belgium	4.0
United Kingdom	3.6
Slovenia	3.4
Germany	3.4
France	3.3
Spain	3.3
Russian Federation	3.3
Estonia	3.2
Portugal	2.4
Poland	2.3
Bulgaria	1.7

Figure 2.4: Trust in political parties (means)
Source: ESS 2008. Trust measures are from 0 (no trust) to 10 (high trust).

Country	Value
Denmark	6.5
Finland	6.0
Switzerland	5.8
Norway	5.8
Sweden	5.7
Cyprus	5.4
Spain	5.0
Belgium	4.6
Germany	4.6
France	4.5
Slovenia	4.4
United Kingdom	4.3
Russian Federation	4.0
Estonia	3.9
Portugal	3.5
Poland	3.0
Bulgaria	1.9

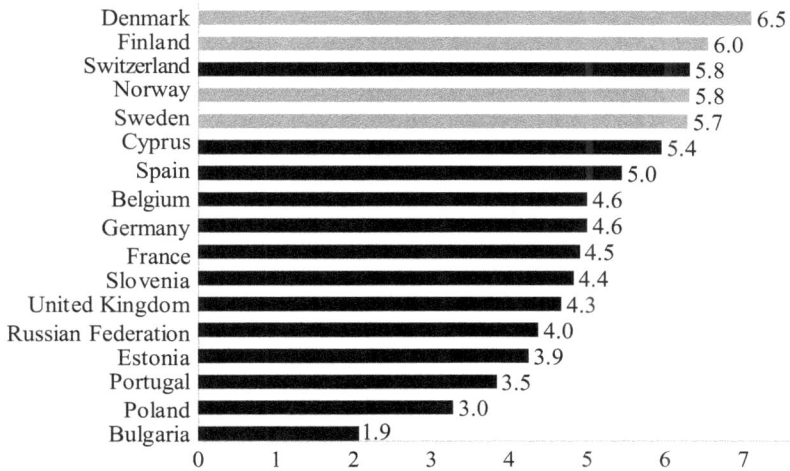

Figure 2.5: Trust in the national parliament (means)
Source: ESS 2008. Trust measures is from 0 (no trust) to 10 (high trust).

Parliamentary democracies

The Nordic countries can today all be characterised as parliamentary democracies and citizens in these countries apparently have high confidence in their parliaments. However, up until relatively recently, Finland deviated from the others, due to the fact that the president possessed a relatively wide range of powers, in particular in the field of foreign policy (Anckar 1992; Nousiainen 2000). These powers have, however, substantially decreased since the beginning of the new millennium and today Finnish democracy can be described as a predominantly parliamentary system (Paloheimo 2003). In all of the five Nordic parliaments political parties are the driving forces and parliaments also tend to be more consensual than confrontational with established committee structures, organised according to policy areas (Heidar and Berntzen 2003).

In order to analyse the dynamics of party democracy and voting behavior in the Nordic countries, it is important to be aware of the specific features concerning parliamentary structure and traditions of government formation, as well as electoral and party systems in the five countries. With the exception of the party systems these will all be discussed in more detail below. Since the party system is perhaps the most crucial element for comprehending voting behaviour, it merits a more thorough presentation, given in Chapter Three. In Chapter Three we will demonstrate that the theory presented by Lipset and Rokkan (1967a) in the 1960s concerning the party system and how it reflects the cleavage structure of the late 1920s still appears to hold true, even though the number of significant exceptions have increased.

The Nordic parliaments

Finland's parliament, the Eduskunta (Riksdagen), has 200 members, and is elected by popular vote every four years. Since 2011, the election takes place on the third Sunday in April (previously on the third Sunday in March), except when an early election is called. An early election is officially called by the President, but since the year 2000, it is done on the initiative of the Prime Minister, after consultations with the parliamentary groups. Prior to 2000, the President could dissolve the Parliament and call an early election, which has happened eight times (not since 1975). The members of the Finnish parliament are elected in fifteen electoral districts, where the number of representatives depends on the population. The exception is the Åland Islands, which is a single member district.

Sweden's parliament, Riksdagen, has 349 members elected from twenty-nine constituencies. Elections are held every fourth year, and always on a Sunday in September. It is possible for an incumbent government to call an extra election if three months have passed since an ordinary election. If an extra election is called within a week from a vote of no confidence, the incumbent government remains in power until the extra election. Extra elections should be held within three months of the decision. The scheduled elections in September, every four years, must, however, still be held. The option of calling an extra election has been used only once, in June 1958.

Denmark's parliament, the Folketing, has 179 members of which two are elected from Greenland and two from the Faroe Islands. The parliamentary election has to be called within a four year term limit, but the prime minister can call it whenever he or she likes, with a minimum of twenty days notice. The election can be held any day of the week, even though Tuesday seems to be popular, as seventeen of the last twenty-two elections were held on a Tuesday. The months of June, July and August have not been used over the last twenty-two elections. Denmark has a proportional electoral system and the country is divided into ten districts (*storkredse*) and ninety-two multi-member constituencies (*opstillingskrese*).

The Icelandic parliament, Alþingi/Althingi, has sixty-three members elected in six constituencies by PR for four years, usually in April or May. The president (on the advice of the prime minister) can call an early election, as in April 2009 – in the aftermath of the bank crash. Early elections used to be common in the Icelandic system, but from 1991–2007 all governments served their full four-year terms. While full proportionality between political parties was achieved in the electoral system in 1987, considerable dis-proportionality between constituencies and regions (malapportionment) has remained, benefiting the countryside – and is much greater than in the other Nordic countries (Harðarson 2002).

The Norwegian parliament, Storting, has 169 members elected for a four year fixed term. Election is held on a Monday in September in the last year of the four year term limit. Extra elections are not possible. The specific Monday is decided by the 'King', which in praxis is a joint decision when the King meets with the government. Usually it is within the first two weeks of September. Norway is divided into nineteen electoral districts corresponding to the nineteen regions which are also responsible for health care (Fylke).

The Nordic electoral system

Voting is not compulsory across the five Nordic countries and citizens over eighteen years old are all eligible to vote. Universal suffrage for national elections for women was introduced in Finland in 1906, Norway in 1913, Denmark and Iceland in 1915 and Sweden in 1921.

The electoral system is a proportional representative system in all five countries with multi-seat constituencies. Denmark has ten constituencies, Iceland six, Norway nineteen, Sweden twenty-nine and Finland fifteen. In Denmark, Sweden, Norway and Iceland 135, 310, 150 and 54 of the seats are distributed in the constituencies whereas 40, 39, 16 and 9 seats respectively, are distributed as adjustment/supplementary seats in order to achieve full proportionality. In Finland, 199 of the 200 seat are distributed directly without any adjustment seats. The final seat in Finland is in the province of Åland which is the only single member district. The D'Hondt method is used in three out of five countries and two others, Norway and Sweden, use the modified Sainte-Laguë method to allocate the seats in the constituencies. The adjustment seats are distributed with the D'Hondt method in Iceland and Denmark. Finland does not apply adjustment seats creating a transparent system, but one with less proportionality and with greater variation between constituencies (Farrell 2001; Elklit 1993; Statistics Denmark 2012).

The electoral threshold for obtaining adjustment seats in Iceland is 5 per cent of all the votes. In Denmark there is a 2 per cent threshold of all votes in order to obtain adjustment seats. Furthermore, a party can also gain adjustment seats if the party receives a constituency mandate or receives, in two of the three electoral administrative regions the country is divided into, as many votes at the average number of votes per constituency mandate. In Norway the electoral threshold is 4 per cent. Finland has no threshold, but the effective threshold can be as high as 12 per cent in some of the smaller constituencies.

The electoral threshold in Sweden is 4 per cent. Only parties that reach more than four per cent on the national level are included in the distribution of the 310 fixed seats. The 39 adjustment seats are utilised in order to make the result more proportional. In practice, this means that all parties that enter the Riksdag are guaranteed a minimum of 14 seats. If a party fails to reach four per cent of the national vote, but receives more than 12 per cent in a constituency, the party will also enter the competition for seats in that specific constituency (which will not guarantee a seat in parliament, especially not in some of the smaller constituencies).

The ballots are quite different in the five countries (*see* Figure 2.6), which is partly due to the great variation in terms of preferential voting. Norway has a closed-list system where the personal votes have almost no influence and it has never happened that the party list has been changed with the voters crossing out or changing the order of the candidates. Sweden and Iceland have a semi-closed system where the personal vote has been seen to change the order of the candidates, however, the impact of the preferential system is still very limited (Oscarsson and Holmberg 2013). In Denmark most lists are open, while a few are semi-closed. The open list in Denmark means that the personal votes determinate the order of the candidates that are elected. Finland has open lists and voters can only cast a vote for a candidate, not a party. In sum, the personal vote in Finland is fully determinate of the ordering of candidates and the total amount of votes for candidates running for a party determines how many seats each party gets. In Denmark it is quite determinate, in Sweden and Iceland only of limited importance and in Norway of no importance.

In Denmark, Norway, Iceland and Finland the government pays for the printing and distribution of the ballots. This is also the case in Sweden, but only if the party has received at least one per cent of the votes in any of the two previous elections. Another observation is that only names are printed on the ballot in Denmark and Iceland, whereas Sweden allows age, employment and residence. Employment and residence are also used on the Norwegian ballots, while in Finland, employment and/or education and residence are also posted on the list of all candidates running in the district, which is posted along with their candidate numbers in the polling booth. On the Finnish ballots you write the number of the candidate you chose to vote for. The numbers are important for voters to remember and are also actively used in the campaigns (e.g. on campaign posters etc.).

This means that, except in Denmark and Iceland, there are important cues provided for voters in the polling booth, which probably, especially for less decisive voters, are used for deciding who to vote for (Holmberg and Möller 1999).

Chapter Six has a detailed account of the electoral system when it comes to the importance of the personal vote and explains, in more detail, the differences between the strictly closed Norwegian and the fully open Finnish system, with the others countries falling somewhere in between.

Government formation in the Nordic countries

Obviously, in the Nordic countries, citizens vote for parties, not governments. Government formation takes place after the elections and is based on the electoral outcome. Historically, the coalitions are largest in Finland and smallest in Sweden and Norway, especially because of the long period with single party Social Democratic governments. In recent Nordic elections there has been a tendency towards stronger pre-electoral alliances which has made the outcome of government formation more predictable than previously. This trend has however been limited to Denmark, Norway and Sweden.

The most common type of government in Norway and Sweden is a single party minority government whereas the surplus majority coalition is widely used in Finland. In Iceland, the minimal winning coalition is used more (*see* Table 2.1). In recent elections, the number of minority coalitions has increased and Denmark has had the largest number of minority coalition governments since 1945. This partly reflects the weakening of traditional cleavages and the increasing number of parties in all the Nordic parliaments since the 1940s and 1950s (Indridason 2005; Bergman 2000; Narud and Strøm 2000; Damgaard 2000; Nousiainen 2000; Harðarson 1995). Finland has had forty-two governments – the largest number of governments among the Nordic countries, but this instability is mostly reflected by high government turnover early in the period (Heidar and Berntzen 2003: 97). As we will see in Chapter Eight – the voters and the government – the incumbency effect is rather small but differ significantly between the Nordic countries. One explanation for this is that the political culture in the Nordic countries to a large extent is consensus based, making it difficult for voters to hold the incumbent government accountable for e.g. the economic development, as many parties (also parties outside the current government) often are part of the coalition that ratifies a specific law.

Norway

Sosialistisk Venstreparti

KOPI

Lisle ved Stortingsvalget i Nord-Trøndelag
9. og 10. september 2001

KOPI

Nr.

1. Daglig leder	Inge Ryan	Namsskogan
2. Lærer	Tone Løwe	Stjørdal
3. Student	Trond Martin Sæterhaug	Levanger
4. Historiker	Runbjørg Bremset Hansen	Nærøy
5. Sykepleier	Morten Sommer	Namsos
6. Avdelingssykepleier	Turid B. Krizak	Verdal
7. Kontorsjef	Arnfinn Monsen	Steinkjer
8. Assistent	Ingegjerd Sandberg	Namsos
9. Gårdbruker	Torgeir Strøm	Fosnes
10. Student	Ranveig Walaunet	Vikna
11. Flyktningekonsulent	Ellen Samuelsen	Steinkjer
12. Høgskolelektor	Per Aunet	Levanger

Veiledning på stemmesedlene til stortingsvaig:
"Vil du endre på stemmeseddelen, kan du:.
1. Stryke kandidater
Det gjør du ved å sette stek over navnet til kandidaten. Du kan stryke så mange kandidater du vil.

2. Endre rekkefølgen på kandidater
Det gjør du ved å sette (nytt) nummer i ruten ved siden av navnet til kandidaten.

Du må endre stemmeseddelen som forklart over. Andre måter å rette på vil ikke telle med i valgoppgjøret,

Bruk blå/svart penn eller   blyant

Vær oppmerksom på følgende:

☒   For at rekkefølgen på kandidatene på valglisten skal bli endret, må rettelse ved samme kandidatnavn gjøres av mer enn halvparten av de velgerne som har gitt valglisten sin stemme.

☒   Ved stortingsvalg er det ikke adgang til å gi noen kandidat tilleggsstemme kumulere)

☒   Det er ikke adgang til å føre opp navn som ikke står på denne stemmeseddelen

Figure 2.6: Ballots in the Nordic countries

Figure 2.6: (Cont'd)
Denmark

Folketingsvalg
Sæt x til højre for et partinavn eller et kandidatnavn. Sæt kun ét x på stemmesedlen
A. Socialdemokraterne
Marie Andersen
Lars Lime Christensen
Akmed Motaqi
Illona Hansen
Nikolaj Mørke
B. Det Radikale Venstre
Rasmus Kristensen
Richard Thompson
Alice Monsanto
C. Det konservative Folkeparti
Anne Søndergaard
Pelle Knutson
Lars Ove Person
Mads Jernvad
F. Socialistisk Folkeparti
Thorstein Flink-Madsen
Andy Krypin
Johanne Krogh Jakobsen
Mads Olesen
K. Kristendemokraterne
Jens Birch
Tina Webber
Johannes Søkjær
O. Dansk Folkeparti
Christian Sørensen
Else Hundevad
Nicki Larsson
Kim Fensdal
V. Venstre
Niels Nielsen
Jacob Melchior
Jens Villumsen
Andy Voigt
Y. Liberal Alliance
Chris Schleck
Morten Viskum
Ø. Enhedslisten
Sini Breschel
Kurt Mogensen
Matthias Lind

Figure 2.6: (Cont'd)
Iceland

☐ B Listi Framsóknarflokksins	☐ D Listi Sjálfstæðisflokksins	☐ F Listi Frjálslynda flokksins	☐ I Listi Íslandshreyfingarinnar	☐ S Listi Samfylkingarinnar	☐ V Listi Vinstrihreyfingarinnar – græns framboðs
Siv Friðleifsdóttir	Þorgerður Katrín Gunnarsdóttir	Kolbrún Stefánsdóttir	Jakob Frímann Magnússon	Gunnar Svavarsson	Ögmundur Jónasson
Samúel Örn Erlingsson	Bjarni Benediktsson	Valdimar Leó Friðriksson	Svanlaug Jóhannsdóttir	Katrín Júlíusdóttir	Guðfríður Lilja Grétarsdóttir
Una María Óskarsdóttir	Ármann Kr. Ólafsson	Helgi Helgason	Lárus Vilhjálmsson	Þórunn Sveinbjarnardóttir	Gestur Svavarsson
Kristbjörg Þórisdóttir	Jón Gunnarsson	Guðrún María Óskarsdóttir	Elsa D. Gísladóttir	Árni Páll Árnason	Mireya Samper
Hlini Melsteð Jóngeirsson	Ragnheiður Elín Árnadóttir	Guðlaug Þóra Kristinsdóttir	Friðrik Ingi Friðriksson	Guðmundur Steingrímsson	Andrea Ólafsdóttir
Ólafur Ágúst Ingason	Ragnheiður Ríkharðsdóttir	Pétur Guðmundsson	Guðrún Einarsdóttir	Tryggvi Harðarson	Karl Tómasson
Sigurbjörn Rafn Úlfarsson	Rósa Guðbjartsdóttir	Atli Hermannsson	Daníel Helgason	Sonja B. Jónsdóttir	Svala Heiðberg
Óli Kárason Tran	Bryndís Haraldsdóttir	Trausti Hólm Jónasson	Margrét Óskarsdóttir	Ásgeir Jóhannesson	Thelma Ásdísardóttir
Guðbjörg Fjóla Halldórsdóttir	Pétur Árni Jónsson	Björn Birgisson	Kristján Kristjánsson	Kristín Á. Guðmundsdóttir	Emil Hjörvar Petersen
Ragnheiður Sigurðardóttir	Sigríður Rósa Magnúsdóttir	Jón Bragi Gunnlaugsson	Auður Matthíasdóttir	Anna Sigríður Guðnadóttir	Wojciech Szewczyk
Svala Rún Sigurðardóttir	Sjöfn Þórðardóttir	Arnar Bergur Guðjónsson	Ingimundur Þór Þorsteinsson	Magnús M. Norðdahl	Ásdís Bragadóttir
Sigurður Hallgrímsson	Þorsteinn Þorsteinsson	Árelíus Örn Þórðarson	Ragnhildur Guðmundsdóttir	Sandra Franks	Hafdís Hannesdóttir
Stefán E. Sigurðsson	Örn Tryggvi Johnsen	Ingvi H. Ingvason	Guðjón Örn Helgason	Ásgeir Runólfsson	Þórir Steingrímsson
Linda Björk Bentsdóttir	Guðni Stefánsson	Jónbjörg Þórsdóttir	Inga Dís Richter	Amal Tamimi	Birgitta Jónsdóttir
Elín Jóhannsdóttir	Gísli Gíslason	Sif Árnadóttir	Páll Daníelsson	Theódór Júlíusson	Þorleifur Friðriksson
Andrés Pétursson	Stefanía Magnúsdóttir	Pétur Gissurarson	Halldóra Traustadóttir	Lísa Sigríður Greipsson	Erlendur Jónsson
Eggert Sólberg Jónsson	Valgeir Guðjónsson	Jóna Brynja Tómasdóttir	Benedikt S. Lafleur	Freyr Árnason	Þóra Elfa Björnsson
Kristjana Bergsdóttir	Hilmar Stefánsson	Hafsteinn Þór Hafsteinsson	Matti Ósvald Stefánsson	Silja Úlfarsdóttir	Sigurður Flosason
Sigurbjörg Björgvinsdóttir	Elín Ósk Óskarsdóttir	Þuríður Erla Erlingsdóttir	Kristín S. Helgadóttir	Helgi Pétursson	Sveinbjörn Markús Njálsson
Einar Sveinbjörnsson	Guðrún Edda Haraldsdóttir	Viggó Eyþórsson	Smári Pálmarsson	Kristján Sveinbjörnsson	Jóhanna B. Magnúsdóttir
Hildur Helga Gísladóttir	Almar Grímsson	Guðmundur Þ. Gunnþórsson	Inga Dóra Jóhannsdóttir	Erna Fríða Berg	Anna Þorsteinsdóttir
Leifur Kr. Jóhannesson	Sigurrós Þorgrímsdóttir	Haraldur B. Sigsteinsson	Halldór Halldórsson	Jón Sigurðsson	Höskuldur Þráinsson
Hansína Á. Björgvinsdóttir	Gunnar Ingi Birgisson	Thitinat Lampha	Hulda Runólfsdóttir	Lúðvík Geirsson	Kristín Halldórsdóttir
Steingrímur Hermannsson	Sigríður Anna Þórðardóttir	Helgi Hallvarðsson	Eyþór Sigmundsson	Rannveig Guðmundsdóttir	Benedikt Davíðsson

Table 2.1: Types of government in the Nordic countries, 1945–2012

	Single-party majority	Minimal winning coalition	Surplus majority coalition	Single-party minority	Minority coalitions	Total
Denmark	-	4	-	14	**18**	36
Finland	-	6	**25**	4	7	42
Iceland	-	**23**	1	3	1	27
Norway	6	5	-	**12**	6	29
Sweden	3	6	1	**16**	3	29
Total (per cent)	9(6)	44(27)	27(17)	49(30)	35(21)	163(101)

Source: Updated and corrected from Gallagher *et al.* (2001: 357).

A comparative case study of the five Nordic countries

Since the book deals with electoral behaviour in the five Nordic countries, our overarching research question aims to explain the electoral behaviour across the five countries through comparison. Essentially, comparative studies are about selecting cases in a way that allows the provision of causal conclusions across cases. The focus on the five Nordic countries provides a case selection that allows exactly that, because on the one hand the countries have several common characteristics, such as similar (but not identical) political systems, culture, language and history. That is, it makes comparison more straightforward, concepts translatable from country to country and, most importantly, common characteristics cannot account for variation across countries in the dependent variable. The common characteristics can, so to speak, be excluded from this list of independent variables, providing the opportunity to focus on the variables that vary between the countries and thus carry the power of explanation.

The five countries differ remarkably when it comes to electoral behaviour, despite their common political system. Sometimes the countries have the same trends in the data, but lagged by time, and sometimes these trends do not seem to follow each other at all. We want to explain these differences with our analyses of the five countries.

Although the Nordic countries share many common traits and, from a broad international perspective, may appear as strikingly similar, it does not take much insight to realise that interesting differences are to be found among this set of five countries – differences that might shed light on the underlying patterns of change that are found. Generally speaking, the study of the Nordic countries is a focus on a small number of cases closely related to one another, observed over time, and the design has the advantage of having several common characteristics, together with much variation on key dependent and independent variables.

Data and key variables

The data applied in this book are primarily the latest publicly available National Election Studies. The latest election surveys are merged into a combined data set including all five Nordic countries. It was a greater hassle than we expected to create such a dataset, mainly because each of the National Election Studies, even through emerging from the same American origin, have developed into their own unique dataset with their own particular question phrasing. The Appendix supplies a detailed account of the variables and their coding use in this book. We have used the same coding in all the chapters.

For convenience and comparability, the same set of independent variables has been used in the concluding multivariate analyses of each empirical chapter, (Chapters Four – Nine). These independent variables are selected in accordance with the classic 'funnel of causality' (Campbell *et al.* 1960) combined with Lipset and Rokkan's (1967a) cleavage structure of the Nordic Countries (e.g. class and urbanisation). That is, the variables included in the analysis are first socio-demographic (gender, age, education, employment (class) followed by public sector employment, civil status and urbanisation). Also included are ideology as (economic) left-right self-placement, indexes of key issues such as size of public sector, moral issues, attitudes to EU, immigration, environment and political knowledge and media awareness (measured as attention to political news in the media).

Conclusion – From a most similar system to a somewhat different system

The five Nordic countries share many aspects of their historical development and also today have strong political, cultural and economic bonds. The countries have some of the most developed and trusted welfare states in the world, but as we saw, the difference between the five Nordic countries is much larger today than in 1990, and at present, the Nordic countries are not the only countries which have strong welfare states.

Analysing the actual process of voting (i.e. the electoral system) we see that there are substantial differences between the Nordic countries. In Finland, voters are obliged to vote for candidates within open lists whereas in Norway, voters cannot alter the ranking made by parties. This is discussed in more detail in Chapter Six.

There are a growing number of minority coalition governments in Nordic countries party due to an increased number of parties represented in the parliaments. The older, main parties are, however, still dominant in the process of government formation.

We have identified a number of differences between the Nordic countries and we will explore these differences in more detail in the following chapters, using these between-country variations to understand more clearly, the Nordic voter.

Chapter Three

The Nordic Party Systems

The party systems of the 1960's reflect, with few but significant exceptions, the cleavage structures of the 1920's. This is a crucial characteristic of Western competitive politics in the age of 'high mass consumption': the party alternatives, and in remarkably many cases the party organisations, are older than the majorities of the national electorates (Lipset and Rokkan 1967b: 50).

Modern representative democracy was reinvented in the late eighteenth century, almost simultaneously in France (Abbé Siéyès) and America (James Madison), even though Ancient Greece and the Italian city-states had elements of representation as well as elections. The main idea is that citizens select their representatives at regular elections (Manin 1997). In between elections, the elected representatives rule by consent of the citizens. If representatives fail, citizens have the option to vote them out of office at the next election. The two processes of *mandate giving* and *democratic accountability* will secure sound governance.

In one important aspect, the Nordic welfare democracies of today are distant from the original invention of representative democracy. Most of the time, the typical role of democratic elections in the Nordic countries is *not* primarily to elect specific individual representatives. Instead, Nordic citizens typically vote for *political parties* and hold *parties* accountable at elections. Consequently, during the strong party era in the twentieth century, Nordic voters have developed emotional bonds primarily to *parties*, not to leaders or candidates.

This chapter gives a short introduction to the historical development and present features of the Nordic party systems. We also present novel comparative analyses of how the system of parties in the Nordic countries is currently shaping party voters' ideological orientations. We map Nordic party voters' positions along the central left-right dimension and along five supplemental issue dimensions, tapping the attitudes towards the size of public sector, the environment, the European Union, immigration, and moral issues. The issue dimensions will eventually play an important role in our analyses of party choice (*see* Chapter Nine).

The history of the Nordic party systems

The point of departure in most analyses of the Nordic party systems is that individual parties exist because of a successful polarisation of underlying social cleavages. The historical-sociological Lipset-Rokkan cleavage model still offers the most popular explanation of why a nation's party system has emerged (Lipset and Rokkan 1967b). Their theory of social cleavages claims that the conflicts between specific socio-demographic groups present in the early twentieth century, to a large extent, can explain party system development thereafter. The alignment of political forces was first accentuated by a centre-versus periphery cleavage, then by an urban-versus rural cleavage, as peasants responded to the industrial revolution (Lipset and Rokkan 1967b).

According to Lipset and Rokkan's famous freezing hypothesis, the backbones of Nordic party systems were formed before the 1920s. The rise of strong parties was a direct result of awakening political protest from farmer and labour movements, the increasing politicisation of social cleavages stemming from the national and industrial revolutions, and the introduction of parliamentary government. In the advent of mass democracy and universal suffrage, it became necessary also for loose intra-parliamentary factions of representatives to coordinate and organise themselves, transforming into modern parties. Long term political opinion formation and modern election campaigns demanded more resources (and more members). So, it is fair to conclude that the twentieth century became the heyday of representative *party* democracy in the Nordic countries.

In the Nordic countries the social cleavages are often said to be divided around three poles: L) Labour, workers (social democratic parties), B) the capital, business owners (conservative parties), and F) rural periphery, farmers (agrarian parties = centre parties) (Rokkan 1987: 81–95). Later these cleavages were supplemented with groupings around urban areas and minor landowners (liberals) and the communists. Thus the Nordic party system has traditionally been classified as a five-party system (Berglund and Lindström 1978; Knutsen 2001; Sundberg 1999; Damgaard 1974; Elklit 1986).

Five parties – a communist, a social democratic, an agrarian centre party, a liberal and a conservative party – are often considered to have been the backbone of the Nordic party system from the advent of universal suffrage in the 1920s until the early 1970s. However, we consider the classic Nordic five-party model to be an oversimplification. If it ever was a good description of the Nordic party system, it can now be said to have been obsolete for decades in most countries, except

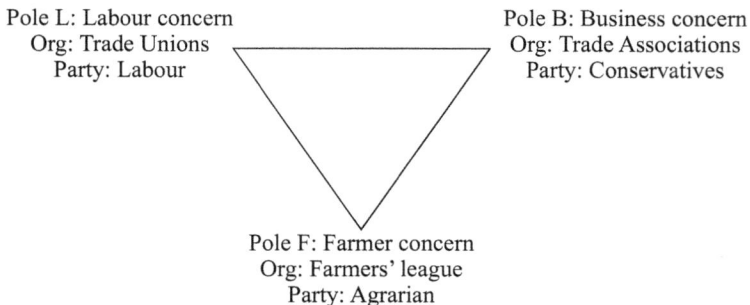

Pole L: Labour concern   Pole B: Business concern
Org: Trade Unions   Org: Trade Associations
Party: Labour   Party: Conservatives

Pole F: Farmer concern
Org: Farmers' league
Party: Agrarian

Figure 3.1: The functional-economic dimension of cleavages and party development in the Nordic region

Source: Lipset and Rokkan (1967a): 93

Figure 2.6: (Cont'd)
Sweden

VAL TILL LANDSTINGSFULLMÄKTIGE

Moderata Samlingspartiet

Du kan personrösta genom att sätta ett kryss för den kandidat du
helst vill ska bli vald. Du kan inte personrösta på fler än en eller
någon annan kandidat än de som står nedan.

- ☐ 1 Johnny Magnusson, 58, Regionråd
- ☐ 2 Lisbeth Sundén Andersson, 60, Biomedicinsk analytiker
- ☐ 3 Agneta Granberg, 59, Kommunalråd, Socionom
- ☐ 4 Johnny Bröndt, 55, Civilekonom
- ☐ 5 Mimmi von Troil, 49, Marknadsekonom
- ☐ 6 Peter Hermansson, 28, Studerande
- ☐ 7 Henrik Ekelund, 33, Politisk sekreterare
- ☐ 8 Johan Fält, 51, Konstruktionschef
- ☐ 9 Kristina Holmgren, 66, Lågstadielärare
- ☐ 10 Magnus Palmlöf, 48, Civilingenjör/Tekn. Dr
- ☐ 11 Erland Lundell, 61, Fiskare
- ☐ 12 Kajsa Olofsson, 32, Originalare
- ☐ 13 Nils-Erik Wangler, 64, Pensionär
- ☐ 14 Susanna Cassberg, 41, Administratör
- ☐ 15 Börje Olsson, 63, F.d polisinspektör
- ☐ 16 Otto Linton, 74, Jägmästare
- ☐ 17 Anna-Maria Raimer, 34, Pol.mag./ Kommunaltjänsteman
- ☐ 18 Paul Flisak, 43, IT-strateg
- ☐ 19 David Josefsson, 27, Ekonom
- ☐ 20 Christina Hjort, 46, Sekreterare
- ☐ 21 Pär Sundaeus, 63, Aukt. revisor
- ☐ 22 Isabella Szajewska, 26, Studerande
- ☐ 23 Linda Arnströmer, 34, Leg. sjuksköterska
- ☐ 24 Andreas Rydbo, 37, Stabschef
- ☐ 25 Göran Larsson, 60, Skyddstekniker
- ☐ 26 Per-Ola Maneschiöld, 44, Universitetslektor
- ☐ 27 Bertil Kärnefelt, 54, Tjänsteman

Finland

Eduskuntavaalit
2011
Riksdagsval

N:o

perhaps in Sweden. Around 1970, the narrative of the development of the Nordic party systems became increasingly complicated. At that point in time, we argue that all reminiscences of a common Nordic five-party structure had already vanished.

For instance, the Christian Democratic Party in Norway (*Kristelig Folkeparti*) had been already founded in 1933. And the Finnish protest party (*Suomen Maaseudun Puolue/Finlands landsbygdsparti*) was in place by 1959. Christian democratic parties were formed in Sweden and Finland in the early 1960s and in Denmark in 1970 (*Kristendemokraterne*). The Christian Democrats were represented in the Danish parliament from 1973 until 1994, 1998–2005 and 2010–2011. They were part of the government in Denmark from 1982–1988.

Partly because the Nordic countries are quite religiously homogeneous (today 84 per cent of Nordic citizens are Christians Protestants) religion only plays a minor role in politics in the Nordic countries.

Right wing populist parties appeared in the 1970s and green parties in the 1980s (Petersson 2005). In Iceland, no liberal, green or popular right parties have established themselves, and it has today a distinctly different party system compared to the other Nordic countries. In fact, the Icelandic party system has basically been a four-party system, even though since 1971, short-lived fifth or sixth parties have entered parliament after most elections; the most successful was the Women's Alliance who gained MPs in four elections, 1983–95 (Kristinsson 2001; *see* the Appendix for more details of the political parties in the Nordic countries).

In only one of the Nordic countries – Sweden – did the five-party system remain intact until 1988, when the environmental green party managed to win representation in parliament. And already in 1991, two new parties, protest party New Democracy and the Christian Democratic Party, passed the four per cent threshold to the Swedish *Riksdag*. Much later than all the other Nordic countries, the stable Swedish five-party system was transformed into a party system with seven to eight parties and, with the successful election of the Sweden Democrats (popular right party) in 2010, the system changed once again; for the first time eight parties were represented in the *Riksdag*.

Features of the Nordic party systems in the twenty-first century

What are the main characteristics of the Nordic party space today? In Table 3.1 below we have collated a range of party system characteristics – such as party system size, polarisation, and dimensionality – that will give a general idea of how the main features of the Nordic party systems contrast with a set of other systems in the world. This comparative outlook will serve many analyses of Nordic voting behaviour in this book. Here, we will address both the issues of exceptionality and similarity when it comes to the Nordic party systems of today.

To begin with, although the number of parties has expanded during the last decades, the Nordic party systems are quite dissimilar as regards popular measures of party system size. *The number of effective parties* (a) are highest in Finland (5.93) and lowest in Iceland (3.55), while Norway, Sweden and Denmark have around five effective parties.

Table 3.1: Six party system characteristics of the Nordic countries in a comparative perspective (rank order in parentheses)

	Effective Number of Parties (a)	Dalton's Party Polarisation Index (b)	Party System Competition (c)	Degree of Uni-dimensionality (d)	Strength of Left-Right Dimension (e)	Weighted Absolute Ideological Congruence (f)
(1) United States 2004	2.18 (4)	2.43 (9)	0.41 (3)	0.37 (15)	1.00 (16)	0.24
(2) Spain 2004	2.99 (16)	4.33 (6)	0.34 (13)	0.60 (12)	1.00 (4)	0.08
(3) Portugal 2005	3.19 (9)	3.44 (4)	0.32 (9)	0.54 (16)	1.00 (15)	0.16
(4) United Kingdom 2005	3.21 (3)	2.37 (8)	0.36 (11)	0.56 (8)	0.50 (7)	0.10
(5) Australia 2007	3.46 (1)	1.96 (14)	0.43 (16)	0.76 (4)	0.40 (10)	0.12
(6) Iceland 2003	3.55 (15)	4.08 (17)	0.48 (17)	0.84 (3)	0.30 (2)	0.08
(7) Canada 2004	3.77 (17)	4.37 (3)	0.31 (6)	0.43 (11)	0.80 (9)	0.11
(8) Germany 2002	3.79 (6)	2.70 (2)	0.27 (12)	0.60 (6)	0.43 (12)	0.14
(9) Ireland 2002	3.95 (2)	2.20 (11)	0.42 (1)	0.25 (5)	0.40 (13)	0.15
(10) Sweden 2002	4.54 (14)	4.07 (10)	0.41 (8)	0.52 (10)	0.75 (8)	0.10
(11) Denmark 2001	4.74 (10)	3.57 (5)	0.34 (9)	0.54 (9)	0.62 (3)	0.08
(12) Norway 2005	5.07 (12)	3.75 (7)	0.35 (15)	0.63 (14)	1.00 (5)	0.08
(13) Netherlands 2002	5.13 (11)	3.64 (13)	0.42 (2)	0.36 (2)	0.18 (1)	0.06
(14) Switzerland 2007	5.86 (13)	4.01 (16)	0.46 (16)	0.60 (13)	1.00 (11)	0.13
(15) Finland 2007	5.93 (7)	2.85 (12)	0.42 (4)	0.37 (7)	0.50 (6)	0.09
(16) France 2002	6.54 (8)	3.29 (1)	0.24 (7)	0.47 (1)	0.00 (14)	0.16
(17) Belgium 2003	10.29 (5)	2.46 (15)	0.45 (5)	0.42 (5)	—	—

Notes: (a) The number of effective parties is the classic Laakso and Taagepera measure (1979) calculated for years around 2000, taken from the Quality of Government (QoG) dataset (Teorell *et al.* 2009). (b) is Russell Daltons' (2008) measure of party polarisation that is based on left-right self placements of party voters taken from the CSES-modules I and II. (c) Party system competition is an additive index based on the questions 'like-dislike party a-i'. If a voter has given a party a score of 6 or higher the variable is coded as 1 and 0 otherwise. The competition index thus indicates the average number of parties in each country that has scored 6 or higher, i.e. is being liked by the voters. (d) In order to obtain a measure for the degree of unidimensionality a multiple unidimensional unfolding procedure has been conducted. The data is voters' evaluations of parties on a like-dislike scale. The unfolding procedure tries all possible orderings of the parties and selects the unfolding model that best fits the evaluation data. An H-coefficient smaller than .30 indicates that the structure in the data is insufficient for the justification of using individual items as indicators of a single latent dimension (van Schuur and Post 1990). Mudfold is distributed by ProGAMMA, P.O. Box 841, 9700 AV Groeningen, The Netherlands. The measure of fit for the unfolding model, the coefficient of scalability (Loevinger's H), varies from 0 to 1 and tells us to what extent voters' preference-orderings of parties are in agreement with a perfect unfolding model (*see also* Dahlberg 2009). The unfolding analysis is based on the questions 'like-dislike party a-i'. The guiding principle in this iterative search has been that each unfolding scale should, if possible, include all main parties. Plausible models, where all the large parties are included, have thus been selected over models with better fit where any of the relevant parties are left out. (e) The strength of left-right dimension is a simple Spearman's rank correlation between the ordering of parties derived from the unfolding model with the ordering of the parties based on voter perceptions of party positions along the left-right dimension; the higher the correlation the more likely it is that the unidimensional structure is based on the left-right dimension. The absolute congruence measure (f) is based on left-right self placements and perceptions of parties' positions along the left-right scale. First, we calculate the average absolute distance between the citizens and the position of the party voted for, where N is the number of citizens and Ci is the ideal point of the ith citizen. *Absolute Congruence* $= \frac{1}{N} \sum_{i=1}^{N} |C_i - P|$. The measure is then weighted according to the relative size of the parties, in terms of percentages of votes, and aggregated into single country measures of congruence. The measure stretches from 0 to 1 where 0 indicates perfect ideological congruence.

Finland is not only the party system with the highest number of effective parties; according to the polarisation measure of our choice, it is also the least polarised system of the Nordic countries. The Dalton polarisation index score (b) for Finland is 2.85, which is in sharp contrast with Swedish and Icelandic party systems that are far more polarised (4.07 and 4.08). Also in respect to polarisation, the Nordic party systems display large variation and do not cluster.

The degree of competition measure (c) shows the average number of parties that individual voters' score higher than six, on an eleven-point dislike-scale. According to this measure, the most competitive party system among the Nordic countries is Iceland (0.48), while the Norwegian and Danish party systems appear much less competitive (0.31 and 0.35).

The degree of unidimensionality (d) is a goodness of fit-measure that shows how well a unidimensional unfolding model fits with the structure in voters' party evaluations, i.e. scores on a dislike-like scale (using CSES-data). The higher the score, the better a unidimensional unfolding model works to reproduce party evaluations. In this analysis, Iceland turns out as the most unidimensional of the Nordic party systems with an excellent fit measure (0.84), while Finland turns out as the least unidimensional.

To assess whether the unidimensional structure is produced by a left-right dimension, we also calculated the rank correlation (rho) between two of the party orderings in the table (d), the first retrieved from the unfolding model, and the second based on voter's mean placements of the parties along the left-right dimension. Results show that, although the Icelandic party system is the most unidimensional, the unidimensional structure is not likely to be produced by the left-right conflict (rho=0.30). There is also a low correlation in Finland (0.50), which suggests that the left-right dimension only, to a smaller extent, is structuring party system competition in the Finnish party space. In Denmark, Sweden and Norway, however, there are more decent correlations which suggest that the unidimensional structure of the systems can be attributed to the left-right dimension.

In one respect, the Nordic party systems seem to form a distinct cluster compared to other systems: ideological congruence. The Nordic systems display a much lower score on the weighted ideological congruence measure (e) than other systems in the analysis. Low scores indicate that there are small ideological left-right distances between voters and their parties (a score of 0 would indicate that all party voters placed themselves on the same ideological position as the party they voted for). This means that in all five of the Nordic multi party systems, ideology plays a more important role in party competition and voting behaviour than in many other established multi party democracies outside the Nordic region.

Parties are still strong in the Nordic countries

Strong parties are still a central feature of the Nordic democracies. Although we can document a profound ongoing dealignment of social cleavages, declining party identification and decreasing party membership (except in Iceland – due

Table 3.2: Distribution of opinion on the necessity of parties in 20 countries (percentages)

Country	Parties are necessary				Parties are not needed	Opinion balance:
	1	2	3	4	5	(1+2)−(4 + 5)
Netherlands	61	29	7	2	1	+87
Norway	68	21	8	2	1	+86
Spain	58	25	9	4	4	+75
Taiwan	59	23	10	3	5	+74
Sweden	61	20	12	4	3	+74
Germany	58	22	14	2	4	+74
Britain	43	33	19	3	2	+71
Romania	65	14	10	5	6	+68
Czech Republic	39	35	20	4	2	+68
Iceland	55	23	11	5	6	+67
Argentina	66	12	10	6	6	+66
Hungary	45	27	19	4	5	+63
Israel	53	20	16	5	6	+62
Australia	43	28	20	5	4	+62
New Zealand	39	32	20	6	3	+62
Poland	38	29	21	7	5	+55
Mexico	56	13	15	7	9	+53
Japan	37	28	21	9	5	+51
USA	25	31	26	12	6	+38
Lithuania	31	24	24	9	12	+34
Ukraine	43	14	17	8	18	+31

Notes: The table is from Holmberg (2003), adding Iceland in 1999. The results are based on data from the Comparative Study of Electoral Systems (CSES; www.cses.org). Entries in columns 1–5 are row percentages. The question asked was: 'Some people say that the political parties are necessary to make our political system work in [country]. Others say that no political parties are needed in [country]. Using the scale on this card, where would you place yourself?'. The scale runs from 1 to 5, coded as 1 for 'political parties are necessary for the functioning of our political system' and 5 for 'political parties are not needed in [country]'; 3 on the scale is a neutral mid-point.

and nuclear power, morality and religion, decentralisation, the European Union, immigration, gender equality and the environment have accompanied the economic left-right dimension in the Nordic countries. Country specialists would agree that a unidimensional left-right description of the party space does not suffice to explain electoral outcomes: perhaps it is a good starting point but at the same time also an oversimplification.

In most comparative analyses, however, generality often triumphs detail. For many decades, a standard question about voter self-placement along the left-right scale has been included in election studies around the world. Although the actual content and interpretations of the left-right division is much debated (Bobbio 1996), the average placements of party voters along the left-right continuum serve to give an immediate idea of the main features of a country's party system (Gilljam and Oscarsson 1996).

In Figure 3.2 we display the average left-right self placements of Nordic party voters. Results show that the line-up of parties is still very alike in the Nordic countries. The far left parties, left socialist parties, social democratic parties and conservative parties have a similar left-right ranking in all countries with agrarian, green and liberal parties placed in-between. The average placements are fairly similar, but there is also considerable variation within party families: social democratic party voters' mean placements range from 37 in Sweden to 46 in Iceland. Voters of liberal parties place themselves in the range 49–67, Christian democratic voters in the range 54–66, and conservative party voters, tight together in the range 71–77. The left socialist party voters place themselves in the range 25–34.

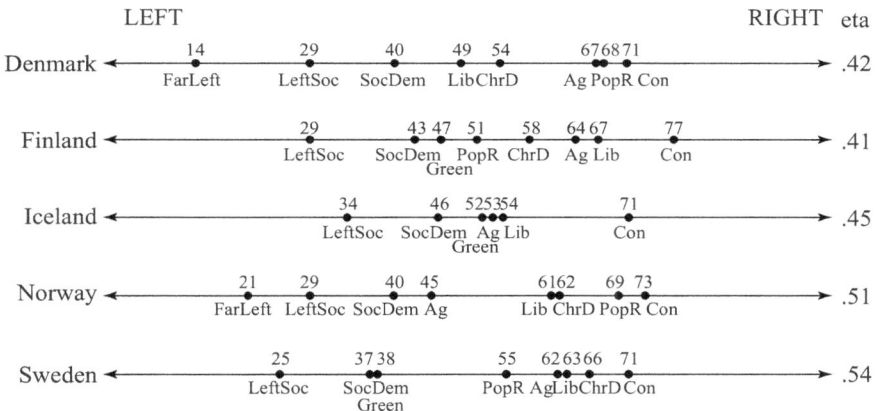

Figure 3.2: Nordic party voters' left-right self-placements (means)

Comment: Data are average left-right self-placements of party voters in Denmark (2007), Finland (2007), Iceland (2007), Norway (2005), and Sweden (2006). In all countries, eleven-point scales ranging from 0 to 10 were used to tap ideological left-right self placement. Averages were multiplied by 10 in order to avoid decimals in the figure. The eta measure of correlation is retrieved from an analysis of variance where left-right self-placement is the dependent variable and the groups of parties, the independent nominal level variable. More specifically, the eta value is the squared ratio of the between party variation (between sum of squares) and the total variation (total sum of squares). Eta ranges between 0 and 1.

There are also distinct differences in the average left-right placements of the green party voters and the populist party voters. The green party voters place themselves in the centre of the left-right dimension in Finland (47) and Iceland (52) but have a much more leftist position in the Swedish party system (38). And the populist party voters consider themselves as clearly right-wing in Denmark (68) and Norway (69) but as centre in Sweden (55) and Finland (51). Parties that are newcomers to the political party space do not share the same left-right positions to the same extent as the old parties. A reason for this is that new parties tend to be based upon ideologically cross-cutting dimensions, and depending on the multidimensional structure of the party system in a country, they will end up having different locations on the left-right dimension.

In this analysis, Denmark comes out as the most polarised Nordic country having the largest distance between the most leftist and the most rightist group of party voters (Wing Party Distance=57). This is not the first time Denmark has come out as the most polarised of the Nordic party systems (Gilljam and Oscarsson 1996). The left-right distance between the wing parties are somewhat lower in Norway (WPD=52), Finland (WPD=48), and Sweden (WPD=46). Iceland stands out as the least polarised party system in terms of left-right distances between wing parties (WPD=37).

Analyses of variance show that the discriminatory power of the left-right ideological dimension, i.e. the correlation of left-right self placements and party choice, is about the same in all the Nordic countries, though higher in Norway (eta=0.51) and Sweden (eta=0.54) than in Iceland (eta=0.45), Finland (eta=0.41), and Denmark (eta=0.42).

Let us now, eventually, turn to some of the supplemental issue dimensions present in the Nordic countries. We have been able to construct five issue dimensions with acceptable comparability that have demonstrated explanatory power in previous nation-specific analyses of voting behaviour in the Nordic countries (Oscarsson and Holmberg 2008; Aardal 2007; Borre 1995). Here, the issue dimensions are constructed differently in each country but we have tried to make use of similarly phrased single or multiple indicators for each dimension (*see* Appendix for details). Our ideological indices have been standardised with a mean of zero and standard deviation of 1, individually for each country.

The five supplemental issue dimensions deal with a) attitudes towards the size of public sector, which can be regarded as a concrete reflection of underlying left-right orientation or, if you will, as a 'harder test' of the relevance of the left-right dimension in the Nordic countries, b) attitudes towards the European Union, c) the environment, d) immigration, and e) moral issues.

For Sweden, Iceland, Denmark and Norway, *the size of public sector*-dimension reveals almost identical party orderings, as the left-right dimension did in the previous analysis (Figure 3.2) For these four countries it is fair to say that the issue of the size of the public sector, lines up consistently with voters' general left-right ideological orientation. However, this is really not the case in Finland. Here, the issue of the size of the public sector yields a rank ordering that is quite dissimilar from the left-right ordering of parties: in Finland, voters from

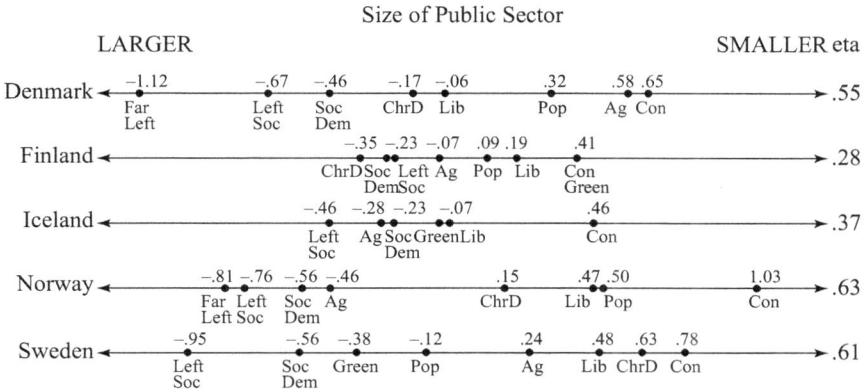

(a)

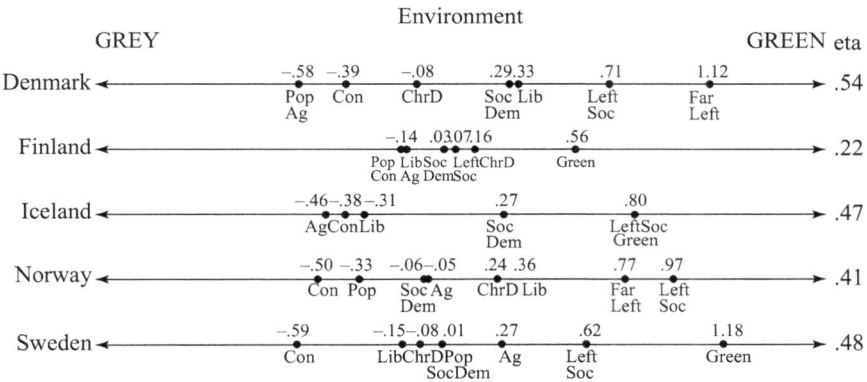

(b)

Figure 3.3a – b: Nordic party voters' positions on supplemental issue dimensions (average)

the Christian democratic party are most in favour of a large public sector and, on the other flank, the green party voters share the same views as the conservative party voters.

The discriminatory power of the *size of public sector*-dimension is stronger in Norway, Sweden and Denmark (eta=0.63, eta=0.61, and eta=0.55) than in Iceland and Finland (eta=0.37 and eta=0.28).

Along the green environmental issue dimension (*see* Figure 3.3b), as expected the green party voters, where present, are the most pro-environment. Voters of the left parties also tend to position themselves distinctly on the pro-environment side while conservative party voters tend to position themselves on the other end of the green issue dimension. In Denmark and Norway there are no green parties. Instead the most pro-environment party voters are the supporters of left socialist and the far left parties.

Figure 3.3c – e: Nordic party voters' positions on supplemental issue dimensions (average)

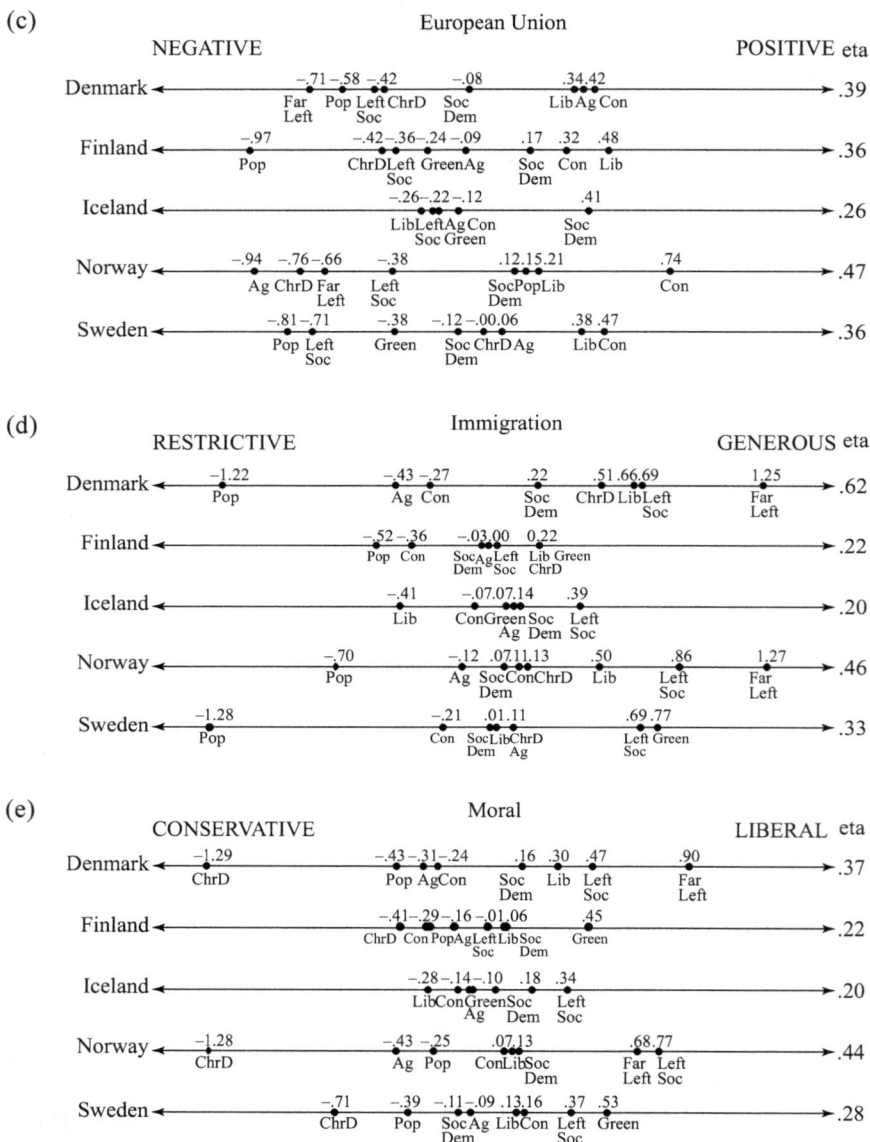

(c)

European Union

NEGATIVE   POSITIVE eta

Denmark ← ... →.39
  −.71 −.58 −.42   −.08   .34 .42
  Far Pop Left ChrD Soc   Lib Ag Con
  Left   Soc   Dem

Finland ← ... →.36
  −.97   −.42 −.36 −.24 −.09   .17 .32 .48
  Pop   ChrD Left Green Ag   Soc Con Lib
            Soc   Dem

Iceland ← ... →.26
  −.26 −.22 −.12   .41
  Lib Left Ag Con   Soc
  Soc Green   Dem

Norway ← ... →.47
  −.94 −.76 −.66   −.38   .12 .15 .21   .74
  Ag ChrD Far   Left   Soc Pop Lib   Con
     Left   Soc   Dem

Sweden ← ... →.36
  −.81 −.71   −.38   −.12 −.00 .06   .38 .47
  Pop Left   Green Soc ChrD Ag   Lib Con
  Soc   Dem

(d)

Immigration

RESTRICTIVE   GENEROUS eta

Denmark ← ... →.62
  −1.22   −.43 −.27   .22   .51 .66 .69   1.25
  Pop   Ag Con   Soc   ChrD Lib Left   Far
                             Dem   Soc   Left

Finland ← ... →.22
              −.52 −.36 −.03 .00 0 .22
              Pop Con   Soc Ag Left Lib Green
                        Dem Soc ChrD

Iceland ← ... →.20
              −.41   −.07 .07 .14   .39
              Lib   Con Green Soc Left
                     Ag Dem Soc

Norway ← ... →.46
         −.70   −.12 .07 .11 .13   .50   .86   1.27
         Pop   Ag Soc Con ChrD   Lib   Left   Far
                       Dem   Soc   Left

Sweden ← ... →.33
  −1.28   −.21 .01 .11   .69 .77
  Pop   Con Soc Lib ChrD   Left Green
                      Dem Ag   Soc

(e)

Moral

CONSERVATIVE   LIBERAL eta

Denmark ← ... →.37
  −1.29   −.43 −.31 −.24   .16 .30 .47   .90
  ChrD   Pop Ag Con   Soc Lib Left   Far
                                 Dem   Soc   Left

Finland ← ... →.22
              −.41 −.29 −.16 −.01 .06   .45
              ChrD Con Pop Ag Left Lib Soc   Green
                            Soc   Dem

Iceland ← ... →.20
              −.28 −.14 −.10 .18 .34
              Lib Con Green Soc Left
                  Ag Dem Soc

Norway ← ... →.44
  −1.28   −.43 −.25   .07 .13   .68 .77
  ChrD   Ag Pop   Con Lib Soc   Far Left
                               Dem   Left Soc

Sweden ← ... →.28
         −.71   −.39 −.11 −.09 .13 .16   .37 .53
         ChrD   Pop Soc Ag Lib Con   Left Green
                     Dem   Soc

Comment: Data are average placements of party voters along five issue dimensions in Denmark (2007), Finland (2007), Iceland (2007), Norway (2005), and Sweden (2006). The discriminatory power of the issue dimensions, they were standardised individually for each country with a mean of 0 and standard deviation of 1. For details on the construction of the issue dimensions in each country, *see* Appendix.

to primary elections) political parties are undoubtedly still at the centre stage in Nordic politics. And, according to the Nordic voters, parties are still considered 'necessary to make the political system work'. A clear majority of voters in the three Nordic countries represented in Table 3.2, (Norway 2001, Sweden 2002, Iceland 1999), answered that parties are necessary (68, 61 and 55 per cent respectively). This puts Iceland, Sweden and Norway among many other party oriented multiparty systems such as the Netherlands, Spain, and Taiwan.

Dimensionality of the Nordic party space

Citizens do not only develop relationships with individual parties but also form experiences with an *entire set* of competing parties, i.e. the *system of parties* that ultimately make up the breadth of political choice options in a political system. In this section, we perform a classic comparative analysis of the Nordic party voter's positions along the 'super' issue dimension of left and right, and five more supplemental issue dimensions that have come to play an important role in shaping the party competition and voting behaviour in the Nordic countries. In party oriented systems, the ideological space is the infrastructure of party competition and thus plays an important role in the fortunes and misfortunes of political parties. The dimensions presented here will be used in explanatory models of party choice in later analyses in Chapter Nine.

By far, the most important analytic tool in studies of Nordic voting behaviour and party competition is the *left-right dimension*. The meaningfulness of a left-right distinction and the dimensionality of the party space have always been points of major controversy in studies of the Nordic party systems and have also been the focus of several studies (Grendstad 2003; Jenssen Pesonen, and Gilljam 1998; Oscarsson 1998; Petersson and Valen 1979). For instance, while Swedish analysts strongly prefer unidimensional approaches, Danish, Norwegian and Finnish scholars often prefer to think of the party system as multidimensional, and in some cases, treat the division of left and right as not one but two or more ideological divisions, such as a public-private dimension or a liberal-conservative dimension. Factor analytic approaches typically tend to produce a large number of issue dimensions that need attention in more detailed empirical studies of Nordic party systems (*see* Holmberg and Oscarsson 2004, Oscarsson and Holmberg 2008a, 2013; Aardal 2011; Hansen and Goul Andersen 2013; Borre 1995, 2003a, 2003b; Harðarson 1995; Reunanen and Suhonen 2009; Grönlund and Westinen 2012).

Thus, in country specific analyses of political change, it is obvious that the idea of a unidimensional political space, where parties are ordered from left to right, do not suffice to make a good description of how the main political conflicts are structured. This is true even for Sweden, a system that often is considered to be one of the most unidimensional party systems in the world (*see* Dahlberg and Oscarsson, 2006) where super-issues such as European unification and the environment have also shaped party competition and voting behaviour in the past decades. So, again, once you go into more detail, the issue space of Nordic countries tends to be multidimensional. For instance, issues of energy production

In Figure 3.3c, Nordic party voters' average positions along the European Union dimension is displayed. It is clear that the EU-dimension represents a cross-cutting dimension in most of the Nordic countries. Furthermore, the party voters' line up tends to be quite different. In Finland, the social democratic voters side with conservative and liberal voters at the EU-positive end. In Norway, the agrarian, Christian democratic voters side with the far left and the left socialist party voters at the EU-negative flank of the dimension. In Iceland, the social democratic voters are by far the most pro-EU, reflecting the fact that their party has been the only party consistently supporting Icelandic EU-membership in recent years.

Not surprisingly, the populist party's voters stand out as being the most anti-immigration (*see* Figure 3.3d). The Danish, Norwegian and Swedish populist parties (*Dansk Folkeparti, Fremskrittspartiet* and *Sverigedemokraterna*) hold extreme anti-immigration positions compared to most other parties. In Denmark, Norway and Sweden the immigration issue dimension shows much stronger correlation with party choice (eta=0.62, eta=0.46, and eta=0.33) than in Finland and Iceland. In 2007, the small liberal party in Iceland, however, presented some anti-immigration policies – their voters are also the most negative on the immigration dimension. All over the board, in general, the leftist party voters generally display the most generous pro-immigration positions in the Nordic countries.

The moral dimension encompasses attitudes towards Christian values, gay marriages, abortions and euthanasia. As expected, the Christian democratic parties in the Nordic countries, where present, have the most moral, conservative positions along the dimension, most notably in Denmark and Norway. It is also in both these countries that the moral dimension shows the highest correlation with party choice (eta=0.37 and eta=0.44).

Conclusion: The Nordic party systems: Stable but increasingly diverse

In this chapter, we have compared the Nordic party systems on six characteristics. The comparative analyses show that the Nordic party systems are neither exceptional nor very similar as regards party system characteristics, such as the effective number of parties, polarisation, the degree of unidimensionality, and party system competition. Only in one respect are the Nordic countries clustered together: the degree of party ideological congruence, i.e., the extent to which party voters place themselves close to their own party along the left-right dimension.

We have also mapped the Nordic party space using the party voters' positions along the main left-right dimension and five supplemental issue dimensions. The analysis reiterates that ideology plays an important role for party competition and voter behaviour in the Nordic multiparty systems: since all issue dimensions have large discriminatory power they should be included in the upcoming analyses of party choice. There exists large ideological distances between leftist parties (socialist left and far left parties) and the conservative parties on all supplemental issue dimensions. These are ideological distances that reflects the same general left-right ordering of parties, although the spaces may actually have very little to do with traditional left-right issues of social equality, the size of public sector or the level of state intervention. This means that much of the ideological variation along the left-right dimension, in practice, also reflects the ideological diversity of issues of immigration, environment and morality.

In an historical perspective, the Nordic party systems are far more stable than many other multiparty systems. The old set of parties in all five Nordic countries are today still the same parties that came out of the 1920s cleavage structure, and they have still a dominating role. Nevertheless, the number of significant exceptions from the 1920s cleavage structure increases over time. That is, today the Nordic countries with regard to their party systems, are more diverse than ever before.

Chapter Four

Voters and Representative Democracy

Scholars of democracy have often seen the Scandinavian democracies as being closer than many others to realizing the ideal type for a strong representative democracy on a solid popular base (Amnå 2006: 587, referring to Putnam 2000).

Introduction

From an international perspective the well being of advanced representative democracies has been topical since the late 1960s and 1970s (Norris 1999). The discussion started of with gloomy crisis theories and has, in the light of the democratic survival and expansion rate, developed into a debate about the challenges that mature democracies are facing (Cain *et al.* 2003). The international discussion did not at first appear as particularly relevant from a Nordic perspective. The Nordic countries were at the time well known for their stability, egalitarianism and high levels of political participation (Goul Andersen and Hoff 2001). However, along with the economic downturn in the 1990s, a gloomier outlook of the functioning of democracy started to spread amongst the Nordic countries as well, not the least due to decreasing levels of turnout, party membership and trust in political institutions. This chapter will take a closer look at the relationship between voters and representative democracy and how well the characterisation of the Nordic countries as 'happy democracies' stands the test, by analysing turnout in elections and satisfaction with democracy.

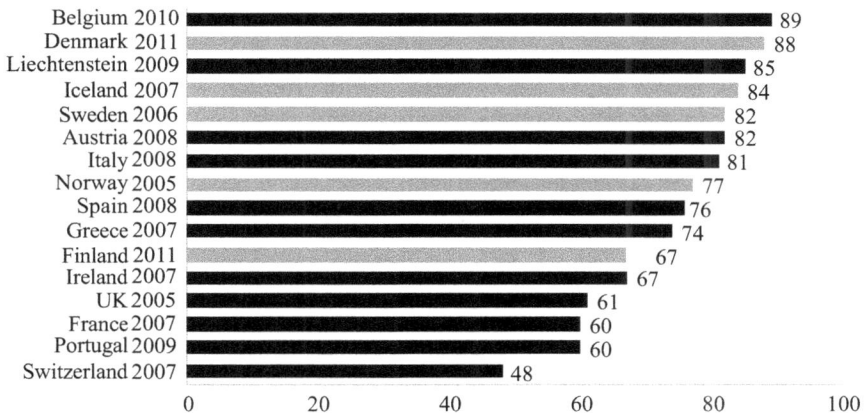

Figure 4.1: Turnout in recent elections (per cent)

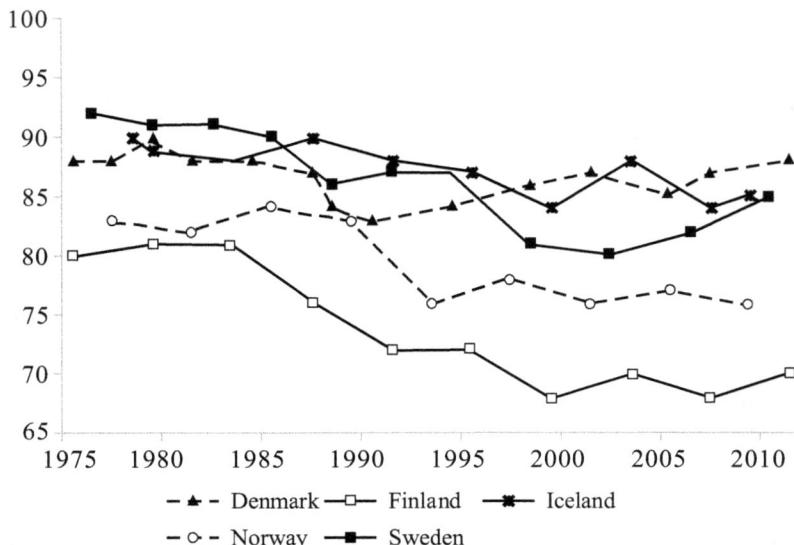

Figure 4.2: Turnout in parliamentary elections since 1975 (per cent)

A comparative outlook reveals that the view of the Nordic countries as a homogenous group of countries with an active citizenry and high levels of turnout is slightly exaggerated. On the contrary, it seems as if there are substantial differences within the Nordic sphere. When looking at the turnout rates in the last parliamentary election held in each Western European country, we indeed find that Denmark, Iceland and Sweden all belong to the top five (Figure 4.1). Moreover, the other countries found in the top all utilise compulsory voting systems, although with varying degrees of sanctions. Norway and, in particular, Finland, do however play in a different league.[1]

As stands clear from Figure 4.2, decreasing levels of turnout in parliamentary elections have indeed hit all of the Nordic countries during the last twenty years. The extent of the decrease and the level of departure are, however, very different from one country to another. The variation between the two extreme cases – Finland on the one hand, and Denmark and Iceland on the other – is quite remarkable. Not only did these three countries enter the period at different levels, but while turnout in Denmark and Iceland has decreased with around five percentage points since

---

1. In the latest Finnish parliamentary election in April 2011 the level of turnout reported was 70.5 per cent of Finnish citizens resident in Finland. Official Finnish statistics does however not, since 1975, include Finnish citizens living abroad. The result presented in Figure 4.1 is the comparative turnout rate used by international IDEA that includes all Finnish citizens that are entitled to vote independently of their country of residence whereas Figure 4.2 only includes Finnish citizens resident in Finland.

1975, Finland has suffered a corresponding drop of twelve points. The pattern for Norway and Sweden falls somewhere in-between. Until 1985, Sweden had the highest turnout of the Nordic countries but the drop between 1976 and 2002 was as large as 10 percentage points. During the last two elections in 2006 and 2010, both of which were close races between two clear government alternatives, turnout figures have, however turned back upwards (84.6 per cent in 2010). The level of turnout in parliamentary elections in Norway has never reached the same high levels as in Sweden, Iceland and Denmark. Until the end of the 1980s it was above 80 per cent, but since then the level has decreased to just above 75 per cent. But as in Sweden, the negative general downturn had stopped during the beginning of the new millennium and even turned into a slight increase in turnout rates.

It has been suggested that one of the reasons why Denmark has the highest turnout among the Nordic countries is due to the well established popular right party in Denmark – The Danish People's Party. This party has a strong base among the less politically interested and engaged voters who otherwise might have stayed at home on election day (Elklit *et al.* 2005, *see also* Chapter Nine). The ability of populist parties to mobilise disengaged voters has also been witnessed in the 2011 Finnish and the 2010 Swedish election, where populist parties (the True Finns and the Sweden Democrats) substantially increased their support.

Nordic audits of power and democracy

A clear sign that the general concern of the state of democracy was increasing during the 1990s are the audits of power and democracy that were set up by the governments of Norway, Denmark and Sweden (Amnå *et al.* 2007: 62). The motive behind these attempts to review the conditions of democracy was the falling turnout rates, but an amplified scepticism towards politics and a steady decrease in party members apparently contributed as well. The audits started of with what seemed as relatively similar changes in the prerequisites for democracy in each of the countries but did, interestingly enough, present rather different conclusions regarding the Scandinavian model of strong participatory democracy.

The report from the Danish audit of power was written in a positive spirit and concluded that that democracy was evolving. The Danish voters were presented as active, capable of taking action, as well as strong on resources. Danish voters' political engagement was described as shifting from collectively based towards more individualised acts – a trend that was considered to decrease rather than increase the distance between the political elite and the voters (Togeby *et al.* 2003: 402).

The statement from the Norwegian audit of power was in turn characterised by very gloomy prospects. The system of rule by the people (*folkestyret*) at the national level was portrayed as eroding due to globalisation, lower rates of activity in party organisations and in elections, less distinct profiles of parties, as well as less distinct political alternatives. Popular participation was found to have changed from long-term organisations such as political parties, to short-term action groups and associations. These changed patterns of political engagement among voters

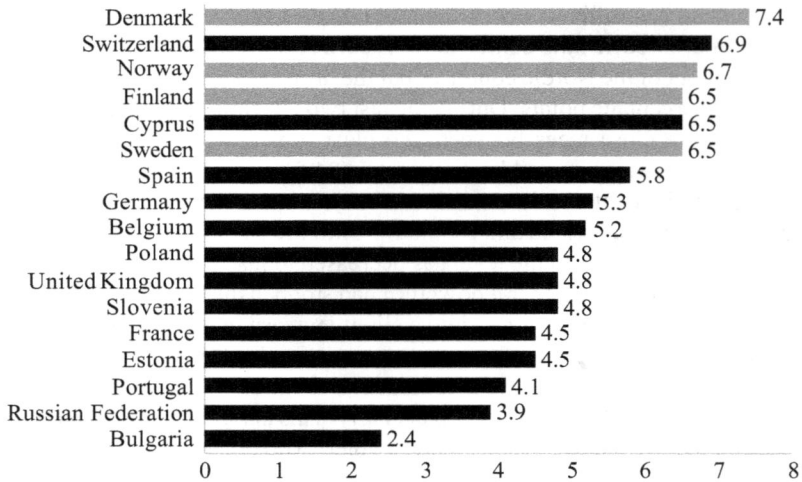

Figure 4.3: Satisfaction with democracy, ESS 2008 (0–10)

were described as complementary, but without the ability to replace or compensate for the weaknesses discovered among the institutions of representative democracy (Østerud et al. 2003: 289–98; Selle and Østerud 2006: 551).

In Sweden a trend of weakening political legitimacy led to the set up of a governmental commission for democracy at the end of the 1990s, and a published report in the year 2000 (Demokratiutredningen 2000: 1). The report more or less discusses the trends and tendencies visible in the Norwegian and Danish audits. Due to its different character, the authors of the Swedish report did not end up with a statement about the state of Swedish democracy, but rather concluded with a normative discussion about what democracy should entail, emphasising the importance of more input in the democratic process on behalf of the voters (Amnå 2006; Demokratiutredningen 2000: 243). The conclusions made by the Swedish democracy commission have been described as falling somewhere in between the gloomy Norwegian and the positive Danish forecasts (Strandberg 2006: 537). In the two other Nordic countries – Finland and Iceland – no large scale audits of power or democracy have been performed so far. However, some work in this direction has however been introduced in the Finnish context, through the *Citizen Participation Policy Programme* introduced after the parliamentary election in 2003. Research also indicates that Finnish democracy on some accounts is under stress with decreasing levels of turnout (Wass and Borg 2012) and a relatively large share of disillusioned citizens (Bengtsson and Mattila 2009; Bengtsson and Christensen 2012). The Icelandic democratic system has also been under considerable strain in recent years, especially since the bank crash in 2008, and the following 'pots and pan revolution' (Onnudóttir and Harðarson 2011).

The three different audits of power and democracy, briefly presented above, clearly end up with different conclusions about the state of democracy. If these diverse conclusions are due to actual disparities, or simply caused by values and predispositions among the members of the audits, is however, hard to tell. Based on previous comparative research and observations it does appear as if the audits might be onto something. The most common conclusion tends to be that Denmark stands out as the healthiest democracy in the Nordic context in terms of its popularity and support, as well as the level of political engagement among its citizens (Goul Andersen and Hoff 2001; Listhaug and Wiberg 1995: 304–5; Dalton 2004: 61; Klingemann 1999: 50). This is supported by international comparative data on political trust and satisfaction with democracy, where Denmark comes out as number one in all national indicators (*see* for example Figure 4.3). However, all of the Nordic countries scored high and from a comparative perspective. Overall, the citizens in the Nordic countries appear as satisfied with representative democracy and its major actors.

Evaluation of regime performance

A positive attitude towards the political system is considered as an important indicator of a healthy democracy (Almond and Verba 1963; Booth and Seligson 2009). In order to interpret how well the relationship between voters and the political elite is perceived as working common to differentiate between different levels of political support, or support for various parts of the political system (Listhaug *et al.* 2009: 311–2). In a conceptualisation by Norris (1999: 12) support is divided into five different levels; support for the political community, regime principles, regime performance, regime institutions and political actors. The main focus of this chapter lies in the third level, i.e. regime performance, that most commonly is operationalised as a question about satisfaction with the way democracy works. This measure can also be described as an instrumental evaluation, as opposed to affective orientation (Almond and Verba 1963; Dalton 1999), or as specific rather than diffuse support (Easton 1965). Although the question is widely accepted as a measure of how well democracy is functioning in practice as opposed to the ideal (Fuchs *et al.* 1995), some reservations can be made; it might also be interpreted as a measure of support for democracy as a value or as tapping satisfaction with the incumbent government (Norris 1999: 11).

The functioning of the democratic system can also be grasped by more detailed questions about input support and output support (Easton 1965). Input support is an assessment of if it is possible to influence the political process and output support, an evaluation of the outcome of the political processes (Listhaug *et al.* 2009). Input support, often labelled external efficacy, measures how responsive or open for influence the political system is perceived to be and is tapped by the question of if it matters who you vote for.[2] One aspect of output support – the

---

2.   This should be considered as a simplified version of external efficacy. The concept is commonly tapped by several different statements concerning beliefs about the responsiveness of governmental authorities to the demands of citizens (Niemi *et al.* 1991: 1407–8).

ability of the political system to produce different policies depending on who is in government, is tapped by a question on if it matters who is in power (Listhaug *et al.* 2009).

Since the ground-breaking study *The Civic Culture* by Almond and Verba (1963), a large number of studies that look at the interplay between institutional design and support for democracy have been published (*see* for example: Klingemann and Fuchs 1995; Kaase and Newton 1995; Anderson and Guillory 1997; Norris 1999). Research focusing specifically on regime performance is however relatively rare. In a global study on democratic development it was found that satisfaction with democracy is higher in highly developed democracies (Klingemann 1999). Others have shown that voters in proportional electoral systems are more satisfied with the way democracy works than voters in majoritarian systems (Lijphart 1997). Moreover, Anderson and Guillory (1997) demonstrate that supporters of government parties (winners) are more satisfied with democracy than those who voted for a party that went into opposition (losers). They also find that the difference between winners and losers is larger in majoritarian democracies than in consensual political systems. However, in a more recent study by Listhaug, Aardal and Opheim Ellis (2009) based on CSES data, no systematic impact of the institutional design is found.

Unfortunately, a great deal of the previous research concerning the interplay between institutional variation and evaluation of democratic performance is of low relevance for our current Nordic perspective. In the context at hand, the variation in terms of electoral systems or the level of democratic development is minimal. The five Nordic countries are all classified as old and well established consensual democracies with proportional electoral systems. However, inside the frame of proportional electoral systems with a consensual profile, there are variations to be found that might influence the way democracy is perceived to function. From this perspective, earlier work by Frederick Weil (1989) appears as relevant. Weil stresses the importance of aspects that might vary inside one country from one time to another, and between countries with similar formal institutional structures, such as party system fragmentation, ideological polarisation, government formation and stability. He concludes that the way institutions develop accountability by means of presenting the voters with real (but not polarised) alternatives is of importance for the confidence voters have in political institutions and the legitimacy of the political system (Listhaug *et al.* 2009).[3]

Another classical argument along the same lines is that if people become indifferent towards party alternatives, they are likely to become less inclined to

---

3. As was presented in Chapter Two, we can find variation between the Nordic countries among some of the factors stressed by Weil (1989). The mean effective threshold, a measure of how hard it is for parties to win a seat in the parliament, varies from slightly over 2 per cent in Denmark to close to 10 per cent in Iceland. And if we look at the most common type of government formation we find that Denmark, Norway and Sweden are used to minority governments with on average between 1.3–2.1 parties in the government. Finland on the other hand, displays an average of 4 parties in the government and a tradition of surplus coalitions while Iceland is used to minimal winning governments with on average 2.3 parties.

vote, even if they are politically engaged (Gilljam and Holmberg 1990; Korpi 1981; Aardal and Valen 1995; Franklin and van der Eijk 1996). A long-term feeling of indifference towards policy alternatives can occur if politics is conceived as unimportant or if parties become increasingly similar, as we might expect them to, according to arguments in line with Kirchheimer's catch-all party theory (1966). Election campaigns that present voters with clear alternatives have also proven to stimulate levels of turnout (Campbell *et al.* 1960; Valen and Narud 1996; Narud 2003; Franklin 2004).

The interpretation of the data presented in Table 4.1 is not self-evident. Among the three indicators presented (regime support, as well as out- and input support), there is no distinct overall pattern. On an overarching level it does however appear as if Denmark is the country in which the most positive evaluation of regime performance can be found. In Denmark, alongside with Norway, the preceptions of democracy is more positive than in the other three countries. In Denmark we also find the highest input support, i.e. the highest belief in that it matters who you vote for. On the other hand, Danish voters appear to have a less enthusiastic view of the importance of who is in power, i.e. the level of output support (*see also* Andersen 2007: 337).

Two countries with more or less the opposite tendencies, compared to Denmark, are Iceland and Finland. Here we find a relatively moderate support for democracy and Finnish and Icelandic voters are not very impressed with the act of voting as a means of making a difference. On the other hand, the level of output support is comparatively high. Icelandic and Finnish voters thus perceive that it makes a difference as to who gains power. Norway displays the most variation concerning the three different measures. Norwegian voters are the most satisfied with the way democracy works, their input support is at a medium level, and their output support is the lowest among the Nordic countries. The puzzling result implies that Norwegian voters consider that democracy works very well, that it is relatively important who you vote for, but they are less enthusiastic about if it makes a difference what party or parties gain power. Swedish voters also display low levels of output support and fall somewhere in between on the other two measures.

The results presented in Table 4.1 might seem scattered at first sight. However, there seems to be a tendency towards a positive relationship between high satisfaction with regime performance (satisfaction with the way democracy works)

Table 4.1: Attitudes towards regime performance (per cent agreeing with)

	Denmark 2007	Finland 2007	Iceland 2007	Norway 2005	Sweden 2006
Satisfaction with democracy	86	76	69	88	79
Matters who you vote for	80	70	72	75	75
Matters who is in power	68	72	76	63	65
n	4 018	1 422	1 541	2 012	1 219

and input support, i.e. that it matters who you vote for. On the other hand countries that score high on these accounts (Norway, Denmark and to some extent Sweden) display lower levels of output support. In order to be satisfied with the way the democratic system functions it thus appears that the feeling that it matters who you vote for – that is, real alternatives to choose from are offered to voters in the election – is more important than the actual results of the political game. This is in line with Weil (1989) who, in his comparative study of political support, concludes that voters are less interested with what the system gives them and care more whether they are presented with real alternatives that respond to their choices.

Finland might serve as an illustration of the opposite relationship, i.e. moderate support for democracy and input support but high levels of output support. In Finland parties are reluctant to discuss in terms of alternative government coalitions during the election campaigns. Bargaining about government positions takes place after the election and parties prefer to keep all doors open during the campaign. As a consequence, it is difficult for voters to predict the impact of their vote on the process of government formation and virtually impossible to use the vote to make a statement about what type of government they prefer. The Finnish culture of consensus and coalition building also implies that the differences between parties, or the way parties strive to distinguish themselves ideologically from each other during the election campaign, is down played. The governments that are formed after the election are traditionally strong surplus coalitions with parties from different sides of the ideological scale and the remaining opposition is very weak. From this perspective it is logical for voters to have – from a Nordic viewpoint – a relatively negative sense of how well democracy is working, and how important it is who you vote for, but on the other hand, to emphasise the importance of who is in power. To some extent, this is also true for Iceland. Usually, minimum winning coalitions are formed, but the coalition system is quite open; virtually all parties can work with all other parties, despite their ideological differences (Harðarson and Kristinsson 2008, 2010a; Indridason 2005).

The results found here also correspond relatively well with the findings by Anderson (2011), in his comparative study based on CSES-data. Although using different and more specific concepts that grasp how well elections, parties or leaders represent voters views, the general tendency is the same. Danish voters score the highest on all accounts while Finnish and Icelandic voters feel less well represented. Results for Sweden and Norway are mixed (Anderson 2011: 217).

The results presented so far, concerning the development in turnout over time as well as evaluations of regime performance by voters of today, reveal some interesting differences. Overall it is stands clear that Danish democracy plays in a league of its own with high levels of turnout and a positive evaluation of democracy made by Danish voters. On the other side of the scale we find Finland, where turnout and the evaluation of regime performance clearly displays more negative values than in most other countries. The patterns concerning the other three countries, Iceland, Norway and Sweden, are less clear cut. So is unfortunately our understanding of the differences between the five countries.

Individual level analyses

In the next section we will look into the individual correlates of two different aspects of how voters relate to the representative democratic system, factors that have been presented and discussed at the aggregate level in previous sections. The first aspect is turnout, an indirect measure of regime performance grasped by the interest to participate in the election of political representatives and formal decision makers in the democratic system. The second, and more direct measure of regime performance, is satisfaction with democracy.

Turnout

Turnout in parliamentary elections is relatively often used as an indicator of the state of democracy, or as Russell Dalton expresses it (2008: 76): 'Without public involvement in the process, democracy lacks both its legitimacy and its guiding force'. In recent decades we have witnessed a decreased interest from citizens to participate in many of the activities strongly related to representative democracy, such as voting and party activity, a trend that has raised a growing worry among political scientists as well as politicians. If voters do not bother to turn out and vote, it is taken as a sign of dissatisfaction or frustration. In order to evaluate the causes and consequences of turnout it is important to look at its sources.

Turnout in elections is a well explored and thoroughly analysed aspect of the literature on elections and voting behaviour. In an often cited study from 1995, Sidney Verba and his colleagues state that voters choose not to participate in elections because: 1) they cannot, 2) they do not want to, or 3) nobody asked. The first reason is concentrated on resources that are needed for participation such as time, skills and money, what is commonly explained by socioeconomic status or the 'SES model'. The second aspect, in turn, deals with the absence of emotional engagement with politics, i.e. a lack of interest, motivation or meaningfulness. The third explanation implies absence of, or isolation from various channels of recruitment such as social networks at the workplace, at church, contacts to a political party or other organisations (Nevitte *et al.* 2009).

Recent research from the Nordic context has, to a large extent, focused on age and more specifically the role that the younger generations play in the, on most accounts, decreasing levels of turnout (Holmberg and Oscarsson 2007; Wass 2008; Bhatti and Hansen 2012a, 2012b). The well established life-cycle effect (Milbrath 1965) has been demonstrated to be complemented by generational effects, referring to long lasting differences in turnout between various age groups. In particular, voters entering the electorate since the 1980s appear to be turning out to vote less frequently than previous generations (Persson and Oscarsson 2010; Wass 2007; Persson, Wass and Oscarsson 2013).

In the following analysis we will compare the importance of resources (age, education, civil status, gender, knowledge and employment) and motivational factors (political awareness, ideology, party identification) for turning out to vote in the five Nordic countries. In order to explore the extent to which there are consistent cross-national patterns, results are presented for each country separately.

When looking at the overall turnout levels in Table 4.2 where turnout for different groups of voters are presented, alongside with 95 per cent confidence intervals and number of respondents, it stands clear that there is a tendency for overreporting and self-selection of high turnout respondents. Compared to the aggregated figures of factual turnout presented in Figure 4.1, the numbers of reported turnout are, in most cases substantially higher. Over reporting is especially a problem in Finland (+15 percentage points), Denmark (+13 percentage points) and Norway (+12 percentage points). In Sweden (+7 percentage points) and Iceland (+1 percentage points) there is less of a problem. In Sweden, where voter turnout is checked against the official statistics the slightly higher turnout rate (+ 7 percentage points) in the election study is thus due to a slightly distorted sample (self-selection of high turnout respondents). In Iceland, the excellent correspondence is, on the other hand, attained without official statistics, which indicates an absence of over reporting. In the three previous cases with an over reporting of more than 10 per cent, it is likely to be due to both distortion and the respondent's reluctance to admit to not having voted. In the case of Denmark, where a high real turnout level is combined with a strong tendency for over reporting (and a more self-selected sample) the reported level of turnout in the election study comes close to 100 per cent. This in turn does strongly limit the possible variation between different groups of voters and the variation of explanation.

This said, we still find many of the well-known patterns of turnout in the descriptive statistics presented in Table 4.2. One of the most apparent differences is found among different age groups, where turnout is increasing relatively substantially between the ages of 18 and 54 and then stabilises, or decreases slightly (*see* Bhatti *et al.* 2012 for an exception to this rule). The variation among different age groups appears to be particularly strong in Finland, where reported turnout among 18 to 24 year olds is as low as 57 per cent, compared to 91 per cent among those who are 65 or older. A similar pattern with low turnout-levels among the youngest is, however, found in Norway and in Iceland as well. Expectations are also confirmed for civil status, where voters who are married or living together with a partner, turn out to vote more frequently than voters who are single (Blais 2000; Wolfinger and Rosenstone 1980; Bhatti and Hansen 2012a, 2012b; Martikainen and Wass 2002; Oscarsson and Holmberg 2013). Here the largest differences are found in Iceland (11 percentage points) and Norway (13 percentage points).

Education is another classic decisive factor included in the SES model, where social economic status is used to explain variation in turnout (the 'cannot'-alternative among Verba *et al.*'s three explanations). The importance of education stands out particularly in Finland, where the difference in reported turnout among voters with low and high education is 18 percentage points; an effect that might be due to the mandatory preferential voting system used in Finland (*see* Chapter Six). According to Gallego (2010), lower-educated citizens are more likely to abstain in elections using open rather than closed lists, due to the higher information costs involved. Also employment seems to matter a great deal in most countries, where the largest difference commonly is found between blue collar and higher white collar workers (20 percentage points in Finland and 10 in Iceland, Norway and Sweden).

Table 4.2: Turnout among different groups of voters

	Denmark 2007			Finland 2007			Iceland 2007			Norway 2005			Sweden 2006		
	%	[CI]*	n	%	[CI]*	n	%	[CI]*	n	%	[CI]*	n	%	[CI]*	n
Gender															
Men	97	[97–98]	1 992	83	[80–86]	721	87	[84–89]	774	89	[87–91]	1 065	88	[86–89]	1 585
Women	98	[97–98]	2 014	82	[79–85]	700	86	[83–99]	767	89	[87–91]	947	91	[90–93]	1 526
Age															
18–24	95	[92–98]	229	57	[48–66]	137	75	[69–81]	228	74	[68–79]	228	83	[79–87]	362
25–34	96	[94–98]	522	75	[69–82]	214	83	[78–88]	265	86	[82–90]	313	88	[85–91]	498
35–44	97	[96–98]	673	75	[68–81]	203	92	[89–96]	293	92	[89–95]	424	88	[86–91]	465
45–54	98	[97–99]	732	89	[85–93]	237	90	[86–93]	292	93	[90–95]	395	91	[89–93]	553
55–64	98	[97–99]	853	89	[85–93]	285	90	[86–94]	240	94	[91–96]	339	91	[88–93]	576
65+	98	[97–99]	989	91	[88–95]	346	84	[80–89]	223	92	[89–95]	306	93	[91–95]	557
Civil status															
Single	96	[95–97]	1 281	79	[76–83]	574	79	[75–82]	497	80	[77–83]	630	85	[83–87]	1 102
Married/living tog.	98	[98–99]	2 737	85	[82–87]	847	90	[88–92]	1044	93	[92–95]	1 382	92	[90–93]	2 009
Urbanisation															
Countryside	97	[96–99]	1 577	88	[82–93]	163	85	[82–88]	636	87	[84–89]	658	88	[86–91]	505
–	98	[97–98]	1 721	82	[79–84]	914	–	–	–	–	–	–	90	[89–91]	2 155
Big city	98	[96–99]	684	82	[77–87]	345	87	[85–89]	905	90	[89–92]	1 352	88	[85–91]	451

(Cont'd)

Table 4.2: (Cont'd)

	Denmark 2007			Finland 2007			Iceland 2007			Norway 2005			Sweden 2006		
	%	[CI]*	n	%	[CI]*	n	%	[CI]*	n	%	[CI]*	n	%	[CI]*	n
Education															
Compulsory	95	[94–97]	781	76	[72–81]	374	80	[77–83]	567	81	[77–86]	300	84	[82–87]	701
Lower secondary	98	[97–99]	2 763	82	[79–85]	781	89	[86–92]	572	86	[84–88]	913	87	[85–89]	1 245
Higher education	98	[97–99]	473	94	[91–97]	266	91	[88–94]	402	96	[94–97]	799	96	[94–97]	1 109
Employment															
Outside labour m.	97	[96–98]	1 510	84	[80–87]	386	83	[80–86]	548	85	[82–88]	660	91	[89–93]	864
Blue collar	96	[95–97]	805	73	[68–78]	300	83	[79–87]	282	84	[79–88]	249	87	[84–90]	403
Self-employed	97	[95–99]	241	86	[79–93]	103	91	[87–95]	169	90	[85–95]	150	85	[79–91]	135
Lower white collar	99	[98–100]	709	86	[81–92]	172	84	[79–89]	238	93	[91–95]	562	94	[92–95]	668
Higher white collar	98	[98–99]	753	93	[89–97]	184	93	[91–96]	304	94	[91–96]	391	96	[94–99]	272
Party identification															
No	96	[95–97]	1 852	73	[69–79]	666	80	[77–83]	796	86	[84–88]	1062	89	[88–91]	1 630
Yes	99	[99–99]	2 158	91	[89–93]	755	93	[91–94]	745	93	[91–94]	950	96	[94–97]	716
Political awareness															
Low	95	[94–96]	1 371	65	[60–70]	464	75	[72–79]	498	75	[71–78]	530	87	[84–90]	656
Medium	99	[98–99]	1 492	88	[85–91]	438	89	[87–92]	558	92	[90–95]	541	94	[93–96]	831
High	99	[98–99]	1 155	92	[89–95]	497	94	[92–96]	485	96	[94–97]	941	97	[95–98]	374

(Cont'd)

Table 4.2: (Cont'd)

	Denmark 2007			Finland 2007			Iceland 2007			Norway 2005			Sweden 2006		
	%	[CI]*	n	%	[CI]*	n	%	[CI]*	n	%	[CI]*	n	%	[CI]*	n
Political knowledge															
Low	95	[93–96]	1 074	64	[58–70]	317	68	[62–73]	298	86	[83–89]	631	85	[82–88]	544
Medium	98	[98–99]	1 488	84	[80–88]	424	90	[88–92]	909	87	[84–87]	715	94	[92–96]	629
High	99	[98–99]	1 456	90	[88–93]	681	93	[90–96]	334	95	[93–97]	666	96	[95–98]	679
Left-right self-placement															
Left	98	[97–99]	1 165	84	[79–89]	206	89	[85–93]	210	91	[89–94]	453	95	[89–94]	476
Middle	97	[96–98]	1 361	84	[82–87]	818	84	[82–86]	1084	88	[86–89]	1242	92	[90–93]	1307
Right	99	[98–99]	1 410	88	[84–92]	301	94	[91–97]	247	93	[90–96]	317	94	[92–97]	323
Ideological extremism															
Low	96	[94–97]	660	82	[77–86]	316	77	[74–81]	551	81	[77–84]	494	90	[87–92]	728
Medium	98	[97–98]	1 665	85	[82–88]	591	91	[89–93]	632	91	[90–93]	987	95	[93–97]	579
High	99	[98–99]	1 611	88	[84–91]	418	92	[89–94]	358	93	[91–96]	531	95	[93–96]	799
Total (all voters)	97	[97–98]	4 018	82	[80–85]	1 422	86	[84–88]	1 541	89	[88–91]	2 012	89	[88–90]	3 111

Note: The data is not weighted (except for Finland which is weighted according to mother tongue). Political knowledge, correct answers to factual political questions. * 95 per cent confidence interval.

When turning to factual political knowledge, relatively distinct differences are found as well (Grönlund 2009; Oscarsson and Holmberg 2013). In Finland reported turnout varies with as much as 26 percentage points from voters with low levels of political knowledge to the most knowledgeable. The variation is almost as large in Iceland (25 per cent), but more moderate in Norway (11 per cent), Sweden (12 per cent) and Denmark (4 per cent). Almost as large a difference in turnout is found for political awareness, which grasps the extent to which voters are interested in politics and follow politics in the media, but as in the previous case, it varies from one country to another. Yet another important factor is party identification. A mobilising effect seems to exist in all of the five Nordic countries, but varying from almost 20 (in Finland) to 3 (in Denmark) percentage points.

In order to control the tendencies found in the descriptive analyses the result of a multivariate regression analysis is presented in Table 4.3. Results confirm that age is an important factor when it comes to determining who turns out at the polls and who stays home. All countries in the first model, which can be described as the pure SES model, has age presenting a significant effect. In the second model, which also includes political attitudes and behaviour, the effect of age is less consistent and preserved only in Finland and Norway. Not surprisingly we find the strongest age effect in Finland. If age increases by a standard deviation around the mean age, the probability for voters to turn out increases by 8 percentage points in model 1 and by 5 percentage points when controlling for political factors. The corresponding effect in Norway is 4 and 2 percentage points. Research from the Swedish context has shown that political knowledge displays a nearly identical curve linear relationship with turnout as age, and hence, extinguishes the effect of age on turnout. Previous research has often described the effect of age on turnout as a curvilinear effect, where turnout increases with age until middle-age, then flattens out in order to decrease slightly among the older age groups. Tests (not displayed here) have shown however, that this is not the case among the five Nordic countries.[4] Analyses of turnout in Denmark and Finland, on validated public records (government's voting lists), do however strongly confirm the curvilinear effect with the exception among the very young (Bhatti and Hansen 2012a, 2012b).

The effect of education, also well documented in the literature, shows a less consistent effect than expected. It strongly increases the probability of voting in Finland, Norway and Sweden but the effect is less consistent in Denmark and Iceland. In Finland, where we find the strongest effect, the probability of turning out increases by 12 (model 1) and 8 (model 2) percentage points respectively, if voters have a high rather than a compulsory level of education. In Norway the increased probability is about half as large and in Sweden slightly lower. Civil status does not show a significant effect in Sweden and Finland, being married or living together as married increases the probability of turning out at the polls in the other three countries. The strongest gender effect is found in Sweden, where

---

4.   Iceland is an exception but for clarity the presented analyses only includes a linear age variable.

Table 4.3: Modelling the probability of turnout – marginal change (percentage points)

	Denmark 2007		Finland 2007		Iceland 2007		Norway 2005		Sweden 2006	
	Model 1	Model 2	Model 1	Model 2	Model 1	Model 2	Model 1	Model 2	Model 1	Model 2
Age in election year	1***	0	8***	5***	3***	1	4***	2***	2***	0
Female	0	-1**	0	2*	0	3	0	2**	4***	4***
Lower secondary edu.	1	0	2	1	4	2	2*	1	1	0
Higher education	1	0	12***	8***	3	0	8***	4***	5***	3**
Civil status (not single)	1***	1**	3*	3	7***	5***	4***	3***	2	1
Self Employed	0	0	0	-2	8***	5**	2	2	-2	-2
Lower white collar	1**	1**	2	1	6**	5**	3**	2*	1	1
Higher white collar	1	0	4	1	11***	8***	3**	1	2	2
Blue collar	0	0	-6***	-3	5*	5**	1	2*	1	1
Degree of urbanisation	1*	1	-4	-6**	1	0	1	1	-1	-1
Public sector	0	0	2	2	2	1	0	-1	0	0
Party ID		2***		7***		3*		1*		2*
Left-right self-placement		0		1		11**		-1		-2
Left-right extremeness		1**		0		7**		1		1
Political awareness		5***		33***		19***		33***		8***
Political knowledge		2***		26***		8***		3**		8***
No. respondents	3 960	3 960	1 171	1 171	1 737	1 737	1 711	1 711	1 398	1 398
McFadden pseudo R^2	0.05	0.16	0.07	0.16	0.11	0.22	0.08	0.13	0.12	0.24
Log likelihood	-436	-385	-428	-386	-451	-395	-373	-355	-576	-496
Chi^2	47.26	148.22	63.45	146.24	114.56	227.31	64.78	101.52	150.89	309.95

Note: *p<0.1,**p<0.05,***p<0.01. Education (Ref category: compulsory schooling); Employment (Ref category: Outside the labour market) Individual weights are used for Finland 2007. The marginal change in percentage points on the dependent variable when the independent variable changes from 0 to 1 with other variables held at their mean. The marginal change for age is the change from ½ standard deviation below the mean to ½ above the mean on age with all other variables held at their mean.

women are more likely to vote than men (Oscarsson and Holmberg 2011). The effect is also positive for Finland and Denmark (Wass 2008; Bhatti and Hansen 2011). Among the different dummy variables controlling for occupation, where outside the labour market is used as a control group, we find a positive effect for white collar workers in several but not all countries.

Three factors turn out as significant throughout the analyses and that is party identification, factual political knowledge and political awareness. The probability for voters who identify with a party, voters with a high level of political knowledge and voters who are politically aware, to turn out at the polls on the election day, is consistently higher than for others. The effect for political awareness is particularly strong in Finland and Norway. In both of these countries the probability of a politically aware voter (a voter that follows media and is interested in politics) to vote is 33 percentage points higher than a voter who scores low on political awareness. Ideological preferences, in turn, only have an impact on turnout in Denmark and Iceland. In Denmark, voters with a distinct ideological preference, either to the left or the right, are more likely to vote. In Iceland the same type of effect is found but it appears to be driven mainly by right-wing voters.

Turnout is a well researched area of electoral behaviour and the factors influencing the tendency for voters to actually vote is often presented as very consistent and stable. From this perspective the relatively great variation found in Table 4.3 is somewhat surprising. Not even the classical variables in the SES model, such as age, education or civil status display similar, consistent effects in all countries. Socio demographic factors influence who turns out at the polls and who stays at home, but the effect varies from one country to another. Instead party identification, the level of knowledge and awareness, display the most consistent and strongest effects, three politically oriented factors which are relatively close to the dependent variable.

Satisfaction with democracy

After analysing an indirect indicator of regime performance – that is if voters bother to turn out to vote or not – we continue with the very direct measure of satisfaction with the way democracy works. According to research on political culture performed in the 1960s, political support is considered as an important element of any political regime, but especially for democracies (Almond and Verba 1963). Crumbling support can, from this perspective, be considered as unhealthy and even dangerous. Since the 1990s, the idea of criticism as a healthy aspect of democracy and as a force for reform has, however, become more widely accepted (Klingemann 1999). According to this view, critique and dissatisfaction constitutes an important part of a true democracy. The consequences of critique and dissatisfaction with democracy and its actors can thus be interpreted in two radically different ways: as a threat or as a stimulator for further development.

According to Dalton (2004) the implications of the public's growing skepticism towards politics, its actors and institutions, ultimately depends on from where it originates. If dissatisfaction has increased mainly among lower-income and less resourceful individuals, it can be considered as a sign that citizens at the margins of society are becoming politically alienated. This, in turn, is likely to have more severe implications if dissatisfaction continues to grow. If voters refrain from the democratic system rather than crave improvement or further democratic development, we might be faced with the crisis of late capitalism predicted in the 1970s and 1980s (Offe 1972; Habermas 1975; Bobbio 1987).

As the results in Table 4.1 showed, there are relatively large discrepancies between the Nordic countries concerning the aggregated evaluation made by voters. The Norwegian and Danish voters show the highest satisfaction rates concerning regime performance, with 88 and 86 per cent satisfied. Sweden and Finland fall in between with 79 and 76 per cent, and Icelandic voters are the least satisfied with 69 per cent. But in order to understand the consequences of dissatisfaction we will, in this section, move beyond these aggregated numbers and analyse the correlates of the evaluation made by voters in each country.

Previous research demonstrate that political support is due to many things. Winning or losing matters. However, winning is less important for satisfaction with democracy in consensual democracies (Anderson and Guillory 1997). On a general level we might also expect citizens who are interested in, and well informed about, the political system to be more optimistic about the way the political regime functions (Anderson and Guillory 1997: 72). Party identification is also likely to matter since party identifiers are more prone to caring about the outcome of the election and to be able to recognise important differences between government alternatives, or parties (Listhaug *et al.* 2009: 328). It is however less clear cut how different socio-demographic factors interplay with satisfaction with democracy.

We begin by looking at the descriptive statistics presented in Table 4.4. Among the socio-demographic variables, education and employment are the only ones that appear to show a relatively consistent effect. Higher education is associated with higher satisfaction rates in all of the five countries and the largest differences between voters with low and high levels of education is found in Sweden (18 percentage points). The impact of education is somewhat weaker in Norway (10 percentage points), Finland (8), Denmark (7) and Iceland (5).

Among the different groups of employment we find that blue collar workers or voters positioned outside the labour market, in general, display lower satisfaction with democracy than white collar workers, with the largest difference found in Sweden (18 percentage points) and Finland (13 percentage points). When it comes to age there is no overall distinct pattern, although it seems as if a relatively linear effect is detectable for Iceland, where voters belonging to the older generations stand out as more dissatisfied than the younger ones.

As expected, we find that party identification, political awareness and political knowledge, in most cases, contribute to a more positive view of the way democracy works. The clearest differences are, however, found among the politically charged variables, both concerning different groups of voters and tendencies from one country to another. The strongest results have to do with ideological preferences and vote choice. Previous research has found that voting for a winner is of importance, and this clearly seems to be the case in all the Nordic countries except

Table 4.4: Satisfaction with democracy (per cent very or rather satisfied)

	Denmark 2007			Finland 2007			Iceland 2007			Norway 2005			Sweden 2006		
	%	[CI]	n	%	[CI]	n	%	[CI]	n	%	[CI]	n	%	[CI]	n
Gender															
Men	88	[87–90]	2 014	75	[72–79]	720	69	[66–72]	774	88	[86–90]	1 065	80	[77–83]	618
Women	84	[82–86]	1 992	77	[74–81]	702	69	[66–72]	767	87	[85–90]	947	79	[75–82]	601
Age															
18–24	86	[82–91]	229	83	[76–89]	139	76	[70–81]	228	86	[81–90]	228	79	[72–86]	148
25–34	88	[85–90]	522	78	[72–84]	217	74	[68–79]	265	87	[84–91]	313	81	[75–86]	187
35–44	87	[85–90]	673	74	[67–80]	193	69	[64–75]	293	86	[83–89]	424	82	[77–87]	218
45–54	86	[84–89]	732	77	[71–83]	226	71	[65–76]	292	91	[89–94]	395	80	[74–85]	202
55–64	86	[84–88]	853	73	[68–79]	285	64	[58–70]	240	89	[86–92]	339	74	[69–80]	240
65+	84	[83–87]	989	76	[71–81]	362	59	[52–65]	223	86	[82–90]	306	80	[75–86]	224
Civil status															
Single	83	[81–85]	1 281	77	[74–81]	582	67	[63–71]	497	86	[83–88]	630	75	[71–79]	404
Married/living together	87	[86–89]	2 737	76	[73–79]	840	70	[67–73]	1 044	89	[87–90]	1382	81	[79–84]	815
Urbanisation															
Countryside	87	[84–89]	1 577	71	[64–79]	163	68	[65–72]	636	89	[86–91]	658	77	[71–83]	457
–	86	[85–88]	1 721	76	[73–79]	914	–	–	–	–	–	–	79	[76–82]	586
Big city	85	[82–87]	684	79	[74–84]	345	69	[66–72]	905	87	[85–89]	1352	84	[79–89]	176
Education															
Compulsory	81	[78–84]	781	75	[71–81]	374	66	[62–70]	567	81	[77–85]	300	69	[64–75]	298
Lower secondary	87	[85–88]	2 764	75	[71–78]	781	70	[67–74]	572	87	[85–89]	913	78	[74–82]	453
Higher education	88	[85–91]	473	83	[78–88]	266	71	[66–75]	402	91	[89–93]	799	87	[83–90]	467

(Cont'd)

Table 4.4: (Cont'd)

	Denmark 2007			Finland 2007			Iceland 2007			Norway 2005			Sweden 2006		
	%	[CI]	n	%	[CI]	n	%	[CI]	n	%	[CI]	n	%	[CI]	n
Employment															
Outside labour m.	84	[82–85]	1 510	77	[73–81]	476	64	[60–68]	548	84	[81–87]	660	78	[74–81]	440
Blue collar worker	85	[82–87]	805	71	[66–76]	418	70	[65–75]	282	84	[79–88]	249	70	[65–76]	227
Self-employed	88	[84–92]	241	79	[72–87]	121	66	[59–73]	169	90	[85–95]	150	81	[71–90]	72
Lower white collar	88	[85–90]	709	76	[69–82]	205	77	[72–82]	238	91	[89–93]	562	84	[80–88]	344
Higher white collar	90	[88–92]	753	84	[79–90]	202	72	[67–77]	304	91	[88–94]	391	88	[83–94]	130
Party identification															
No	85	[83–86]	1 852	70	[67–74]	666	65	[61–68]	796	87	[85–89]	1062	77	[74–80]	828
Yes	87	[86–89]	2 158	82	[79–85]	756	73	[70–77]	745	88	[86–89]	950	84	[80–87]	391
Political awareness															
Low	84	[82–86]	1 371	67	[62–72]	464	68	[64–72]	498	83	[80–86]	530	77	[72–81]	286
Medium	87	[86–89]	1 492	78	[73–82]	483	70	[66–74]	558	90	[87–93]	541	82	[79–86]	416
High	87	[85–89]	1 155	82	[79–86]	497	69	[65–73]	485	89	[87–91]	941	82	[77–87]	194
Political knowledge															
Low	82	[80–84]	1 074	69	[63–75]	317	64	[58–69]	298	86	[83–88]	631	71	[65–76]	251
Medium	87	[86–89]	1 488	76	[71–80]	424	69	[66–72]	909	88	[85–90]	715	83	[78–87]	301
High	88	[86–89]	1 456	80	[77–84]	681	73	[68–78]	334	90	[87–92]	666	86	[83–90]	339
Left-right self-placement															
Left	77	[75–79]	1 165	67	[60–74]	206	48	[41–55]	210	92	[89–94]	453	82	[78–87]	210
Middle	89	[87–90]	1 874	77	[73–80]	818	67	[67–73]	892	88	[86–89]	1242	82	[79–85]	651
Right	94	[92–95]	897	86	[82–90]	301	82	[77–86]	439	83	[78–87]	317	84	[79–90]	178

(Cont'd)

Table 4.4: (Cont'd)

	Denmark 2007			Finland 2007			Iceland 2007			Norway 2005			Sweden 2006		
	%	[CI]	n	%	[CI]	n	%	[CI]	n	%	[CI]	n	%	[CI]	n
Distance from mean left-right self-placement /Ideological extremism															
Low	83	[80–85]	660	71	[65–76]	316	64	[60–68]	892	86	[83–89]	494	79	[75–83]	357
Medium	89	[88–91]	1 665	79	[75–82]	591	72	[69–76]	509	89	[88–91]	987	85	[81–89]	294
High	85	[83–86]	1 611	80	[76–84]	418	70	[65–75]	140	86	[83–89]	531	83	[80–97]	446
Voted for a winner															
No	80	[79–82]	2 573	68	[65–72]	728	59	[56–63]	733	83	[81–85]	1 141	76	[73–79]	703
Yes	96	[95–97]	1 445	87	[84–90]	694	78	[75–80]	808	94	[92–95]	871	84	[81–87]	516
Turnout															
No	72	[64–81]	101	66	[60–72]	234	59	[52–65]	213	82	[76–87]	217	70	[62–78]	126
Yes	86	[85–87]	3 917	79	[76–81]	1 188	71	[68–73]	1 328	88	[87–90]	1 795	80	[78–83]	1 093
Total (all voters)	86	[85–88]	4 018	76	[74–79]	1 422	69	[67–71]	1 541	88	[86–89]	2 012	79	[77–82]	1 219

Note: The data is not weighted (except for Finland that is weighted in order to control for an oversample of Swedish speaking voters). Political knowledge, correct answers to factual political questions. * 95% Confidence interval.

in Denmark. The strongest effect is found in Finland and Iceland (+19 percentage points). Concerning ideology, we find that right-wing voters, in most cases, are far more satisfied with democracy than voters with a preference to the left. In Iceland less than 50 per cent of those having a distinct left-wing preference are satisfied with the way democracy works. The corresponding share among right-wing voters is 82 per cent (+34). A result in the same direction, but more modest to its extent, is found in Finland (+21 percentage points for right-wing voters) and Denmark (+17 percentage points). However, in Norway we find the opposite result, with left-wing voters being more satisfied than right-wing voters (-8).

A logical explanation might be that the results are due to the ideological colour of the government in power. This interpretation would certainly fit the consistent effect found for winners/losers, where those who voted for a party that formed the government after the election are more satisfied than those who voted for a party that lost the election. And indeed the pattern is consistent for Finland, where a right-wing-centre dominated coalition came into power as a result of the election in 2007 and for Norway, where a left-wing-centre coalition was formed in 2005. It cannot, on the other hand, explain the widespread dissatisfaction found among left-wing voters in Iceland since the two winning parties, i.e. the two parties that constituted the government after the election, were the Social Democratic Alliance (*Samfylkingin*) and the right-wing Independence Party (*Sjálfstæðisflokkurinn*).

In order to get a more nuanced picture of the tendencies displayed in the descriptive table, multivariate analyses are performed and presented in Table 4.5. Most of the tendencies can be confirmed in the multivariate analyses but some new are unravelled as well. Concerning the socio-demographic variables such as age, gender, civil status, employment and education, it is hard to detect consistent results throughout all of the Nordic countries. Age, for example, displays a significant effect in all countries except in Sweden. The probability of being satisfied with the way democracy works is, however, higher among young voters in Denmark, Finland, and in Iceland, while it is lower in Norway. In Norway and Sweden we find that voters with a high level of education are more likely to be satisfied with democracy, while there is no significant effect of education in Denmark, Finland and Iceland. A corresponding pattern is found for white collar workers in Denmark and Norway (and to some extent in Sweden), but not in Finland and Iceland. Voters employed in the public sector are not only more negative about the way democracy works in Denmark, but also in Sweden.

When we turn to the variables included in model 2 we find stronger effects and a slightly more consistent pattern. Voting for a winner has a significant effect on satisfaction with democracy in Finland, Iceland and Norway, a result that was expected based on the findings in Table 4.4. The tendency for right-wing voters to be more positive about the democratic process also holds. The strongest effects by far are found among Icelandic voters where the probability of being satisfied with the way democracy works increases by an astonishing 53 percentage points if you have a right-wing rather than left-wing political preference. A corresponding, but weaker, result is found in Denmark and Finland. The tendency for left-wing voters in Norway found in Table 4.4 can also be confirmed. Being knowledgeable

Table 4.5: Modelling the probability of satisfaction with democracy (very or rather satisfied) – marginal change (percentage point)

	Denmark 2007		Finland 2007		Iceland 2007		Norway 2005		Sweden 2006	
	Model 1	Model 2	Model 1	Model 2	Model 1	Model 2	Model 1	Model 2	Model 1	Model 2
Age in election year	-1**	-2***	-2*	-5***	-5***	-6***	3***	2**	1	-1
Women	3**	1	3	2	-1	4	-1	-2	2	2
Lower secondary	4***	2	0	-2	5*	4	3	3*	4	4
Higher education	3	0	5	-3	5	4	6**	5**	10***	8**
Not single	3**	1	-2	-3	2	0	0	0	4	3
Self employed	1	-1	2	-1	-4	-10*	3	3	-1	-1
Lower white collar	3*	2	-3	-4	7	2	7***	6***	7**	5
Higher white collar	5***	3**	6	1	1	-4	6***	5**	5	2
Blue collar	0	0	-7**	-3	-3	-5	2	2	4	3
Degree of urbanisation	-2	0	4	4	-1	-3	-3	-2	5	5
Employed in Public sector	-5***	-2*	0	-1	-1	1	03*	2	-7**	-7**
Left-right self-placement	/	13***	/	18***	/	53***	/	-3	/	-3
Left-right extremism	/	-5***	/	-3	/	-4	/	-5	/	3
Political awareness	/	4	/	22***	/	-4	/	3	/	-10*
Political knowledge	/	6***	/	9	/	2	/	0	/	19**
Did vote	/	4**	/	9***	/	4	/	4	/	4
Voted for a winner	/	12***	/	12***	/	12***	/	7***	/	1
Party ID	/	2**	/	5**	/	6**	/	0	/	4

(Cont'd)

Table 4.5: (Cont'd)

	Denmark 2007		Finland 2007		Iceland 2007		Norway 2005		Sweden 2006	
	Model 1	Model 2	Model 1	Model 2	Model 1	Model 2	Model 1	Model 2	Model 1	Model 2
No. respondents	3 960	3 960	1 398	1 398	1 171	1 171	1 737	1 737	832	832
McFadden pseudo R^2	0.02	0.11	0.02	0.09	0.01	0.09	0.03	0.06	0.03	0.05
Log likelihood	-1,556	-1,413	-755	-699	-698	-642	-609	-591	-363	-357
Chi^2	57.93	342.33	27.17	138.69	20.43	132.07	39.68	75.36	24.79	37.55

Note: $*p<0.1, **p<0.05, ***p<0.01$. Education (Ref category: compulsory schooling); Employment (Ref category: Outside the labour market) Individual weights are used for Finland 2007. The marginal change in percentage points on the dependent variable when the independent variable changes from 0 to 1 with other variables held at their mean. The marginal change for age is the change from ½ standard deviation below the mean to ½ above the mean on age with all other variables held at their mean.

and/or being aware of what is going on at the political arena indicates a higher satisfaction with democracy in Denmark and, in particular, in Sweden where the probability of being satisfied with democracy increases by 19 percentage points if a voter has a high level of political knowledge rather than a low one. Politically aware voters are more satisfied in Finland.

The overall conclusion is that the factors influencing the extent by which voters are satisfied with the democratic process vary from one country to another. The younger voters do not seem to be more critical than the older ones. On the contrary, it is the middle-aged population which has the most critical perception of the way democracy works in most countries. There are also some indications of higher social status contributing to a more positive view, the exact indicators do, however, vary from one country to another, and the effect is not large. We can thus conclude that there appears to be no strong threat caused by less resourceful individuals at the margins of society in becoming alienated from the democratic system as such.

In line with expectations (Anderson and Guillory 1997) we find that there is a general tendency for politically integrated voters, i.e. voters who are aware, knowledgeable or identifiers of a specific party, to be more satisfied. However, in line with Dalton's statement that the implications of dissatisfaction depend on from where they originate, the result concerning ideology might be considered as troublesome. Right-wing voters are distinctly more positive towards the democratic process than left-wing voters in three out of five countries.

Conclusions

To present the five Nordic countries as exceptionally strong and stable democracies based on popular participation is a slight exaggeration. Indeed they do still, to some extent, stand up to their reputation – at least some of them, and at least to a certain extent. From a comparative perspective it is clear that rates of trust in political actors and institutions is high – with Iceland as the exception (*see also* Chapter Three). In this chapter we have also been able to show that voters in the Nordic countries are comparably satisfied with democracy as a system. However, when it comes to turnout in elections we find relatively large differences from one Nordic country to another. While the electorate in all of the five countries over time has become less active, the development has been far less dramatic in Denmark and Iceland than in Norway and, in particular, in Finland. With regard to turnout for the Danish Parliament (*Folketing*) it has actually been stable with small increases over the last three elections. Not only do the Nordic countries today have very different levels of turnout, the differences were already there when the decreasing trend began in the 1980s. Moreover, the determinants of turnout at the individual level vary from one country to another.

It appears as likely that the variation in turnout has some of its origin in how voters perceive the link between the election results and how politics is run after the election. At least this interpretation holds for the Finnish case, where the oversized and ideologically wide coalitions, common in Finnish politics since the 1980s, have made elections less decisive and hence less interesting for the general voter. Interestingly enough there is no straight line between turnout and satisfaction with democracy, since the least satisfied voters are found in Iceland and the most satisfied in Norway. However, all in all, it appears as if the Danish power study (Togeby *et al.* 2003) was on to something. Danish democracy certainly seems to stand strong and founded on several strong pillars. Danish citizens are comparatively satisfied with the way democracy works, they are politically interested, trust their political actors and institutions, and participate actively both in elections and in other forms of political activities (Goul Andersen and Hoff 2001).

The implications of dissatisfaction with the democratic regime are hard to speculate about. The fact that the differences according to socioeconomic status are relatively marginal in most countries is, however, comforting. It is not the least resourceful citizens in terms of socioeconomic attributes that are the most critical, but rather it appears as if the political resources are more important. In line with previous research, belonging to a winning team matters for how satisfied with democracy voters are in most of the Nordic countries (Anderson and Guillory 1997). This, in turn, indicates that satisfaction with democracy does not stick, but rather that it changes as government alters. Perhaps not very surprising but potentially more troublesome, is the finding that politically well integrated voters are more satisfied than others. Groups at the margins of politics are less likely to mobilise and become politically involved, and might constitute a stable group of dissatisfied, disengaged voters that constitute a problem for the healthy democratic system even if they are not identifiable by the typical socio-economic indicators.

The overall impression is that Nordic democracy from a comparative perspective stands strong, but also that it is a less homogenous group of countries than is often assumed. Much of the Nordic reputation, as strong and vivid democracies, rests on the shoulders of Denmark. In particular, Finland and to some extent Sweden, Norway and Iceland can, on most accounts, be considered as any other stable Western European democracy, nothing more, and nothing less.

Chapter Five

Party Identification in the Nordic Countries

Most Americans have this sense of attachment with one party or the other. […] the strength and direction of party identification are facts of central importance in accounting for attitude and behavior (Campbell *et al.* 1960: 121).

Introduction

Because of the strong party-based democracy in the Nordic countries, the vertical ties between the masses and the political elites were not based mainly on relationships between individual citizens and representatives but rather between well-defined social groups and political parties. In the early twentieth century, interest organisations (e.g. labour unions) and political parties managed to successfully link their political endeavours to well-defined social groups, securing their electoral support. This way, patterns of voting behavior became highly associated with the socio economic structure. And consequently, voters developed stable and strong bonds to particular parties. Group based loyalties to specific parties were then strengthened through the mechanisms of political socialisation-processes of social learning that still structure political preferences and party choice in the Nordic electorates.

The concept of *party identification* is by far the most well known concept referring to the ties between voters and parties (Holmberg 2007). Originally, the Michigan model of party identification was introduced from social psychology and social identity theory, referring to individuals' affective orientation towards a political party (Campbell *et al.* 1960; Miller and Shanks 1996: 120f). This psychological attachment to a particular party was primarily based on emotions and feelings of group belonging, and was therefore expected to be a very stable and lifelong entity. Later, alternative definitions have politicised the concept, highlighting that party identification may also have cognitive and short-term components, depending on the voter's judgements of party policy and retrospective political evaluations (Fiorina 1981).

Since the 1960s, a large number of different measures of party attachment/ adherence/identification/sympathy/closeness belong to the standard set of survey instruments in election studies around the world (Dalton and Weldon 2007). However, in spite of the great impact and popularity of the Michigan model, there has never been a universal standard for asking about party attachment or party identification. Comparative research is problematic since the extent to which citizens in various countries self-identify with a party depends heavily on the exact wording of the question. Minor changes in question wording have been shown to generate very different estimates of the proportion of voters that feel attached to a specific party (Blais *et al.* 2001)

In the Comparative Study of Electoral Systems (CSES), voters are (in most of the countries) asked whether they think of themselves as close to any party. This is a softer measure of partisanship than the classic Michigan measure, since it has been adapted to the conditions of large scale comparative studies of the rich variation of electoral democracies around the world. However, some of the participating countries in the CSES collaboration have occasionally or systematically deviated from the CSES standard instrument, which makes country comparisons tricky.

In Table 5.1 we present a comparative overview of the proportion of party-attached voters in 46 countries in the period 1995–2010. As expected, given the party oriented political culture in the Nordic countries, in a comparative perspective, the proportions of party-attached voters in the Nordic countries in the period 2000–2005 are high and, within a very tight margin, very close to 50 per cent. On average across the three waves of the CSES, the proportion of party-identified voters was the highest in Denmark (52.6) followed by Iceland (52.2 per cent), Finland (51.0), Sweden (50.5), and Norway (47.3).[1]

The country comparison shows that the Nordic countries do not, in any way, stick out but rather group together in mid-range when it comes to the level of party-identified voters. The Nordic countries are at the same level as countries such as France, Canada, Spain, Portugal and Great Britain, where the proportion of party identifiers also score around 50 per cent. Of the old established Western democracies – which we think are most reasonable to compare with in this case – only Australia shows a distinctly *higher* proportion of party-identified voters (84.0 per cent) than the Nordic countries. In countries as Belgium, Germany, the Netherlands, and Ireland, the proportion of party identifiers average in the range 30–40 per cent.

Dealignment in the Nordic countries

The invention of the party identification concept had a particularly great impact on Scandinavian research on voting behaviour. Shortly after the introduction, adapted versions of the Michigan model were introduced by scholars in Norway, Denmark, and Sweden (Campbell and Valen 1961; Särlvik 1970; Listhaug 1988; Holmberg 1994; Borre and Goul Andersen 1997; Berglund 2004) – and a few years later in Iceland (Harðarson 1995). When crossing the North Atlantic, the *directional component* of party identification became almost useless in analyses of political behaviour since the correlation with party choice most of the time exceeded .90 (Thomassen 1976; Holmberg 1994). Instead, there was a full analytic focus on the *strength component*, i.e. whether voters feel weakly or strongly attached to a party or feel unattached. Voters' strength of party identification was a useful analytic tool because it contributed to the explanations of many types of political behaviour.

---

1. Estimates from the European Social Survey 2002 showed a somewhat different rank order of the Nordic countries with Sweden (68.5 per cent 'feel close to a party'), Denmark (66.9 percent), Norway (59.7 percent), and Finland (55.0 percent). *See* Dalton (2013) for more details.

Table 5.1: Party attachments in 46 countries (percentage that are close to any party)

Nation	CSES I 1996–2000	CSES II 2000–2005	CSES III 2005–2010	Average CSES I–III
Australia	83.5	83.9	84.5	84.0
Uruguay	–	–	80.0	80.0
Slovakia	–	–	71.8	71.8
Ukraine	70.5	–	–	70.5
France	–	55.8	71.1	63.5
Greece	–	–	61.3	61.3
Estonia	–	–	59.8	59.8
Israel	64.2	62.4	45.4	57.3
United States	57.0	56.1	–	56.6
Czech Republic	48.8	63.7	–	56.3
Russian Federation	56.1	–	–	56.1
New Zealand	56.3	55.7	48.2	53.4
Denmark	51.4	50.0	56.3	52.6
Mexico	48.2	51.9	56.9	52.3
Iceland	51.6	54.2	50.9	52.2
Canada	52.1	–	–	52.1
Spain	42.8	61.3	–	52.1
Finland	–	46.6	55.4	51.0
Sweden	53.1	48.8	49.5	50.5
Austria	–	–	49.7	49.7
Portugal	51.8	51.8	45.3	49.6
Poland	53.7	41.8	52.8	49.4
Brazil	–	–	48.0	48.0
Norway	52.9	41.3	47.8	47.3
Romania	47.1	–	–	47.1
Great Britain	48.8	44.9	–	46.9
Hungary	35.8	52.6	–	44.2
Bulgaria	–	42.7	–	42.7
Taiwan	33.8	42.8	51.3	42.6
Brazil	–	49.4	33.4	41.4
Croatia	–	–	41.2	41.2
Germany	37.4	37.2	49.1	41.2
Japan	37.5	–	44.9	41.2

(Cont'd)

Table 5.1: (Cont'd)

Nation	CSES I 1996–2000	CSES II 2000–2005	CSES III 2005–2010	Average CSES I–III
South Korea	–	–	40.5	40.5
Switzerland	36.7	42.5	40.3	39.8
Belgium	–	36.1	–	36.1
Republic of Korea	27.3	40.0	40.5	35.9
Lithuania	34.6	–	–	34.6
Ireland	–	27.7	31.4	29.6
Netherlands	27.9	–	–	27.9
Peru	22.8	–	–	22.8
Slovenia	21.7	–	21.7	21.7
Chile	20.7	–	–	20.7
Hong Kong	7.9	28.1	–	18.0
Thailand	21.5	17.7	6.9	15.4
Belarus	11.7	–	12.7	12.2

Source: Results from CSES I and CSES II are taken from Dalton and Weldon (2007). Results for Iceland and Denmark in the years 2005–2010 are appended to the data from the March 2010 edition of the CSES III. The question wording used in the CSES is 'Do you think of yourself as close to any particular party? Which party is that? Do you feel very close to this party, somewhat close, or not very close? Some countries have used a different question wording, notably Australia ('Generally speaking, do you usually think of yourself as Liberal, Labor, National or what', Brazil ('In general, is there any party that you like?'), Mexico ('[…]do you sympathise with any political party in particular?'), Netherlands ('Do you think of yourself as an adherent to a certain political party?'). (Examples are all from the CSES III-wave.) Results are weighted individually for each country. The countries have been ranked in order according to the average proportion of party identifiers in the three waves of the CSES (Note, however, that the comparability of indicators is not perfect across years within countries). If a country participated twice in the CSES III-module, we have chosen to display results from the most recent election.

The secular decline of the strength of party identification in established democracies is one of the most well known trends in the social sciences (Dalton 1984; Dalton and Wattenberg 2000). The explanations of the decline are many. According to Dalton, party attachments play a less important role in democracies as parties are less prone to focus on social group representation. The mass media is carrying out most of the information functions once performed by the political parties. Cognitive mobilisation and increasing levels of individualisation have turned electorates into being less dependent on political parties (Dalton and Weldon 2007).

Admittedly, in most advanced democracies, the emotional ties between voters and parties have weakened during the post war period, and also in most newly democratised countries. Among the five Nordic countries, the dealignment trend has been most pronounced in Sweden. Here, the proportion of party identifiers – using the stricter original measure of partisanship – has dropped almost linearly from 65 per cent in 1965 to 29 per cent in 2010. Also in Norway the share of party-identified voters has dropped from 71 per cent in 1981 to 50 per cent in 2005, but since party identification in Norway recovered in the 1980s, most of the decline is more recent than in Sweden (*see* Figure 5.1).

However, the three remaining Nordic countries – Iceland, Denmark and Finland – deviate somewhat from a general secular trend of continuously weakening party identification. In these countries, we have seen clear signs of a recovery in the levels of party identification in the last decade. In the first election survey in Iceland in 1983, party identification – in the stronger sense – was weaker than in Norway and Sweden at the same time. A downward trend in the 1980s and 1990s (a drop from 49 per cent in 1983 to 38 per cent in 1999) came to a stop in the 2000s. In the 2009 election, 39 per cent of the Icelandic voters identified with a political party – which is the same level as ten years ago. A similar development is visible in Denmark

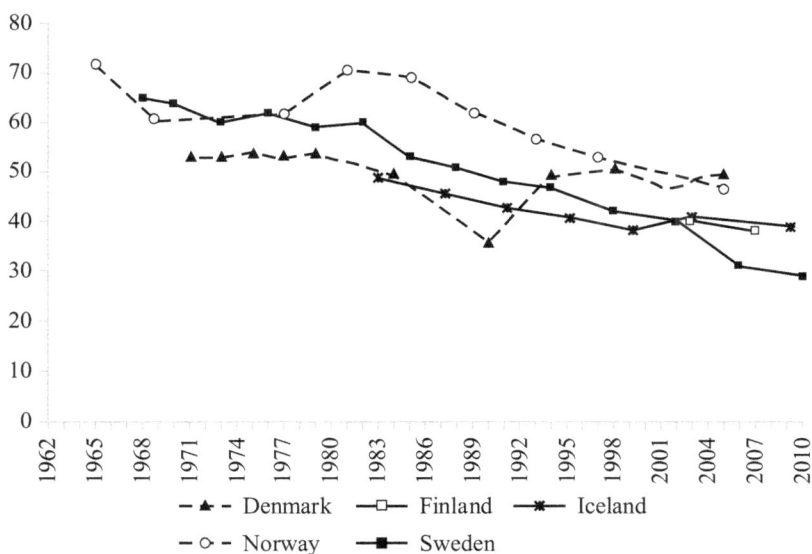

Figure 5.1: Proportion of voters that consider themselves a supporter of a particular party in the Nordic countries 1965–2010 (per cent)

Notes: Data are from the Nordic National Election Studies 1965–2010. Question wording Sweden: 'Many think of themselves as partisans of a specific party. But there are also many that do not have such a relation to a party. Do you usually think of yourself as a partisan of a specific party or don't you have such a relation to any political party?'. Question wording Iceland: 'Many people consider themselves supporters of political parties or organisations while others do not feel a solidarity with any party. Do you in general consider yourself as a supporter of any political party or organisation?'. Question wording Denmark: 'Do you in general feel attached to a specific party?'. Question wording Norway: 'Many people think of themselves as adherents to a particular party, while others feel no affiliation with any party. Would you say that you in general think of yourself as a Conservative, a Labourite, a SV supporter, etc, or don't you consider yourself affiliated with any particular party?'. Question wording Finland: 'Do you think of yourself as close to any particular party?'.

where the proportion of party identifiers did plummet from 54 per cent in 1979 to 36 per cent in 1990. Here, the proportion of party-identified voters recovered fast, and in the 2007 Danish general election, 47 per cent of the party voters claimed to be attached to a particular party – a level which is only marginally lower than in the 1960s. And finally, Finland has experienced a small rise in party identification from 47 to 53 per cent between the 2003 and 2007 elections.

When it comes to the recent levels of party-identified voters in the Nordic countries, Sweden stands out as a deviating case with only about 30 per cent party-identified voters while about 40 per cent of Icelandic and Finnish voters and about half of the electorates in Denmark and Norway claim they feel attached to a specific political party.[2]

In the literature, there are two main views on what drives the macro level of party identification in a democracy: One view is that the processes of *modernisation and cognitive mobilisation* have rendered party identification less useful for voters when they make up their minds on how to vote (Dalton and Wattenberg 2000). A more individualised electorate grows more independent of collectives in general and political parties in particular. The growing proportion of well educated, politically knowledgeable and cognitively sophisticated voters would be less inclined to develop strong psychological attachments to specific political parties. This process is quite slow since it is based on long term socialisation. According to this view, as time goes by, generational replacement will eventually and inevitably lead to lower levels of party identification. Eroding emotional ties to particular parties can be expected to pave way for higher electoral volatility, the development of multiple party identification, a higher proportion of late deciders, and more leeway for short term campaign effects on the final vote decision.

A second view is that it is shorter term political contextual factors – such as the *degree of ideological polarisation* at the times of elections – that affect voters psychological attachment to parties (Schmitt and Holmberg 1995). The modes and themes of election campaigns and the character of party competition can vary across elections within the same country, thus producing different levels of party identification. In contexts where intense campaigning and polarised debates revolve around highly salient political issues, a given voter may quite quickly develop stronger emotional bonds to a particular party. Under these circumstances we will experience rising levels of party identification.

A full blown test of short term and long term effects on aggregate levels of party identification is beyond the scope of this study. Our examination of the Nordic countries does not encompass contextual data on many elections. Instead, we perform indirect tests of these two main hypotheses. We call them *the modernisation/cognitive mobilisation hypothesis* and *the ideological polarisation hypothesis*. The micro level version of the modernisation/cognitive mobilisation

---

2.   Norway 2001 is left out of the time series analysis in Figure 5.1 because the NNES did not use the Michigan question of party ID in that year. The CSES estimates for Norway 2001 is found in Table 5.1.

hypothesis is that it is the more educated, politically aware and knowledgeable voters who will display lower party identification. And the micro level version of the polarisation hypothesis is that voters with clear and strong ideological predispositions will tend to have stronger party identification than voters with weak or ambivalent predispositions. In the following section we will put these hypotheses to a test with data from recent elections in the five Nordic countries.

Who is party-identified?

We begin with a tabular analysis of the proportion of party-identified voters in different voter groups in the five Nordic countries. The purpose is to get an overview of what categories of voters are more party identified than others and to discover differences between countries. Table 5.2 displays the proportion of party identifiers in the five Nordic countries (with confidence intervals in parentheses) among different voter groups. We present the results for the same standard set of social and political variables as in all other empirical chapters of this book.

Noticeably, there are quite a few bivariate relationships between the SES-variables and party identification that turn out significant. Overall, the results show only small differences between e.g. single and married voters and voters occupied in the public and private sector. No clear pattern emerges when it comes to occupational status. Rural voters show a robust tendency to be more party identified than urban voters but the differences are too small to be statistically significant.

As regards party identification among male and female voters, the Nordic countries display interesting discrepancies. There exists no gender gap in party identification in Finland and Sweden. However, in Denmark, Iceland and Norway, men are more party identified than women.

One striking result of the bivariate analyses is the clear positive relationship between generation/age and the level of party identification that exists in all the Nordic countries. Older generations have stronger party ID than younger generations. We highlight the age relationship because it will be quite important in the coming analyses. As will become clear later on, in a multivariate analysis, the strong positive relationship between age and party identification most often disappears, one reason being that older generations tend to score lower on level of education and education is negatively correlated with party identification: the higher the education levels the weaker the emotional bonds between voters and parties.

Longitudinal data can demonstrate that the downward trend in party identification is a pattern consistent with what one would expect if it were mainly driven by a process of generational replacement. For instance, cohort analyses of Swedish data illustrate quite clearly that younger generations do not develop strong emotional ties with political parties during their life span as the older generations did earlier in life (Persson and Oscarsson 2011). The result may well be used as an indirect support for the modernisation hypothesis introduced earlier. The prediction for the Swedish case is that the aggregate level of party identification will most

Table 5.2: Proportion of party-identified voters in the Nordic countries (percentages with confidence intervals)

	Denmark 2007		Finland 2007		Iceland 2007		Norway 2005		Sweden 2006	
	%	CI	%	CI	%	CI	%	CI	%	CI
Gender										
Men	57	[54–59]	54	[50–57]	52	[49–56]	51	[48–54]	31	[29–34]
Women	51	[49–53]	53	[49–57]	44	[41–48]	43	[40–46]	30	[27–32]
Age										
18–24 years	45	[38–51]	42	[33–51]	47	[41–54]	39	[33–46]	19	[14–23]
25–34 years	43	[39–48]	44	[37–51]	43	[37–49]	37	[32–43]	23	[19–27]
35–44 years	47	[43–51]	40	[32–47]	47	[42–53]	45	[40–50]	27	[22–31]
45–54 years	52	[48–55]	53	[46–60]	46	[41–52]	47	[42–52]	30	[26–35]
55–64 years	56	[53–60]	60	[54–66]	53	[46–59]	53	[47–58]	35	[31–40]
65+	66	[63–69]	66	[61–71]	56	[49–62]	59	[54–65]	44	[39–49]
Marital status										
Single	52	[50–55]	54	[50–59]	46	[41–50]	45	[41–49]	29	[25–32]
Married/living tog.	54	[53–56]	52	[49–56]	50	[47–53]	48	[46–51]	31	[29–34]
Degree of urbanisation										
Country side	55	[51–59]	56	[48–64]	49	[45–53]	51	[48–55]	34	[29–38]
Small community	54	[52–56]	52	[49–56]					30	[28–32]
Big city	51	[48–55]	55	[48–61]	48	[45–51]	45	[43–48]	29	[24–34]

(Cont'd)

Table 5.2: (Cont'd)

	Denmark 2007		Finland 2007		Iceland 2007		Norway 2005		Sweden 2006	
	%	CI	%	CI	%	CI	%	CI	%	CI
Education										
Compulsory schooling	56	[52–59]	53	[48–59]	47	[43–51]	52	[46–58]	41	[37–45]
Lower secondary school (student)	54	[52–56]	52	[48–56]	49	[45–53]	50	[46–53]	29	[26–32]
Higher education (univ., teachers, nurses)	50	[46–55]	58	[51–64]	50	[45–55]	43	[39–46]	26	[23–29]
Employment										
Outside the labour market	59	[56–61]	59	[54–63]	50	[45–54]	52	[48–55]	34	[31–37]
Self-employed	56	[50–63]	65	[56–74]	52	[45–60]	51	[43–59]	27	[20–35]
Lower white-collar worker	49	[45–52]	49	[42–57]	45	[39–51]	40	[36–44]	27	[24–31]
Higher white-collar worker	51	[47–55]	59	[51–66]	53	[47–58]	48	[43–53]	26	[20–31]
Blue collar worker (incl. unskilled w.)	51	[47–54]	43	[37–48]	42	[36–48]	49	[43–55]	33	[29–38]
Sector										
Private sector	55	[53–57]	54	[51–58]	48	[45–52]	48	[45–51]	30	[28–32]
Public sector	50	[46–53]	46	[39–53]	50	[45–55]	47	[43–51]	31	[28–34]
Political awareness										
Low	44	[41–47]	27	[22–31]	31	[27–35]	34	[30–38]	23	[20–26]
Medium	57	[54–59]	56	[51–61]	49	[45–54]	47	[43–52]	33	[30–36]
High	62	[59–65]	72	[68–76]	65	[61–69]	55	[51–58]	46	[41–51]

(Cont'd)

Table 5.2: (Cont'd)

	Denmark 2007		Finland 2007		Iceland 2007		Norway 2005		Sweden 2006	
	%	CI	%	CI	%	CI	%	CI	%	CI
Political knowledge										
Low	47	[44–50]	40	[34–46]	34	[29–40]	44	[40–48]	23	[20–27]
Medium	53	[51–56]	53	[48–58]	50	[46–53]	47	[44–51]	33	[30–37]
High	60	[57–62]	60	[56–64]	58	[52–63]	50	[46–54]	38	[34–42]
Left-right self-placement										
Left	57	[54–60]	68	[61–75]	58	[51–64]	60	[55–64]	50	[46–55]
Middle	45	[42–47]	45	[41–49]	40	[37–43]	39	[36–41]	22	[20–25]
Right	69	[66–72]	76	[71–82]	78	[73–83]	62	[57–68]	43	[37–48]
Left-right extremeness										
Middle	42	[39–46]	32	[27–37]	30	[27–34]	33	[29–37]	18	[15–21]
Somewhat to the left/right	44	[40–48]	51	[44–57]	46	[41–51]	41	[37–46]	28	[24–31]
Far to the left/right	60	[58–62]	66	[63–70]	65	[61–68]	56	[53–59]	47	[44–51]
Vote stability										
Party switcher	29	[26–31]	35	[31–38]	31	[27–34]	33	[31–36]	16	[14–18]
Stable party voter	66	[65–68]	73	[69–76]	68	[64–71]	63	[60–67]	49	[46–52]
Total	54	[52–55]	53	[50–56]	48	[46–51]	47	[45–49]	31	[29–32]

Note: Data are from national election studies in Denmark (2007), Finland (2007), Iceland (2007), Norway (2005), and Sweden (2006). Results for Finland are weighted. Note that in this table, we are using the CSES-measure of party attachment ('close to any party') in the results for Iceland (*see* Table 5.1). For details on the coding of variables, see Appendix.

likely continue to drop in coming elections due to generational replacement, unless short term political contextual effects, such as ideological polarisation or realignment processes can counter this development.

As regards the bivariate analyses, the modernisation/cognitive mobilisation hypothesis that highly educated voters should be the least party identified is clearly supported in Norway and Sweden. For instance, Swedish voters with university degrees are less party identified (26 per cent) than voters with compulsory schooling (41 per cent). However, in Denmark, Finland, and Iceland, there is no apparent relationship between education level and levels of party identification.

However, having a university degree may not be the ideal proxy for cognitive mobilisation. Instead, we see that other indicators of cognitive capability – *political knowledge* – show much more convincing correlations with party identification. However, the bivariate relationship is in the wrong direction to what we would expect! In all the Nordic countries, it is the more politically knowledgeable voters that display a higher degree of party identification. Political sophistication goes hand in hand with a stronger attachment with political parties, most notably in Finland, where the proportion of party identifiers is 60 per cent among the most knowledgeable, compared to 40 per cent among the least knowledgeable.

The polarisation hypothesis stated that voters with stronger ideological predispositions should have a stronger party identification than voters with weak or ambivalent predispositions. We find strong evidence in support of this hypothesis in all the Nordic countries. Voters that have more extreme ideological orientations do have a much stronger attachment to political parties than voters oriented towards the middle of the ideological left-right continuum.

Interestingly, the relationship between left-right ideology and party identification varies among the Nordic countries. In Denmark, Finland and Iceland, right-wing voters are significantly more party identified than leftist voters. For example, in Iceland, the proportion of party identifiers is 78 per cent among rightist voters compared to only 58 per cent among leftist voters. In Norway, the leftist and rightist voters are equally party identified. And in Sweden, the relationship is the opposite: leftist voters display a higher proportion of party identifiers (50 per cent) than rightist voters (43 per cent).

Furthermore, there is another political variable that shows robust correlations with party identification: we learn that the politically involved voters – that report a strong interest in politics and expose themselves to political news-tend to be much more party identified than voters with less political awareness. Again, Finland shows the largest gap in party identification between the voters that score low on political awareness (27 per cent identified) and voters that score high on political awareness (72 per cent).

The final, 'behavioural check' with vote stability in Table 5.2 turns out positive in all the Nordic countries. As expected, the proportion of party identified voters is much higher among stable voters (49–73 per cent) than among party switchers (16–29 per cent). A strong emotional attachment with a party may still be a stabiliser of individual voting behaviour. At the same time, there is a far from perfect correlation between psychological attachment and the behaviour of party switching.

Multivariate tests

The next step of the analysis is to perform multivariate tests of the model. As in the other chapters of the book, the regression analyses are performed in two stages for each country, first a model with a standard set of SES-variables and then a second model that also includes political variables such as ideological predispositions, political awareness and political knowledge. To be able to get a more straightforward interpretation of the logistic effects, we report the changes in predicted probabilities when all other independent variables are kept at their mean level (*see* Table 5.3).

The multivariate tests confirm that the set of socio-economic background variables perform weakly in predicting whether a given voter identifies with a party or not. The model fit of the pure SES-model is quite poor. The effects of age and education on party identification are the only SES-effects that eventually survive in the second stage of the regression analysis. The positive age effects are robust and significant in all the Nordic countries but Iceland. The interpretation of the age effects are not as straight forward as the other variables in the model because it is the only continuous variable: for instance, a one standard deviation change in the age variable (equals to about 18 years) will, on average, result in a 4–6 percentage points higher party identification. The education effect is perhaps more impressive: having a higher education has a negative effect (–10 to –14 percentage points) in Denmark, Iceland, Norway and Sweden. However, in Finland there are no statistically significant effects of education on the probability of being a party identified voter.

The political variables in model 2 show stronger effects. The effects of political awareness skyrocket to 60 percentage points in the case of Iceland, and even higher (77 per cent) in Finland. Being attached to the political world in terms of interest and high exposure to political news turns out to be the strongest determinant of party identification in the Nordic countries. Indeed, political awareness is close to the dependent variable in this case, and the causal direction can be discussed. Most likely, the relationship between emotional bonds to political parties and the habit of consuming political news is reciprocal.

The ideological predisposition variables also show strong and robust effects. The multivariate analysis confirms that in Denmark and Iceland, right-wing voters are the strongest party identifiers while in Sweden and Norway, it is the leftist voters that tend to have a higher proportion of party identifiers. The effects of left-right extremism are, however, in the same direction in all countries: voters in the centre of the political space have a lower propensity for party identification than voters that place themselves far to the right or far to the left.

Interestingly, the bivariate effects of knowledge on party identification (*see* Table 5.2) is cancelled out in all the multivariate models. All things being equal, there exists no direct effect of political knowledge on party identification. More politically knowledgeable voters are not, *ceteris paribus*, more inclined to be attached to political parties.

Table 5.3: Modelling the probability of having a party identification in the Nordic countries (marginal change in predicted probabilities – percentage points)

	Denmark 2007 Model 1	Denmark 2007 Model 2	Finland 2007 Model 1	Finland 2007 Model 2	Iceland 2007 Model 1	Iceland 2007 Model 2	Norway 2005 Model 1	Norway 2005 Model 2	Sweden 2006 Model 1	Sweden 2006 Model 2
Age in election year	7***	6***	9***	5***	1	-2	6***	6***	7***	4***
Women	-6***	-3	0	-6*	-10***	-2	-7**	-2	-2	0
Lower secondary	-4**	-7***	-2	-7*	-2	-8**	1	-3	-3	-7**
Higher education	-6**	-10***	4	-4	-2	-10**	-5	-13***	-8**	-14***
Not single	2	0	-1	-4	3	2	1	0	0	2
Self employed	-3	-4	9*	7	-4	-14**	-1	-1	-5	-5
Lower white collar	-5*	-5*	-2	-4	-7	-9	-6*	-9**	-2	-2
Higher white collar	-4	-6**	3	-2	-2	-6	0	-3	-1	1
Blue collar	-3	0	-9**	-8*	-16***	-15***	-3	0	4	5
Degree of urbanisation	-1	-4	1	-9*	-2	-4	-4	-6**	-2	-6
Public sector	1	0	-7	-8	1	0	1	-1	-1	-3
Left-right self-placement		9***		-8		21**		-15**		-30***
Left-right extremeness		32***		48***		44***		44***		49***
Political awareness		42***		77***		60***		41***		26***
Political knowledge		5		14		8		5		12*
No. respondents	3 960	3 960	1 398	1 398	1 171	1 171	1 737	1 737	1 711	1 711
McFadden pseudo R²	0.02	0.07	0.04	0.20	0.02	0.14	0.02	0.09	0.03	0.12
Log likelihood	-2,673	-2,534	-929	-775	-798	-694	-1,173	-1,094	-1,055	-957
Chi²	121.45	398.01	75.74	383.07	26.60	234.29	57.26	216.03	62.27	258.03

Note: Education (Ref category: compulsory schooling); Employment (Ref category: Outside the labour market) Individual weights are used for Finland 2007.
*p<0.10, ** p < 0.05, *** p < 0.01

Conclusion: Weakened ties but they are still there

In this chapter we have analysed Nordic voters' relations to the political parties. Results show that the emotional ties between voters and parties in the Nordic countries still need to be taken under serious consideration in analyses of voting behaviour. Party loyalties still play an important role in the Nordic countries, since in four out of five countries, about 50 per cent of the voters claim to be attached to a specific political party. In this regard, the Nordic countries do not in any way stand out in a comparative analysis but rather group together in mid-range when it comes to the level of party-identified voters.

In addition, the strong dealignment trends of past decades seem not to have continued after the year 2000. There exists no apparent short term downward trend of weakening ties in the past decade. Interestingly, the Swedish voters deviate from this general picture in two ways: the proportion of party identifiers is clearly lower (30 per cent) than in the other Nordic countries, and the secular trend in party identification is very pronounced with a monotonic linear downward trend for decades.

Chapter Six

Candidate Voting

Voters prefer to hold an individual accountable for government performance (or, occasionally, for the performance of the opposition), rather than an abstract institution or political ideal (McAllister 2007: 580 referring to Bean and Mughan 1989).

Introduction

The composition of representative bodies is often discussed simply in terms of the strength of political parties. Nevertheless, parliaments are not made up of anonymous party organisations, but rather of individual politicians representing each of these parties. The role played by individual politicians behind the party leadership, so called backbenchers, does however vary a great deal from one country to another, which is very apparent among the Nordic countries. In some countries backbenchers are relatively anonymous to the general public and only attract a very low level of media attention. In other countries they are well known personalities, almost celebrities, and seen as spokesmen of their own constituency. The relatively extensive differences in the importance of backbenchers among the Nordic countries can, at least to some extent, be attributed to the differences in

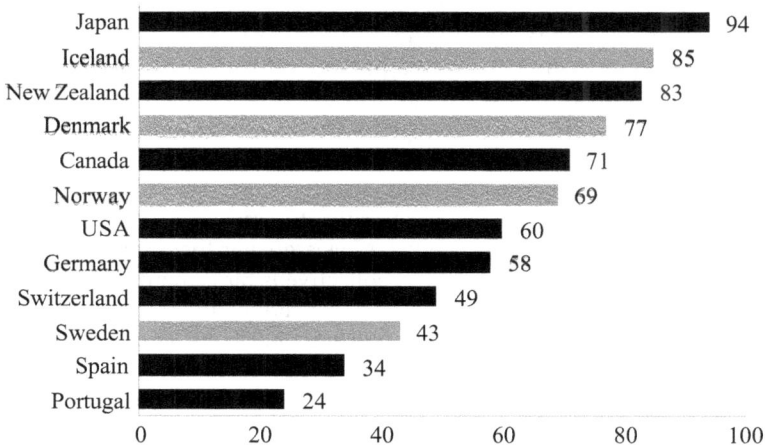

Figure 6.1: Candidate recognition (per cent)[1], CSES module 1

1.   Share of respondents that can recall the name of at least one candidate in their home district/

the electoral systems, or more specifically the opportunities for preferential voting that are provided in each country.

One straightforward way of comparing the importance attributed to individual politicians by voters is to ask about candidate recognition. If voters are not familiar with the candidates that are running in their constituency, it is unlikely that the individual personalities' political profile, or the competence of the candidates will have an impact on the outcome of the election (Holmberg 2009). The question about candidate recognition can hence be considered as a rudimentary indicator of the importance of candidates in the electoral arena. Figure 6.1 clearly demonstrates that the Nordic countries should not be considered as a homogenous group of countries. On the contrary, we find that while Iceland has a very high level of candidate recognition, the level is far less impressive among Swedish voters.

Personalisation of politics

In the literature it is often stated that the importance of individual politicians have increased in advanced democracies. The development is considered as a natural consequence of the rising importance of television in election campaigning, decreased party identification among voters, and a more volatile electorate (*see* Chapters Five and Seven). This trend is generally labelled 'personalisation' (McAllister 2007) or 'presidentialisation' (Poguntke and Webb 2005) of politics. As political ideas, ideologies and party labels appear to have lost some of their previous importance; it is assumed that voters are becoming more focused on individuals, human beings of flesh and blood. Or as Dalton with colleagues puts it: 'As partisanship in the electorate has weakened, it stands to reason that voters would have to substitute other factors in their decision-making process' (2000: 49).

When it comes to scientific proof, the situation appears less clear cut. Previous research has not been able to demonstrate a significant trend towards a more personalised political arena. The overarching impression from the studies performed is thus that the talk about a personalisation of politics is exaggerated (Holmberg and Oscarsson 2011; Bartle and Crewe 2002; Brettschneider and Gabriel 2002; King 2002; Karvonen 2010). On the other hand, it stands clear that personalisation as a political phenomenon can be very difficult to grasp and to compare between different institutional arrangements. One of the most apparent comparability issues to deal with concerns the differences between parliamentary and presidential regimes, where the latter has a greater focus on the president as an individual actor, while the party as a collective is far is more prominent among parliamentary regimes. Large discrepancies concerning the role played by parties versus individual political actors can, however, be found among parliamentary regimes as well, which will be discussed later on.

Research on the personalisation thesis in the Nordic context has so far provided a rather straightforward answer. Independently of what operationalisation has been applied,[2] the overarching interpretation of the studies performed is that

---

constituency. Data for Finland is not available.

2. In most countries research is focused on party leaders, their importance and characteristics.

the importance of individual politicians in determining voters' decisions on the election day has not increased over time (Karvonen 2010; Curtice and Holmberg 2005; Holmberg and Oscarsson 2011; Andersen and Borre 2003; Thomsen and Elklit 2007; Elklit 2008b; Hansen and Hoff 2013; Bengtsson 2012). The decision made by voters is no more dependent on leader evaluation today than it was 20 years ago (Curtice and Holmberg 2005). Neither do voters appear more interested in influencing who becomes an elected representative for a certain party by means of using the possibility to cast a preferential vote (Karvonen 2010; Elklit 2011; Hansen and Hoff 2013). In a comprehensive study by Karvonen (2010) one of the few examples in support of the personalisation thesis is found in Finland, where the share of the electorate that considers candidates as more important than parties when they make their electoral choice has increased slightly over time (2010: 51, see Table 6.1).[3]

In fact, it appears as if the most visible signs that point towards a trend of personalisation of politics can be found, not in the behaviour of voters, but rather in various actions taken by central actors or institutions such as parties or parliaments – not to forget the media's contribution. In Denmark, we find that parties over time have provided voters with more incentives to cast a preferential vote with the increased use of open lists, where the personal votes decide the ranking order of the candidates. Nevertheless, the level of preferential voting has been stable around 50 per cent in Denmark (Thomsen and Elklit 2007: 308–9). Other visible signs have been changes in the electoral systems of Sweden and Iceland towards greater possibilities for preferential voting and in Norway, a development in the same direction has been under intensive debate (Narud and Valen 2007: 64–7).

Despite the fact that most research results indicate that the significance of individual politicians or party leaders have not increased over time, it stands clear that the role played by individual political candidates is not an irrelevant one. One of the aims of this chapter is to give an introduction to the role played by individual politicians in the five Nordic countries with an emphasis on the electoral choice made by voters.

Yet another objective is to analyse what characterises voters that emphasise and care about candidates in the electoral process. Unfortunately this analytic task is not very straightforward. The differences in the electoral systems utilised in the Nordic countries have had a substantial impact on the electoral research performed. As a result, the way of posing survey questions about the importance and influence of candidates running for election varies a great deal from one country to another. While the role, evaluation and effect of party leaders have attracted a great deal of interest in most countries, political representatives at a lower level in the hierarchy, and candidates running for election, are less prominent fields of research. This suggests that we are forced to focus our analyses on different aspects of candidate importance in different contexts, a problem that will be discussed in more detail later.

Finland deviates from the others with the greater emphasis on voters' views on candidates and the role they play in the electoral choices made by voters.

3. The trend was however broken in the most recent parliamentary election in 2011, which becomes clear in Table 6.1.

Preferential voting in the Nordic countries

The Nordic countries are often considered as the archetypes of party-dominated systems that leave limited room for individual candidates (Granberg and Holmberg 1988). However, the role that individual politicians play varies greatly from one Nordic country to another depending on the institutional arrangements. Even though all Nordic countries are parliamentary democracies and use proportional electoral systems that pool votes for parties (or lists) the possibilities for voters to decide who should represent the party in parliament, varies to a large extent from one country to another. We have at our hands five very different systems, ranging from closed party lists to fully developed preferential voting. The variation in institutional arrangements concerning preferential voting can almost be considered as maximised.

According to Karvonen (2004: 208) preferential voting in the Nordic countries can be classified into three different categories which all use list systems that pool votes at the party level:

1. *Strong preferential voting:* Open party lists. Individual legislators are elected on the basis on preference votes only. (Finland)

2. *Weak preferential voting:* Mixed list system. The list order and preference voting both play a role in determining which legislators are elected. The effect of preference voting is clearly limited by the list order. (Denmark, Sweden, Iceland)

3. *No preferential voting:* Closed party lists. The election of individual candidates is based only on the list order, which is decided by the party. (Norway)

In the first category with strong preferential voting we only find one of the five Nordic countries, that is Finland. Finland has, since 1955, used an open list system with mandatory preferential voting (Karvonen 2010: 49). The 200 seats in the *Eduskunta* (Riksdagen in Swedish) are distributed in 14 (15 including Åland) constituencies using the D'Hondt method. The ranking of the candidates running for each party is determined solely by the amount of votes each candidate receives. The ballot paper only contains an empty circle in which voters write the number of their preferred candidate. The parties most commonly present their nominated candidates in alphabetic order, even though this is not a legal requirement (Raunio 2005: 478). Parties are allowed to nominate a maximum of 14 candidates in each constituency unless more representatives are to be elected. If so, the maximal number of nominees corresponds to the amount of representatives to be elected (Raunio 2005: 477).

Despite strong preferential voting, the Finnish electoral system is still a party centred system. All votes are pooled at the party level in each constituency and the total amount of votes given to all candidates running for a party determines how many seats are allocated to the party. The seats are then filled with candidates according to the number of preferential votes that they have received. This may result in popular candidates from small parties not being elected, while less

Table 6.1: The relative importance of party vs. candidates for the vote choice of Finnish voters (per cent)

	1983	1991	2003	2007	2011
Party	52	51	49	48	55
Candidate	42	43	47	51	44
Don't know	6	6	4	1	1
Total	100	100	100	100	100
(n)	(993)	(1 141)	(1 004)	(1 172)	(1 124)

Sources: Finnish Social Science Data Archive (FSD1011, FSD1088, FSD1260, FSD2269, FSD2653).

popular candidates running for parties that receive a large share of the votes in the constituency win a seat.[4] The latter candidates are in fact elected with the help of more popular candidates running for the same party.

About half of the voters consider the party to be more important than the candidate when they decide how to vote. Until the election in 2007, there was a weak but consistent trend towards a more personalised political arena, where the importance of parties decreased and the candidates became more important. This trend was however broken in an extraordinary election in 2011 where the populist party, the True Finns, more than doubled their support and had a large impact on the election campaign (Bengtsson 2012).

Three Nordic countries are found in the middle category with weak preferential voting: Denmark, Iceland and Sweden. Despite the fact that the countries are found in the same group, the preferential voting systems diverge from each other to a rather large extent. Among the three, Denmark stands out as the country with the strongest feature of preferential voting. Both Iceland and Sweden have in recent years introduced greater opportunities for preferential voting and are to be considered as newcomers in the category.

In Denmark the 179 seats in the *Folketing* are distributed in several steps and at several geographical tiers, with a highly proportional outcome (Elklit 2008a: 465).[5] When dealing with the aspect of preferential voting, and the amount of preferential votes that are cast, there are two steps to take into account. The first

---

4.   The tendency for this to happen varies strongly from one constituency to another depending on how many seats are distributed. The number of seats that are distributed in each constituency is determined by the population. In the election in 2007 the number of seats varied from 7 to 34 on the Finnish mainland. As a result, the effective threshold varies greatly from one constituency to another. In the 2007 election the highest effective threshold was 14.3 and the lowest 2.9. This discrepancy has led to an intense debate about electoral reform. As of today, the Finnish system does neither utilise a set electoral threshold, nor nationally distributed compensation seats.

5.   Of these 179 seats, two are distributed in the autonomous region of Greenland and two in the Faroe Islands.

Table 6.2: Open lists and preferential voting in Denmark since 1950s (per cent)

	1950s	1960s	1970s	1980s	1990s	2000s
Open lists	n.a.	13	44	52	76	88
Preferential voting	52	42	47	47	50	49

Sources: See Karvonen (2010: 46).

step involves the nomination made by parties, where there are two different types of lists available for parties to choose from. The first option is a list where the ranking of the candidates is decided by the party, i.e. a closed list or 'standing by district' (*kredsvis opstillning*). The second alternative is a list which gives voters a possibility to cast a preferential vote, an open list or 'standing in parallel' (*sideordnet opstilling*).

If parties opt for a closed list, voters' preferential votes are of limited effect. When parties present their voters with an open list it is the proportion of personal votes in the constituency that determines the ranking of the candidates. Nevertheless, a preferential or party vote is possible in both types of lists even though the influence of a personal vote is much greater with the use of open lists.

Concerning the first step – a party's decision to present voters with open or closed lists – there has been an increase in the amount of open lists over time; a trend that has given more power to the hands of the voters that cast a preferential vote (Karvonen 2010: 46). As becomes apparent in Table 6.2, the share of open lists has doubled since the 1970s when less than half of all lists were open. The second factor that determines the extent of preferential voting – the actual amount of preferential votes casted by voters – has however been rather stable over time at about 50 per cent. In the 2005 election 50 per cent and in 2007, 51 per cent, opted for this alternative (Thomsen and Elklit 2007: 309). Thomsen and Elklit explain the relatively low share of respondents casting a preferential vote in parliamentary elections with the fact that many voters have a limited knowledge of local candidates running for election.[6]

Sweden did, until the 1998 general election, elect the 349 representatives to the *Riksdag* using Saint-Laguë, national compensation seats, a threshold at four per cent and closed party lists. However, in 1997 a new electoral law was passed that allowed for voluntary preferential voting.[7] In practice, parties still present their candidates on the ballot in their preferred order of rank. Voters can, since

---

6.   This assumption is supported by the fact that the share of voters that cast a preferential vote is considerably higher in elections to the European Parliament, an election where the whole country constitutes one constituency and everyone has the possibility to vote for well-known candidates. In the 2004 election to the European Parliament as many as 82 per cent used the opportunity to vote for a specific candidate (Thomsen and Elklit 2007: 309).

7.   Prior to the new law, the system with preferential voting had been tried out in some municipalities in the local election of 1994 and in the election to the European Parliament in 1995 (Holmberg and Möller 1999: 92).

Table 6.3: Candidate recognition in Sweden 1956–1970 and 1985–2006 (per cent)

Year	1956	1960	1964	1968	1970	–	1985	1991	1994	1998	2002	2006	2010
	60	55	56	60	49	–	48	44	45	44	40	41	38

Comment: Share of respondents that could name a candidate from their own constituency among those who voted in the election. Source: Oscarsson and Holmberg 2013.

the election in 1998, choose to opt for an altered order by means of marking their preferred candidate with an X on the ballot. If 8 per cent[8] of the party's voters in a constituency have casted a preferential vote for the same candidate it will overrule the ranking made by the party. The candidates that have received more than 8 per cent personal votes are hence placed on the top of the list. If there is more than one candidate with enough preferential votes to overrule the order decided by the party, the amount of votes determines the ranking of the candidates.

When the system was introduced in the national election in 1998 about 30 per cent of the voters gave a preferential vote. Since the introduction, the popularity of preferential voting has decreased. In the 2006 election the share was 22 per cent (Oscarsson and Holmberg 2008a) and in the 2010 election, 25 per cent (*Valmyndigheten*). The effects on the outcome of the election have so far been relatively limited. In the first election, in 1998, 12 out of 349 seats were filled with candidates that did not follow the preferred rank order by the parties. In the election in 2006 the amount decreased to six seats only to increase to eight seats in 2010 (Karvonen 2010: 47; Oscarsson and Holmberg 2008: 273; *see also* Oscarsson and Holmberg 2013).

On the whole, candidates do not seem to have a very prominent position among Swedish voters. Not only have the effects of the newly introduced system of preferential voting been limited, the share of voters that can name a candidate running for election in their own constituency has also decreased substantially since the 1950s, from 60 to around 40 per cent.

Iceland elects 63 representatives to the *Althingi* from 6 multi-member constituencies, using national compensations seats (9), and an electoral threshold set at 5 per cent. The opportunity for preferential voting has changed over time in Iceland but since 1916, Icelandic voters have had the formal right to change the order of candidates on party lists, either by striking out a candidate's name or re-arrange the ordering of candidates. During the period 1987–1999, Iceland was classified as having no preferential voting (Karvonen 2004). During this period the rules were similar to the ones applied in Norway, that is, 50 per cent of the voters had to strike out a candidate's name on their preferred party list in order to change the ranking order – and in such a case the candidate in question would be removed from the list altogether.

---

8.   The threshold was lowered to 5 per cent in 2010 (*Valmyndigheten*).

Table 6.4: Participation in primaries, Iceland (per cent)

	1983	1987	1991	1995	1999	2003	2007	2009
	28.8	18.5	16.6	18.5	27.8	14.9	30.5	32.1
(n)	(992)	(1 783)	(1 491)	(1 721)	(1 631)	(1 446)	(1 595)	(1 339)

Sources: ICENES 1991, ICENES 1995, ICENES 1999, ICENES 2003, ICENES 2007 available at: www.fel.hi.is/en/icelandic_national_election_study_icenes

A new eletoral system was introduced in the 2003 *Althingi* election. The previously used Borda rule (Saari 1990) was re-introduced as a measure for re-ranking the candidates on party lists.[9] With the current system, the parties preferred order of rank is presented on the ballot. Voters have the option of changing the order of a list in two ways; they can choose to cross out a name of a candidate that they do not want elected, and they can change the order of the candidates. In both the 2007 and the 2009 general elections such changes had an effect on the ranking of two candidates that were degraded one step on the list. There were, however, no real consequences for the outcome in neither of the two elections, since both of the degraded candidates ended up on an eligible place (Harðarson and Kristinsson 2008).

Interestingly enough, the Icelandic voters are very active when it comes to participation in primaries which are often close races (Harðarson and Kristinson 2008). Since 1991 the share of voters participating in primaries has varied between 15 and 31 per cent (Table 6.4). In general, primaries are considered to be far more decisive for the selection of MPs than the preferential voting taking place in the election.

Norway is an unproblematic case, since it represents the category without preferential voting. The transformation of votes into the 169 seats in the *Storting* is done by closed party lists using Saint-Laguë, a 4 per cent threshold and national compensation seats. The highly proportional system has been relatively stable throughout the democratic period (Narud and Valen 2007: 55–63). Technically, the Norwegian voters are permitted to change the list by crossing out the name of one or more candidates on the party list of their choice. However, in order to have an impact on the outcome, that is, to overrule the ranking made by the party, a majority of the party's voters must opt for the same revision. Since this system was introduced in 1920, voters have never succeeded with changing the parties' rank ordering at *Storting* elections. During recent years there has been a relatively intense debate about introducing some element of preferential voting in the Norwegian electoral system. But so far the debate has not lead to any concrete

---

9. The adapted version of Borda means that in most cases a candidate is moved down a seat if 15–25 per cent of voters for a party list strike out a candidate's name (*see* Helgason 2006: 35). This greatly increased the probability of preference voting having an impact on the final ranking order. Earlier versions of the Borda rule have been used during the period 1916–1986 (Helgason 2008).

Table 6.5: Candidate recognition in Norway (per cent)

Year	1969	1985	1997
	64	67	68

Comment: 1969: a candidate on the list that you voted for. 1985 and 1997: a candidate in the constituency.

reforms and it appears as if a majority of the electorate is against a change in this direction (Narud and Valen 2007: 64–67).

Quite unexpectedly the level of candidate recognition appears to be higher in Norway than in Sweden. Unfortunately the data for Norway only covers three elections, with approximately a fifteen year gap in between each time point. It does, however, appear clear that the share of voters that are able to name a candidate running for election in their constituency has not decreased over time. A potential explanation of this difference is constituency size. When fewer MPs are elected from a constituency, as is the case in most of the Norwegian constituencies, it is likely that politicians become more closely connected to voters, and that they, hence, are easier for voters to recognise and recall.

Potential effects of preferential voting

It is not far-fetched to assume that the different possibilities for preferential voting present in the Nordic countries may have an impact on the daily functioning of politics, as well as on voters' attitudes towards the political system. Previous research provides several potential effects of candidate-centred electoral systems, not the least the effects concerning the relationship between candidates and voters, which are of main interest in this chapter. The most important will be presented briefly below, alongside a discussion about to what extent they can be confirmed in the current context.

Preferential voting tends to increase contacts between representatives and voters (Bowler and Farrell 1993),[10] and can on a general level be argued to provide greater incentives for political representatives to act as citizen intermediaries (Curtice and Phillips Shively 2009: 175–76). It is thus more likely that political representatives in systems with strong preferential voting, and where re-election is dependent on personal popularity, will have more contact with voters in the constituency and take on a more active role as delegates (Farrell 2001: 171).[11]

---

10. The study by Bowler and Farrell is performed on the European Parliament, an institution to which members from different member states are elected using a great variety of methods.

11. While single member districts traditionally have been considered to provide the best prerequisites for an active and sincere local contact on behalf of the representatives, Curtis and Phillips Shively argue for an even stronger incentive for candidate contact in multi-member districts with preferential voting. Their argument is based on the fact that there are no 'safe' seats in multi-member districts (Curtice and Phillips Shively 2009: 176). The empirical results presented by Curtice and Phillips Shively do not, however, support their assumptions. Instead the results confirm the more

Based on the information given by the MPs themselves, it is, however, unclear if this finding can be supported in the Nordic context. According to Esaiasson (2000) who compares how Nordic MPs define their political task, there appears to be no systematic variation that lines up with expectations. Nordic MPs from countries with preferential voting are no more inclined than others to emphasise the importance of pursuing the interests of the constituency or the interests of individual voters (Esaiasson 2000: 59).

Preferential voting is also held to have a substantial effect on the electoral campaign, since the incentives to conduct individual election campaigns increase alongside with the feature of preferential voting (Karvonen and Söderlund 2008). The difference becomes evident when we compare electoral campaigns in Finland with the ones in Sweden and Norway (*see also* Chapter Seven). In Finland the individual candidates run intensive campaigns and newspapers are filled with personal ads in the weeks before an election. The campaigns run in Sweden and Norway are, on the other hand, clearly centralised and dominated by the parties and the party leaders.

As a natural consequence of more frequent contact and more intensive individual campaigning, we would expect the degree of candidate recognition to be higher in systems with preferential voting. If voters in times of election are forced (as in the Finnish case) or encouraged (as in systems with weaker elements of preferential voting) to think in terms of candidates, and if their representatives conduct personal campaigns and are active in constituency work in between elections, it appears very likely that it makes voters more aware of who their MPs are. Results by Holmberg 2009, (*see also* Curtice and Phillips Shively 2009) show that the recall of candidates on average is the highest in mixed systems, almost as high in majority/plurality systems and lowest in PR-systems using multi-member districts. However, there is a great variation from one country to another, and the effect of preferential voting on recall among countries using different types of list system have, to our knowledge, not been studied. As was shown in the introduction (Figure 6.1) and discussed in the previous section, there is a relatively great variation in candidate recognition. The pattern is however not entirely in the expected direction and unfortunately there is no data on candidate recognition from Finland.

Moreover, a recent study by Karvonen and Söderlund (2008) shows that net volatility in party-centred systems is lower than in systems with strong preferential voting, such as the Finnish. The higher level of volatility is alleged to be caused by the fact that discontented voters in closed list systems are faced with the only option of switching party. In a system with open lists frustrated voters also have the less radical option of casting their vote for a different candidate representing the same party. The trend in net volatility among the Nordic countries is presented

---

common assumption, i.e. that single member districts encourage representatives to act as citizen intermediaries (Curtice and Phillips Shively 2009: 190). Unfortunately, their study does not include any of the countries classified as having strong preferential voting and PR list systems (Finland, Greece, Italy, Luxembourg [Karvonen 2004]), a fact that is likely to have influenced the results.

in Chapter Seven covering the theme of voters and election campaigns. At first impression it is hard to draw any clear conclusion in favour of the findings by Karvonen and Söderlund. Apart from the turbulent period in the 1970s with, for example, the earthquake election in Denmark (1973), the general trend points towards an increasing level of net volatility. However, it also becomes apparent that the country with the strongest feature of preferential voting, i.e. Finland, displays a relatively low volatility-level throughout the period.

Yet another potential effect of preferential voting has to do with voters' satisfaction with how the democratic system works. Farrell and McAllister (2006) find greater satisfaction with democracy in systems with preferential voting than in systems that do not offer this opportunity to voters. Their analyses show that such systems promote a greater sense of fairness about election outcomes among citizens, which in turn is a major component of the public's satisfaction with the democratic system (Farrell and McAllister 2006: 742). Based on this we would expect voters' satisfaction with democracy to be the highest in candidate-centred Finland, and lowest in Norway, where voters have virtually no say in *who* becomes their elected representative. The effect is, however, disputed and Curtice and Phillips Shively conclude that '*type of electoral system has little or nothing to do with satisfaction with democracy*' (Curtice and Phillips Shively 2009: 190).

Once more, it seems like the effects are far from settled, but if we consider the results presented in Chapter Four on voters and representative democracy, it stands clear that the hypothesis in favour of a positive relationship between preferential voting and satisfaction with democracy cannot be confirmed in the Nordic context. Rather the contrary, since the Finnish voters are the least satisfied with the way democracy works.

Preferential voting, empirical analyses

Previous research on the effects of preferential voting referred to above, clearly gives new and interesting angles to future research endeavours. However, the empirical analyses of the chapter will not be able to take on these challenges but will, instead, concentrate on the use of preferential voting. This involves the questions of, to what extent preferential voting is used by voters when the opportunity is provided, and what kind of voters are interested in individual candidates.

We will start by presenting some descriptive information about the use of preferential voting in the five countries at hand. Due to the strong differences in the five countries, we are confronted with unfortunate problems of comparison. The question about if a voter *casts a preferential vote in the last election* works fine in three countries, i.e. Denmark, Iceland and Sweden, where it is possible for voters to choose between casting a pure party vote, and a vote where they state which candidate they prefer. In the other two countries at hand, Norway and Finland, this question is not suitable and has not been used in the election studies that have been carried out. As was mentioned in the introduction, Norway will be excluded from the analyses due to the absence of a preferential voting system. In Finland a problem of the opposite type exists. Since the Finnish use a mandatory preferential voting system, voters are not able to vote without casting a preferential vote. Consequently, it is impossible to single out those voters who give higher weight to some candidates from others, based on their actual voting decision. In order to handle this aspect, a question that grasps the subjective weight given to parties versus candidates when voters decide how to vote, will be applied. Hence, instead of asking voters if they have cast a preferential vote, Finnish voters were asked if they *considered the party or the candidate as the most important for them when making their vote choice.* This measurement deviates in its meaning and contents from the one applied to Denmark, Iceland and Sweden. It can, however, be considered as a fairly good measure of the relative importance given to candidates by voters.

Looking at the descriptive statistics presented in Table 6.6 we can see that there are distinct differences concerning the frequency with which voters cast a preferential vote in the Nordic countries. It goes without saying why Norway only is represented by missing cases in this table. Among the three countries that employ voluntary preferential voting, i.e. Denmark, Sweden and Iceland, the Danish voters are the most active. 57 per cent of the respondents in the Danish electoral study state that they cast a preferential vote in the 2005 election. The corresponding share for Sweden (where the possibility for preferential voting was introduced in the late 1990s) was 18 per cent in the 2006 election. The Icelandic voters are, based on their own reports, the least interested in deciding who represent the parties in the *Althingi* since only 5 per cent of the voters choose to give a preferential vote in 2007. But, as was described previously, close to one-third state that they participated in a primary election, where the ranking of each of the party lists was determined. Among the Finnish voters slightly more than half of the voters (52 per cent) declare that the choice of candidate was more important than the choice of party for their electoral decision. The figures presented in Table 6.6 reinforce the impression from the introductory description of the electoral systems used in the five countries, where Finland and Denmark stood out as the most candidate-oriented countries.

Table 6.6: Preferential voting in the Nordic countries, per cent (n)

	Denmark 2007	Finland 2007	Iceland 2007	Norway 2005	Sweden 2006
Cast a preferential vote in the election*	57 (3 918)	52 (1 172)	5 (1 418)	– (1 680)	18 (2 780)

*Due to the mandatory preferential voting system in Finland, the question used for Finland represents a subjective evaluation of what is the most important for voters when they decide on how to vote; the candidate or the party.

The next question deals with the characteristics of those who in their electoral behaviour are interested in candidates and if it is possible to find patterns in the way voters prioritise in this matter. Yet another interesting query deals with the matter of cross-country differences. If there are systematic differences between different groups of voters concerning the importance they attribute to individual candidates, do these patterns look the same throughout the Nordic countries? In order to find the answer to these questions two sets of analyses will be performed; a descriptive analyses of the frequency by which different groups of voters use the opportunity to make a preferential vote (or as in the Finnish case, if there are differences in terms of the subjective importance voters give to candidates) and multivariate analyses in order to single out the overall behavioural patterns of voters.

In the first analysis, presented in Table 6.7, the factors included can be divided into two overarching groups. The first group represents socio-demographic and economic background and involves such aspects as gender, age, civil status, education, employment, urbanisation and sector of employment. The second group consists of variables such as political knowledge and politically awareness, as well as political attitudes and behaviour, measured as ideological leaning on the left-right scale and if they are stable voters or not.

Previous research from the Swedish context indicates that preferential voting can be considered as one of the most equal forms of political behaviour in Sweden, due to its low correlation with socio-demographic background. Political sophistication does, however, play a part in determining who gives a preferential vote and who does not, which has been confirmed by resent research from the Belgian context (André *et al.* 2012). Voters with higher education, more political information and a greater interest in politics are more inclined than others to add a personal vote to their ballot. As in many other forms of political activity, the political resources a person possesses influences how active he or she is, on average (Holmberg and Möller 1999: 249–53).

Interestingly enough, research from the Finnish context points in the opposite direction. Among the Finnish electorate it appears as if the voters that can be characterised as having a low level of political sophistication, and that are not well integrated in the political system are the ones that emphasise the choice of candidate over that of the party. Voters without, or with a low sense of party identification, voters who do not trust the political parties, and who have an on average lower level of knowledge about politics, tend to state that the candidates were more important than parties when they decided on how to vote (Bengtsson and Grönlund 2005: 230–38). Results from the Swedish and Finnish environments thus point in opposite directions. A less than far-fetched assumption is that the contradictory tendencies are effects of the electoral system, as well as the way the survey questions are phrased. If this is the case, we would expect the patterns concerning preferential voting in Denmark and Iceland to resemble the ones found in Sweden.

The results presented in Table 6.7, at least partly, confirm previous findings from Finland and Sweden. In Finland, political indicators such as party identification, political awareness and knowledge, as well as ideological extremism display a

Table 6.7: Preferential voting, descriptives

	Denmark 2007			Finland 2007			Iceland 2007			Sweden 2006		
	%	[CI]	n	%	[CI]	n	%	[CI]	n	%	[CI]	n
Gender												
Men	59	[57–61]	1 952	52	[48–57]	594	6	[4–8]	713	18	[16–20]	1 388
Women	54	[52–56]	1 966	51	[47–55]	578	4	[3–6]	705	18	[16–21]	1 392
Age												
18–24 years old	38	[32–45]	217	53	[41–65]	83	7	[3–11]	176	21	[17–26]	299
25–34 years old	45	[41–50]	504	58	[50–66]	168	4	[2–7]	234	22	[18–25]	437
35–44 years old	50	[47–54]	656	56	[47–65]	146	7	[4–10]	282	19	[16–22]	499
45–54 years old	55	[51–58]	721	59	[51–66]	202	5	[2–7]	285	17	[14–21]	503
55–64 years old	64	[61–67]	844	49	[43–56]	252	5	[2–7]	232	15	[12–18]	523
65 years and older	65	[62–68]	966	44	[38–49]	321	3	[1–5]	209	18	[14–21]	519
Civil status												
Single	50	[47–53]	1 237	52	[47–57]	455	4	[2–6]	422	19	[16–21]	941
Married/living together	59	[58–61]	2 693	52	[48–58]	717	6	[4–7]	996	18	[16–20]	1 839
Urbanisation												
Countryside	61	[58–65]	696	55	[46–64]	142	4	[2–5]	586	22	[18–26]	466
–	57	[55–59]	2 531	52	[48–55]	746	–	–	–	17	[15–19]	1 938
Big city	52	[48–56]	668	50	[43–57]	284	6	[4–7]	832	21	[17–25]	396
Education												
Compulsory schooling	53	[49–57]	749	50	[44–57]	293	4	[2–6]	494	15	[12–18]	592

(Cont'd)

Table 6.7: (Cont'd)

	Denmark 2007			Finland 2007			Iceland 2007			Sweden 2006		
	%	[CI]	n	%	[CI]	n	%	[CI]	n	%	[CI]	n
Lower secondary school	58	[56–60]	2 718	53	[49–58]	598	6	[4–8]	536	17	[15–19]	1 080
Higher education	54	[49–58]	463	49	[43–56]	281	5	[3–7]	388	21	[19–24]	1 061
Employment												
Outside the labour market	57	[55–60]	1 467	47	[42–52]	429	4	[2–6]	507	20	[18–23]	766
Blue collar worker	53	[50–57]	777	56	[50–62]	287	7	[4–10]	245	18	[15–23]	351
Self-employed	61	[55–68]	236	52	[41–62]	108	4	[1–7]	161	21	[13–28]	115
Lower white collar worker	53	[49–56]	702	57	[49–65]	163	6	[3–9]	210	17	[14–20]	625
Higher white collar worker	60	[57–64]	742	51	[43–58]	185	5	[2–7]	295	25	[20–30]	272
Party identification												
No	48	[46–51]	1 784	67	[63–72]	475	5	[3–6]	717	17	[15–19]	1 453
Yes	63	[61–65]	2 139	41	[37–45]	697	5	[4–7]	701	26	[22–29]	684
Political awareness												
Low	47	[44–50]	413	60	[54–66]	316	5	[3–7]	413	12	[10–15]	571
Medium	59	[56–61]	1 437	52	[47–57]	384	5	[3–7]	532	21	[18–24]	785
High	64	[61–67]	1 142	46	[41–51]	453	4	[3–7]	473	29	[25–34]	361
Political knowledge												
Low	44	[41–47]	1 023	59	[51–66]	204	5	[2–8]	230	17	[14–21]	464
Medium	57	[55–60]	1 466	56	[51–61]	352	5	[4–7]	863	18	[16–22]	592

(Cont'd)

Table 6.7: (Cont'd)

	Denmark 2007			Finland 2007			Iceland 2007			Sweden 2006		
	%	[CI]	n	%	[CI]	n	%	[CI]	n	%	[CI]	n
High	65	[62–67]	1 441	47	[43–51]	616	5	[3–7]	326	23	[20–26]	655
Left-right self-placement												
Left	56	[53–59]	1 141	36	[28–43]	173	3	[1–6]	193	22	[18–26]	453
Middle	55	[52–57]	1 832	58	[54–62]	688	5	[4–7]	987	20	[17–22]	1 201
Right	62	[58–65]	884	42	[35–48]	266	6	[3–9]	238	20	[16–25]	304
Ideological extremeness												
Low	51	[47–55]	638	59	[52–65]	256	5	[3–7]	487	19	[16–22]	652
Medium	55	[54–59]	1 632	54	[50–59]	505	6	[4–8]	594	21	[17–24]	549
High	59	[57–62]	1 587	40	[34–45]	366	4	[2–7]	337	21	[18–24]	757
Stable voter												
No	47	[45–50]	1 254	65	[59–70]	452	4	[3–6]	684	16	[14–16]	1 447
Yes	61	[59–63]	2 676	43	[37–45]	720	6	[4–8]	734	21	[19–23]	1 333
Total (all voters)	57	[55–58]	3 918	52	[49–55]	1 172	5	[4–6]	1 418	18	[17–20]	2 780

negative pattern with candidate importance. They also, alongside with voting stability, appear to be the most decisive factors. Among the socio-demographic and economic factors differences are smaller. That is, voters who can be considered as less well integrated into the political system attribute a greater importance to candidates than parties when deciding on how to vote, while socio-economic status is of less importance.

As expected, the pattern looks rather the opposite in Sweden, at least concerning the political factors. Party-identifying voters, voters who are politically aware, knowledgeable, stable in their voting behaviour and who have a distinct ideological preference far from the centre, are more active in casting a preferential vote than others. That is, while the strongest interest or focus on which candidates are elected is found among the least politically integrated in Finland, the trend is the reversed in Sweden. In Sweden two other aspects appear to be of importance as well, that is age and education. The younger voters are more frequent preferential voters and the same goes for the highest educated. While the effect of education is predictable, and in line with the results for political resources, such as political knowledge and awareness, the tendency for the younger to be more active candidate selectors, probably is due to the relatively recent introduction of the preferential voting system. Young voters, without longstanding and stable patterns of voting can be expected to be keener on adapting to new rules and opportunities.

Turning to Denmark, a country with a long tradition of preferential voting and where a substantially larger share of the voters use the opportunity to vote for a specific candidate (51 per cent in the 2007 election), we find many of the same effects as in Sweden. Party identifiers, stable voters and voters who are politically knowledgeable and aware, make better use of the opportunity to cast a preferential vote. And as in the Swedish case, voters with a distinct ideological leaning far from the centre on the left-right scale are also more active candidate voters. The young Danish voters are, on the other hand, not very interested in deciding which candidates are representing the party they vote for. Among eighteen to twenty-four year olds, less than 40 per cent cast a preferential vote, compared to 65 per cent for voters who are sixty-five years or older. We also find that women, voters who are married or living together with a partner, and those living at the countryside are more active preferential voters. The more socially integrated Danish voters are, the more likely they are to cast a preferential vote. Yet another interpretation is that there might be some confusion among voters in Denmark and Sweden whether their votes count the same if they simply vote for a party, or if they vote for a candidate that does not succeed in getting elected. That is, a highly political, sophisticated voter might better understand that a preferential vote always at minimum will count the same as a party vote whereas others might believe that it would be lost.

The Icelandic results provide us with more of a challenge to interpret since it contributes few distinct patterns. This might of course be due to the fact that preferential voting is rather uncommon in Iceland. One of the most interesting results is that voters leaning to the right on the ideological scale are more inclined to vote for a candidate than left-wing sympathisers. A weak effect is also found for gender, civil status, age and urbanisation. Men appear to be more frequent preferential voters than women, as are some of the younger age groups, voters who are married or living together with a partner and voters in urban areas. The same goes for blue collar workers and lower white collar workers. It is, however, difficult to find distinct patterns in line with traditional explanatory models such as socio-economic resources or political marginalisation.

In order to find out which results are robust, we will, in Table 6.8, present multivariate analyses for each country. Included in the analyses are, with a few exceptions, the same variables as in Table 6.7. On most accounts the strongest tendencies found in Table 6.7 are confirmed by the multivariate analyses. For Finland, we find that only two of the demographic or socio-economic variables turn out to be significant in the first model, which is age and urbanisation. However, as we see in model 2 for Finland, it is the politically related factors that are of importance in determining who, among Finnish voters, emphasise the choice of candidate over the choice of party. Absence of a closer bond towards a specific party and a volatile vote choice (concerning party) are two important factors. Voters who lack party identification are 18 percentage points more likely than party identifiers to state that the candidate is more important than the party when they decide on how to vote. Yet another variable that correlates positively with candidate centrality is the absence of a distinct ideological leaning. Finnish voters who place themselves in the middle of the ideological scale are 23 percentage points more inclined to give greater importance to the choice of candidate rather than the party, compared to a voter at the endpoint of the ideological scale. On the other hand, we also find that right-wing voters are more candidate oriented than left-wing sympathisers.

The analysis on preferential voting among Danish voters provides very distinct results. Age clearly is a central factor. In model 1 we find that if age increases by a standard deviation around the mean age, the probability that the voters cast a preferential vote increases by 8 percentage points. Under control for political variables in model 2 the effect declines to 5 percentage points. We also find a higher tendency to vote for a candidate among married voters, voters living in rural areas, the politically knowledgeable, aware, party identifiers, and among right-wing voters. In particular, the effect of ideological leaning stands out. Right-wing voters are 29 percentage points more likely to cast a preferential vote than their left-wing counterparts. On the other hand the analysis reveals that blue collar workers are slightly more inclined than others to vote for a candidate, as are voters with low levels of education. It is likely that the latter results, to some extent, are related to the life-cycles pattern found in the analysis.

The recently introduced opportunity to cast a preferential vote in Sweden appears to have become more popular among the younger voters. When controlling for political factors in model 2 we find that if age decreases by a standard deviation around the mean age, the probability of voters to cast a preferential vote will increase with 4 percentage points. As in Denmark, the strongest effect is found for political awareness. The probability for Swedish voters who are politically interested, and who keep track of what is happening through different channels of mass-media, to cast a preferential vote is 26 percentage points higher than among politically unaware voters. The positive relationship between political awareness

Table 6.8: Modelling the probability of voting for a person - marginal change (percentage point)

	Denmark 2007		Finland 2007		Iceland 2007		Sweden 2006	
	Model 1	Model 2	Model 1	Model 2	Model 1	Model 2	Model 1	Model 2
Age in election year	8***	5***	-5***	-2	1	-1	-1	-4***
Women	-4**	0	-1	1	-2*	-2	1	3
Lower secondary	0	-2	2	2	1	1	1	0
Higher education	-4	-7**	-3	0	0	0	6*	3
Not single	7***	6***	-3	-2	1	1	-4*	-4*
Self employed	3	2	3	7	-1	-1	1	1
Lower white collar	-2	-2	7	6	1	0	-5*	-4*
Higher white collar	5**	4	3	3	-2	-0.02	3	3
Blue collar	0	3	4	6	0	1	-6*	-6*
Degree of urbanisation	-4*	-5**	-9*	-6	4***	3***	-5	-7**
Public sector	3	1	4	2	2	2	2	2
Party ID	/	9***	/	-18***	/	0	/	6**
Stable voter	/	6***	/	-14***	/	2	/	4*
Left-right self-placement	/	7**	/	18**	/	6	/	3
Left-right extremeness	/	3	/	-23***	/	-3	/	2
Political awareness	/	29***	/	4	/	7**	/	26***
Political knowledge	/	8***	/	-12	/	-3	/	-1
No. respondents	3 874	3 874	1 137	1 137	1 070	1 070	1 602	1 602
McFadden pseudo R²	0.03	0.06	0.01	0.08	0.04	0.06	0.02	0.05
Log likelihood	-2,575	-2,495	-777	-723	-214	-209	-799	-770
Chi²	150.08	311.16	20.60	130.21	18.13	27.83	28.19	86.29

Note: *p<0.1,**p<0.05,***p<0.01. Education (Ref category: compulsory schooling); Employment (Ref category: Outside the labour market).

and preferential voting is found in all countries, even though it is not statistically significant in the Finnish case. An effect in the same direction, although more modest, is found for party identifiers and stable voters. In Sweden there is also, as in Denmark and Finland, a tendency for voters in urban areas to be less candidate centred than voters living in the country side. However, contrary to the Danish case, we also find a negative (however, in most cases not significant) effect of blue collar workers in Sweden. That is, voters belonging to other categories of employment tend to be more likely to cast a preferential vote, at least higher white-collar and those outside the labour market.

As in the descriptive table, the most striking result for Iceland is the absence of a distinct pattern for preferential voting. In the performed analyses only three variables reach conventional levels of statistical significance. In model 1 we find that men have a 2 percentage point higher probability to cast a preferential vote and that the corresponding increase is 3 percentage points for voters living in urban areas. When the political variables are included in model 2 the gender effect disappears. Instead we find an effect of political awareness in the same direction as in Denmark and in Sweden, although much weaker. The probability of politically aware voters casting a preferential vote is 7 percentage points higher than for politically unaware voters. It should, however, be noted that the fact that such a limited share as 5 per cent of the voters casting a preferential vote, makes it far more difficult to reach statistically significant results, since the variance that is to be explained is very small. An analysis of the same kind, but performed on participation in primary elections provides a more distinct result (not presented here). Perhaps not very surprisingly, we find that party identifiers and stable voters are more inclined to participate in party primaries. The same goes for politically aware voters and voters who lean to the right on the ideological scale. No socio-economic or demographic effects are found when it comes to the Icelandic party primaries.

Conclusion: Voters and the candidates in the Nordic countries

As this chapter has revealed, the relationship between the voters and the candidates that are running for election, looks substantially different in the Nordic countries. Behind the often mentioned similarity in terms of proportional electoral systems, lies an almost maximised variation in the possibilities for preferential voting. Finland has compulsory preferential voting – voters have to vote for a candidate – and Norway has the opposite where no preferential voting is allowed – voters can only vote for the parties. In-between is Denmark with clear effects of preferential voting, Sweden with only minor effects and Iceland with very small effects of the elements of preferential voting.

The large discrepancies concerning the possibilities for preferential voting among the Nordic countries also means that these countries, from an international perspective, can by no means be claimed to constitute a group of their own or be seen as exceptional. On the contrary, we have shown that the level of candidate recognition varies substantially among our countries, where Iceland and Denmark score high from a comparative perspective, while Sweden scores considerably lower and amongst the lowest of the countries used as a reference point. The different systems used, also imply that it is difficult to compare them. However, based on the different indicators presented in the chapter, it appears as if the patterns over time, concerning the importance of candidates, deviate among the five countries. While Icelandic voters have become more inclined to participate in primaries, we have seen that candidate recognition has decreased significantly in Sweden. In Norway, Denmark and Finland it appears as if changes over time are more moderate.

It is also evident that the extensive variation in the systems for preferential voting, hidden under the umbrella of seemingly similar proportional electoral systems, has a real impact on the part that candidates or individual politicians play in public life, as well as in electoral campaigns. It makes the relationship between candidates and voters qualitatively different. It also stands clear that the differences concerning the possibilities for preferential voting have an impact on what type of voters emphasise individual candidates on election day. When preferential voting is optional resources count. Voters who are politically integrated in the sense that they have knowledge, information, and a distinct preference concerning parties as well as ideology, might also be willing to go one step further and decide, not only on how, but also by whom they would like to be represented in the parliament.

When preferential voting is compulsory as in Finland, other factors come into play. Compulsory preferential voting forces candidates to have a visible profile and to focus on their own, rather than merely the party's central electoral campaign. A strong candidate-focus can also cause lower party cohesion due to the many different individual candidate campaigns that are run inside each of the parties. This is in turn likely to make the profile of each party less distinct and less straight forward for voters to evaluate parties as single units. When individual candidates are visible and provide a face to, or if you wish – personalise – a political arena that otherwise might be difficult to sort out in terms of party politics, it is understandable that less resourceful voters, and voters without a distinct party preference, jump on the train.

Our results also indicate that younger voters are more open to adapting to new means of influencing politics. For the recently introduced preferential voting system in Sweden we find that voters of a younger age are keener on casting a preferential vote, opposite to the older Danish system, where it is the older generations that use the possibility more frequently. Although impossible to say with certainty from analysing only one election, it appears as if the results in the Danish case are caused by a typical life-cycle effect, where preferential voting increases with age, independently of what generation you belong to. In Sweden it seems more likely that we are dealing with a generational effect, caused by the newly introduced system. If this interpretation holds, the use of preferential voting is likely to increase over time in Sweden, as new generations and more active preferential voters enter the electorate. The behaviour of parties and individual candidates is, however, likely to determine the fate of the preferential voting system in Sweden. If no individual campaigns are run, voters are likely to lose interest.

Chapter Seven

Voters and the Election Campaign

Someone who holds no strong opinions on politics and hence makes up his mind late in the campaign may very well be susceptible to personal influences because he has learned as a child to take them as useful guides in unknown territory (Lazarsfeld *et al.* 1944: 19).

Introduction

The Nordic countries with their multi-parties, proportional electoral systems infused with a strong welfare state model are often considered as being quite similar when it comes to the conduct of elections, and their political culture, in general. However, there are some remarkable differences between the Nordic countries when it comes to their political campaigning. The CSES collection of elections across many democracies illustrates this point also, especially when it comes to campaigning. Figure 7.1 shows that voters across twenty-five democracies follow the election campaign quite differently. Australian voters follow the campaign intensely whereas voters in Belarus follow it very minimally. When it comes to the Nordic voters we also see differences across the five countries. Iceland and Norway are in the top five of all the twenty-five countries where close to 70 per cent of the voters have followed the campaign closely. In Denmark about 60 per cent of voters follow the campaign closely and in Sweden and Finland only about 50 per cent of the voters do so. This illustrates the point that we should be reluctant to simply group the Nordic countries when trying to understand how campaigns work in these countries.

The election campaigns in the five Nordic countries have developed and matured quite differently and core variables, such as volatility and the number of late deciders, show remarkable differences. In addition, the characteristics of the late deciders show some interesting differences and similarities. This chapter attempts to explain these differences.

Across the Western democracies we have seen increased campaign spending. This tendency is evident also in the Nordic countries, but due to various restrictions on political advertising spending, they are still much behind what we have seen in the latest American election campaigns.

Professionalisation of the election campaign in the Nordic countries

Nordic election campaigns have previously been rather different. The Finnish election campaigns were professionalised early with the use of campaigners, opinion polls, focus groups etc. whereas Danish campaigns were conducted

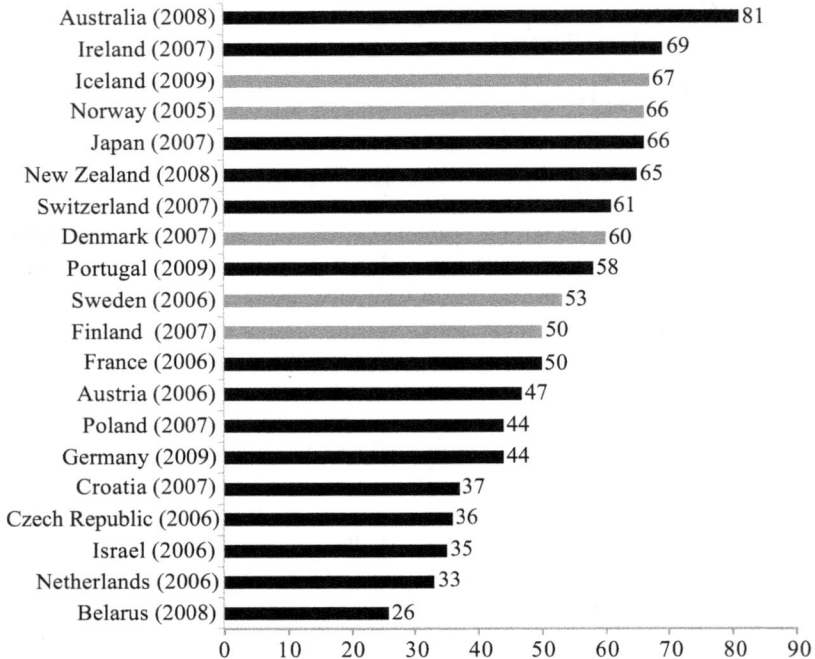

Australia (2008)   81
Ireland (2007)   69
Iceland (2009)   67
Norway (2005)   66
Japan (2007)   66
New Zealand (2008)   65
Switzerland (2007)   61
Denmark (2007)   60
Portugal (2009)   58
Sweden (2006)   53
Finland (2007)   50
France (2006)   50
Austria (2006)   47
Poland (2007)   44
Germany (2009)   44
Croatia (2007)   37
Czech Republic (2006)   36
Israel (2006)   35
Netherlands (2006)   33
Belarus (2008)   26

Figure 7.1: Percentages following the election campaign (very closely and fairly closely)

Source: CSES Module 3

mostly by the party activists and the candidates themselves (Bille *et al.* 1992; Sundberg and Högnabba 1992). However, within the last decade, the campaigns have been somewhat professionalised levelling the differences between the countries. The literature defines a professionalised campaign as being centralised and by applying techniques such as telemarketing, direct-mail, election research, opinion polls, focus groups and use of external consultants, as well as hiring staff with training in communication and campaigning (Gibson and Rommele 2009; Strömbäck 2009).

In Denmark, prior to the 2007 election, all parties except the Danish People's Party and the first-time-running party '*New Alliance*', commissioned some kind of private polling before the election. Social Democrats, Conservative, Social Liberal, Socialist People's Party and *Venstre* also conducted focus groups combined with major public opinion surveys. The parties' budget for campaigns had increased not only with the use of polls, but also with the employment of many trained employees in professional polling, communication and campaigning (Hansen 2008; Hansen and Pedersen 2008).

In Finland, this development had come almost twenty years earlier along with a massive increase in public party support allowing the parties to buy ads, consultancy services and to conduct their own polls. For example, up to the 1991 Finnish election both the Social Democrats, the Centre Party and the National Coalition commissioned private opinion surveys (Sundberg and Högnabba 1992). Since then, the amount spent on campaigning has increased substantially, not the least due to the large expense of television campaigning (Borg and Moring 2005). During the same period funding from individuals and companies has expanded (Moring 2006). The development appears to have peaked in the 2007 election (Moring and Mykkänen 2012). Harsh critique from the Group of States Against Corruption laid the groundwork and an incautious comment by a Finnish MP set off a far reaching political funding scandal with consequences for parties, individual politicians as well as the possibilities of private funding in the latest 2011 general election (Mattila and Sundberg 2012).

In the Norwegian parliamentary election campaign of 1989 the parties sporadically used some opinion polls and did conduct systematic media training for the candidates. In the planning of the 2001 election campaign, all parties commissioned some kind of poll, however only the largest parties commissioned comprehensive polls whereas the smaller parties, with less funding, only conducted some single issues polls. All parties but the Centre Party and the Progress Party conducted focus groups in order to validate their campaign message. The 2001 campaign was more focused on political leaders; it was more centralised and had fewer messages than ever before (Aardal *et al.* 2004; Karlsen and Narud 2004).

In Sweden the Social Democrats started early in the 1960s with a somewhat more professionalised campaign. The Conservatives made a real go at things in 1968 but since the election became a major defeat, they did not move towards professionalisation until the 1990s. The Social Democrats were the first to hire external consultants in the 1994 election and by 2006, all the Swedish parties used opinion polls, had campaigning headquarters, started planning the campaign at least six months before the election and all but one, applied focus groups. Furthermore, hiring advertising agencies have also become the norm among most parties (Ekengren and Oscarsson 2009; Strömbäck 2009).

In Iceland, election campaigns have mainly been fought on a national level through the mass media. Candidates from all parties present their views in the national newspapers and frequently take part in discussions both on private and public radio and TV, whereas the impact of local party papers and rallies has decreased. The election campaigns in Iceland have become increasingly professionalised since the 1980s. Political advertisements are allowed both on public and private radio and TV and the first campaign marked by TV advertisements was in 1987. Besides, most political parties have increasingly used services from professional communication specialists, pollsters and hired staff, while the role of party workers has decreased. The professionalisation of the Icelandic campaigns has greatly increased the election expenses of the parties. As there was no law on party financing or campaign spending until 2007, detailed accounts of campaign costs, and the parties' sources of income, were not available until recently. However it was clear that increasingly generous public financing played an important role. Many observers thought this was also the case for private contributions, especially from the business community.

A peculiarity of Icelandic election campaigns is the widespread use of primaries, since the early 1970s, as a method for the selection of candidates. In 2007 and in 2009, around 30 per cent of voters participated in party primaries. The primaries are in many cases quite expensive for individual candidates, who have to organise their own personal campaigns and networks. As a result, party membership has increased in the last decade to an amazing 25–30 per cent of the voting population – the only activity of most party members is, however, simply taking part in a primary. Until recently, the primary candidates were not obliged to publicly reveal expenses or incomes for their personal campaigns. However, it has been revealed that parties and individual candidates have received enormous private contributions, before the 2007 legislation on party financing. This law imposed rather strict restrictions on private contributions to parties. As a result, the parties reached a voluntary agreement on maximum spending on several types of advertising. Due to the new law on party financing, loud criticism of private contributions, and the poor conditions of the economy, campaign advertising in 2009 was more modest than had been the case for many years.

Another common trend, and part of the more professionalised campaigns in the Nordic countries, is a development to focus campaigns more and more on party leaders rather than on parties. Along with the professionalised campaign we have also seen a strong increase in campaign budgets. For example, the rough estimates are that the campaign budgets in Denmark have close to doubled from 2001 to 2007 with spending now well above 100 million DDK. In Finland the trend was similar between the 2003 and 2007 elections when the central campaign budget for the five main parties almost doubled and reached some 5.2 million Euros (Moring and Mykkänen 2007). This sum does not, however, include individual candidate spending that clearly generally exceeds the amount spent by the parties as central organisations (Pesonen *et al.* 1993; Borg and Moring 2005). A successful personal campaign in the election of 2003 did, on average, amount to €27,000 and in 2007 €38,000, an increase of about 40 per cent (Moring and Mykkänen 2007). Furthermore, there is very little control of the use of public or private money that parties can spend during a campaign in the Nordic countries with the exception of Iceland.

Generally speaking we have seen a similar development in the Nordic countries towards a more professionalised campaign even though this development came first in Finland and last in Denmark.

In many ways the political campaigns in the Nordic countries (except Iceland) are unique compared to other western countries because of the ban on political advertisements on TV, and partly also on public radio (Leroy and Siune 1994; Moring 2006; NOU 2004; Petersson *et al.* 2006: 52; Siune 1987; Siune 1994). In 2009, in connection with the European Election, TV ads were allowed for the first time in Sweden (Dahlberg 2010). This ban is probably one major reason why the professionalisation of the campaign has been lagging behind many other countries and negative campaigning was kept at a minimum (Hansen and Pedersen 2008).

Table 7.1: Some elements of the Nordic election campaigns

	Denmark	**Finland**	**Iceland**	**Norway**	**Sweden**
Election date fixed	no	yes	no	yes	yes
Short intensive campaign	yes	yes	yes	yes	yes
Early professionalisation of campaign	no	yes	no	no	no
TV ads allowed	no	yes (only commercial TV)	yes	no	yes (from 2009)
Free slot for parties on TV	yes	no	yes	no	no

Do campaigns matter?

Research on political campaigns has suggested various models for understanding the insensitivity of political information during a campaign. From the literature on campaign effects, Hansen (2008) sums up six competing hypotheses:

1. The *civic engagement* effect that argues that people will learn and become more politically engaged due to the campaign (Craig *et al.* 2005; Freedman *et al.* 2004; Norris *et al.* 1999).

2. The *priming studies* argument that campaigns affect what issues the voters evaluate the parties and leaders on and sequentially their vote (Iyengar and Simon 1993; Johnston *et al.* 1992; Togeby 2007).

3. The *minimal effect models* argue that campaigns only mobilise existing prepositions and voters only seek to confirm their intermediated vote choice (Berelson *et al.* 1954; Campbell *et al.* 1960; Lazarsfeld *et al.* 1944; Schmitt-Beck 2007: 753).

4. The *memory based models* argue that the vote choice is based on sampling of the available information filtered through the voters' predisposition and in the light of their political awareness and sophistication (Price and Zaller 1993; Sciarini and Kriesi 2003; Zaller 1992).

5. *Online based models* argue that voters continuously incorporate the political discourses in their vote choice and then soon forget these discourses (Bizer *et al.* 2006; Lodge *et al.* 1989; Lodge *et al.* 1995).

6. The *shortcut based models* highlight the various shortcuts to political choice (e.g. basic likes and dislikes) (Lau and Redlawsk 2001; Popkin 1991; Sniderman *et al.* 1991).

If we turn our attention to the voters in the five countries, when it comes to the number of voters making decisions during the campaign we see some interesting similarities and differences.[1] The development of the number of voters making

---

1. There has been some discussion on whether or not self-reported decision time after the election is held is a reliable measure of decision time. However self-reported time of vote choice seems quite reliable in parliamentary systems like the Nordic countries, with relative short, well-defined

decisions during the campaign gives us some tentative indications on whether or not the campaigns seem to affect the vote choice (*see* Figure 7.2). We are aware that this is an indirect measure and that there are other elements such as media exposure, a declining interest in politics and the weakening parties ties, in general, that also cause an increase in the number of late deciders. It also needs to be emphasised that even though the question on the number of late deciders is identically phrased, the answer is related to five different electoral systems.

In Denmark a voter can either vote for the entire party (party-vote) or for a specific candidate on the parties' list. In 2007, 50.8 per cent of the voters decided to place their vote next to a candidate and 49.2 next to the party. This 50/50 split has been quite stable over time. Denmark is divided into ten electoral districts. The list of candidates varies between these ten districts. In Sweden, like in Denmark, voters have the opportunity to vote for the entire party or a candidate on that list. In 2006, 22.6 per cent of the Swedish voters crossed a candidate. However, the effect of the personal vote is much stronger in Denmark compared to Sweden, as the ordering of the candidates being elected to parliament is, for almost all lists, determined by the personal votes. In Sweden a candidate must get 8 per cent of the party vote in her constituency to come to the top of the list, this means that the actual effect of the personal vote system in Sweden is very limited. In 2006, only six out of 349 Swedish parliamentarians got their mandates because of the system. In Iceland, the voter votes for a party list, which is ranked by the party, however the voter can change the ranking order of the candidates, but the effect is quite limited. In Finland, the voter must vote for a candidate, and not only vote for the party, whereas in Norway it is the direct opposite. There the voter must vote for the entire party and cannot cast a personal vote. The voters in Norway are permitted to change the list by crossing out the name of one or more candidates. However, in practice, such deletions by individual voters have never affected the result, as the majority of the voters need to do the same changes in the ordering. To sum up, the personal vote in Finland is fully determinant on the ordering of candidate. In Denmark it is quite determinant, in Sweden and Iceland only of limited importance and in Norway of no importance. *See also* Chapter Two and Chapter Six on these issues.

When voters answer the question on when they decided how to vote, it is a mixture of deciding to vote at all, what party to vote for and which specific candidate to vote for. In comparing the five electoral systems about the potential effect of the personal vote, we would expect a positive relationship between effect of personal voting and the number of late deciders. That is, the order of the countries should be Finland, Denmark, Sweden, Iceland and Norway. However this is apparently not the case when we investigate Figure 7.2, with the trend of the number of late deciders across the five countries. Thus, we must reject the

and intensive campaigns, where the candidates are well known in advance of the campaign. The vote options (which running parties and candidates to vote for) are, so to speak, known before the election campaign (Fournier *et al.* 2001; Fournier *et al.* 2004).

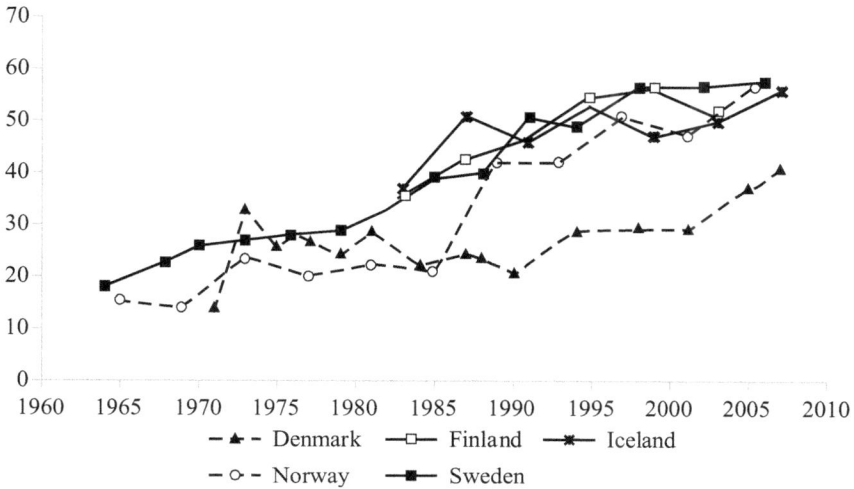

Figure 7.2: Time of vote choice (per cent deciding during the campaign)

hypothesis that the effect of a personal vote is directly related to the number of late deciders.

All countries tend to follow the same pattern of an increased number of late-deciders as we have seen across the West-European democracies (Norris *et al.* 1999: 178). The share of the electorate that state that they decide on how to vote during the election campaign, has clearly increased in four out of five countries included in the study.

The trend is most distinct in Sweden and Norway.[2] In both of these countries in the 1960s, less than 20 per cent made up their mind about how to vote during the election campaign. Today close to 60 per cent of the voters decide on how to vote during the election campaign. The Finnish data, which covers the period between 1983 and 2003, also displays a rather large increase in late deciders, from around 35 to slightly over 50 per cent. An increase has also taken place in Denmark, but in this case the change is more modest and today the level of late deciders constitutes around 40 per cent of the Danish electorate. Thus across the five countries we have seen a continuous increase in late deciders.

Several hypotheses can be set out to understand the development of the close race and how it might increase the number of late deciders, as voters wait until the last minutes to vote for a preferred alliance of parties supporting a particular

---

2.   The large increase in the number of late deciders in Norway from 1985 to 1989 is partly explained by an increased polarisation of Norwegian politics, where the extremes parties on both the left and the right gained support. The increased polarisation made it more difficult for voters to see clear government alternatives, which eventually led to late decisions (Foss 1990; Valen *et al.* 1990). This also explains why so many Norwegians changed party in the 1989 election (*see* Figure 7.2).

prime minister. The easier the access new parties have to the electoral arena (e.g. electoral threshold, how parties are eligible to run for office and media norms of exposure) the more (new) parties there might be for voters to choose between, and become acquainted with during the campaign, thus, extending the time needed to make a final vote choice. We might also believe that the particular issues on which the campaign is focused can affect the number of late deciders. Finally, we could speculate that if there is a large number of new candidates running, or if the major officeholders are not rerunning, i.e. if the present Prime Minister is not running again, then voters might need more time in order to make a final choice. If any these hypotheses are relevant in understanding the development of the increasing number of late deciders in the Nordic countries, then we should see Denmark deviate on some of these mentioned independent variables. However when comparing Denmark with the others Nordic countries, Denmark does not seem to stand out when it comes to any of the above mentioned variables. Thus we have to look elsewhere for the explanation. It is more likely that the late professionalisation of the campaign in Denmark, compared to the other Nordic countries, is the key to understanding the development in the number of late deciders. We will thus expect that the number of late deciders in Denmark will catch up to the other Nordic countries if the professionalisation of campaigns in Denmark remains high.

Since some parties believe elections are won or lost in the last weeks of the campaign, they tend to come up with new policies and pledges very late in the campaigns. As the voters might be aware of this it seems irrational to decide early. Finally, the parties are clustered closer together on the political left-right scale than ever before, causing a party shift to be less politically fundamental than earlier. If we take this further we could create four types of voters.

Partisans, who decide early and believe their vote counts, the *calculated voters* that decide during the campaign and believe their vote counts, the *disengaged* voters that decide early, but do not think their vote matters and finally the *capricious* voters that decide late and do not think their vote matters. The table below shows the distribution for all the Nordic countries taken together.

Table 7.2: Voters divided on time of vote decision and whether they believe their vote counts (per cent, all Nordic countries)

	Decided before campaign	Decided during campaign	Total
Vote believed to matter much	*Partisans*	*Calculated*	
	23	18	41
Vote believed not to matter much	*Disengaged*	*Capricious*	
	27	32	59
Total	50	50	

Note: Weighted N=4.095. *See* McAllister (2002) for a similar distinctions. Chi2-test of independence p<0.01.

Table 7.3: Voters divided on time of vote decision and whether they believe their vote counts (per cent)

	Decided before campaign	Decided during campaign
Vote believed to matter much	**Partisans**	**Calculated**
	Denmark: 29	Denmark: 17
	Finland: 11	Finland: 18
	Iceland: 28	Iceland: 19
	Norway: 21	Norway: 18
	Sweden: 20	Sweden: 21
Vote believed not to matter much	**Disengaged**	**Capricious**
	Denmark 30	Denmark: 24
	Finland: 25	Finland: 46
	Iceland: 25	Iceland: 28
	Norway: 29	Norway: 32
	Sweden: 23	Sweden: 36

Note: Weighted about n=1.000 for each country.

The smallest group is the calculated voter with 18 per cent whereas the capricious voters account for almost one-third of the votes. Denmark with the fewest late deciders should stand out. Looking at Table 7.3, this shows that Denmark is at an extreme in all four groups, as it has the most partisans, the most disengaged and the fewest calculated and capricious voters.

Finland's results with the very candidate-focused elections, explains why the country has so few partisans and such strong competition between candidates in elections and it might also explain why the country has so many capricious voters. Finally, the traditional, very broad coalitions in Finland cause many Finns to believe that their votes do not matter much, which also helps us understand the large number of capricious voters in the country (Arter 2009).

Denmark seems to be an outlier in the sense that Denmark has significantly fewer campaign deciders than the other four countries. On the other hand Denmark is the 'prototypical forerunner', i.e., the first country to experience a shock to the political system with the earthquake-election of 1973 along with increases in volatility (Goul Andersen and Hoff 2001: 66). Furthermore, Denmark is also the only country of the five where the development of professionalised campaigns has been slowest. That is, it could be argued that there might be a positive relation between the degree of campaign professionalisation (and the factors leading to this) and the number of voters deciding during the campaign, as suggested by Strömbäck (2009). This explanation goes hand in hand with the fact that Denmark professionalised late and has the fewest campaign deciders.

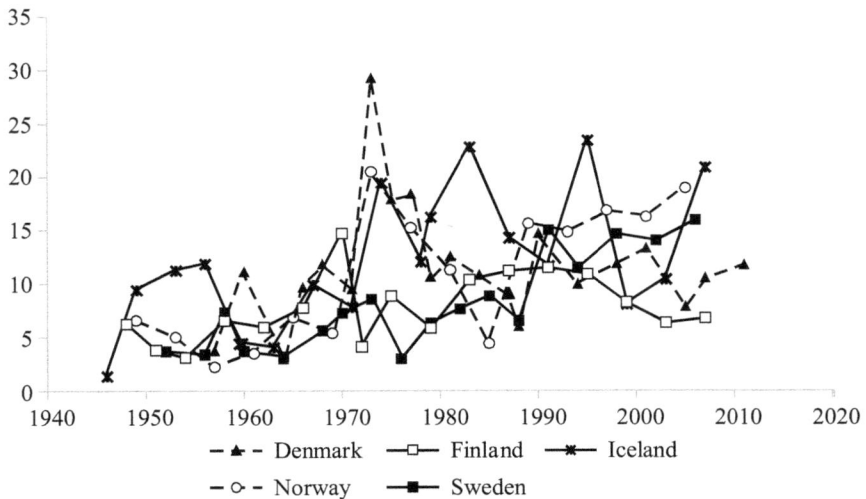

Figure 7.3: Volatility (Pedersen's index)

Another way to gain an understanding of the electoral change is to analyse the voters' volatility. Volatility is measured by summing the absolute values of all parties gains and losses dividing by two (also known as Pedersen's index) at each election (Pedersen 1979). The volatility for each of the Nordic countries over the past sixty years is reported in Figure 7.3.

With the emerging of many new parties and the merging of existing parties, Iceland stands out with high, fluctuation volatility in the entire period. The Danish earthquake-election of 1973 stands out in Figure 7.3 as it did in Figure 7.2 on decision-time, where volatility jumped close to an index value of 30. This general development follows the tendency among Western democracies, i.e. a slight increase in volatility since a more stable period in the 1950s and 1960s (Dalton and Wattenberg 2000; Gallagher *et al.* 2006: 294). However, looking at the individual countries, large fluctuations are shown where Norway and Sweden, in the last three elections, have had a minor increase in volatility whereas Finland has had a minor decrease.

Comparing the volatility (Figure 7.3) with the development in time-of-vote-choice (Figure 7.2) provides us with yet another interesting finding. The (Pearson) correlations between the two are, in Sweden 0.9, Norway 0.7, Denmark 0.2, Iceland -0.3 and in Finland -0.4, however, only statistically significant ($p<0.05$) in the Swedish and Norwegian cases. Thus, we have a strong positive relation between time-of-vote choice in Norway and Sweden and an inconclusive relationship in Finland and Denmark. Accordingly, we see a development in Sweden and Norway where an increased number of late deciders goes hand in hand with increased volatility.

It is generally held that the comparatively low rates of volatility but high degree of late deciders in Finnish politics, at least partly, is due to the fact that voters can be volatile in their vote choice without having to change party. By voting for a different candidate than in the previous election, they are able to show dissatisfaction without the need to change party. Furthermore, it might be the case that in Finland and Denmark the campaign tends to reinforce and mobilise existing values and the relationship between values and vote choice. In this sense, the campaigns in Denmark and Finland cause voters to stay with the same party, whereas the campaigns in Sweden and Norway tend to provide alternatives and challenge existing values and the values' relationship to political choices, and in this sense, the campaigns cause voters to change party.

With this interpretation, the campaigns should work differently in the different countries. We have already seen from Table 7.1, that Sweden and Norway are identical on all five institutional variables regarding the campaign. That is, Sweden and Norway are the two countries, which have the most institutional regulations on the parties' campaigns in their effort to reach the voters with a total ban on ads on TV, without giving the parties free slots on TV. Such regulation should encourage parties to focus their campaign activities on other fields such as direct advertising and direct contact between voters and politicians. Nevertheless, Table 7.4 seems to tell another story when it comes to how the campaigns work in the five countries, according to the national election surveys (*see* Table 7.4).

Sweden is the outlier on all three questions. The voters in Sweden tend to be less persuaded by others for a particular party, participate less in campaign activities and are the least contacted by a party or candidate. Norwegians also tend to be relatively less inclined to participate in campaign activities or to be contacted by a party or candidate, compared to Iceland, Denmark, and Finland.

That is the hypothesis so far, that the campaigns in Norway and Sweden reach fewer, and have an effect on fewer, voters compared to the three other Nordic countries. The campaigns in Sweden and Norway reach fewer voters because of the stronger regulation on the media, and furthermore, the parties are apparently less able to reach voters and mobilise voters during the campaigns.

In this light, the voters in Sweden and Norway are more left to themselves during the campaign than in the three other countries. Less interference from parties seems to increase the relationship between volatility and number of campaign deciders. On the other hand, the stronger interaction from parties in

Table 7.4: Voters relationship with the campaign (n)

	Denmark	Finland	Iceland	Norway	Sweden
Tried to persuade others to vote for a particular party or candidate in the election? (index: 0–100)	17 (2 019)	8 (1 191)	15 (1 441)	11 (2 034)	8 (1 058)
Participated in the campaign e.g. meeting, posters etc. (index: 0–100)	6 (2 023)	7 (1 188)	10 (1 435)	4 (2 035	2 (1 058)
Contacted by party or candidate (%)	24 (2 022)	21 (1 192)	28 (1 438)	15 (2 035)	7 (1 058)

Source: CSES model 2. Index is a mean of 0=Never, 33=Rarely, 67=Occasionally, 100=Frequently. The groups are statistically significantly p<0.01 (ONE-way-ANOVA).

Denmark, Iceland and Finland tends to mobilise preexisting political values and consequently, removes any relationship between volatility and time-of-vote-choice-decision.

Who decides during the campaign?

If these aggregated, suggestive explanations are true we should find some of the same patterns for individual voters across the Nordic countries. Table 7.5 shows the bivariate relationship between campaign deciders and key demographic and other key variables.

Generally speaking, we have more voters deciding during the campaign in Finland and the fewest deciding at that time in Denmark, and despite these differences, the independent variables show many of the same relationships. One exception is gender. In Finland more women and men decide during the campaign, whereas it is the opposite in the four other countries. This suggests that the specific elections count for the differences rather than general country explanations because of the very similar patterns on all the other variables. On age, education, employment, party ID, political awareness, political knowledge, civic status and urbanisation, we find the same general tendencies across the five Nordic countries.

The older the voter the less likely is it that the decision on how to vote will be made during the campaign. Inglehart's (1990) hypothesis that political choice is socialised among young voters and then becomes more stable as the voter becomes older, seem to be confirmed also in these analyses.

The higher the education level the more likely it is that the final decision on how to vote is taken during the campaign. The more educated are more likely to be campaign deciders because education causes more openness to new information. They are likely to be more rational, in the sense of waiting until the last minute in order to be able to include as much information in the vote choice as possible. This suggests that education helps to open up party choice rather than simply relying on the inheritance of a specific party choice based on social class (Hansen 2009b; Oscarsson 2007).

White collar workers tend to be more campaign deciders. Higher political knowledge and more political awareness facilitate fewer campaign deciders suggesting that political knowledge and awareness help people make up their minds before the campaign starts.

Not surprisingly, party identifiers depress campaign deciders as many of these voters are very robust to outside influences and information in their party choice. With regard to civil status, urbanisation and public/private employment there are no general differences.

Another interesting finding is that many campaign deciders are clustered around the middle of the left-right political scale where the density of the parties is highest, i.e. on the middle of the scale where many parties fight a political battle for potential voters. The finding suggests that there seems to be good reason for this as many of the voters who place themselves on the middle of the scale decide relatively late, compared to voters who place themselves at the extremes, who decide earlier.

Table 7.5: Voters deciding how to vote during the campaign

	Denmark 2007			Finland 2003			Iceland 2007			Norway 2005			Sweden 2006		
	%	n	CI	%	n	CI	%	n	CI	%	n	CI	%	n	CI
Gender															
Men	38	1 937	[36–40]	66	519	[62–71]	44	774	[41–48]	51	951	[47–54]	55	1 308	[53–58]
Women	44	1 918	[42–46]	61	502	[57–65]	58	767	[54–61]	60	844	[57–64]	60	1 330	[58–63]
Age															
18–24 years old	62	214	[55–68]	84	113	[77–91]	68	228	[61–75]	68	168	[60–75]	75	272	[69–80]
25–34 years old	50	495	[45–54]	81	153	[74–87]	65	265	[58–71]	64	268	[58–70]	71	407	[67–76]
35–44 years old	47	647	[44–51]	69	177	[62–76]	57	293	[51–63]	60	390	[55–65]	62	469	[58–67]
45–54 years old	40	701	[36–43]	62	190	[55–69]	46	292	[41–52]	56	366	[51–62]	55	481	[51–60]
55–64 years old	37	829	[33–40]	52	203	[45–59]	41	240	[35–47]	47	317	[41–52]	53	506	[49–58]
65-years old and older	33	958	[30–36]	47	185	[39–54]	32	223	[25–38]	41	282	[35–47]	41	503	[37–45]
Education															
Compulsory schooling	38	731	[34–42]	52	279	[45–58]	49	567	[45–54]	49	244	[43–56]	46	557	[42–50]
Lower secondary school (student)	41	2 675	[39–43]	69	542	[65–73]	49	572	[45–53]	53	786	[49–57]	60	1 010	[57–63]
Higher education (university, teachers, nurses)	45	460	[40–50]	68	199	[62–75]	56	402	[51–61]	59	765	[56–63]	64	1 026	[61–67]
Employment															
Outside the labour market	39	1 452	[37–42]	63	463	[59–68]	46	548	[42–50]	50	561	[45–54]	55	732	[51–59]
Self-employed	38	232	[31–44]	61	89	[50–72]	50	169	[42–57]	51	135	[42–60]	63	107	[53–72]

(Cont'd)

Table 7.5: (Cont'd)

	Denmark 2007			Finland 2003			Iceland 2007			Norway 2005			Sweden 2006		
	%	n	CI	%	n	CI	%	n	CI	%	n	CI	%	n	CI
Blue-collar worker (incl. unskilled workers)	40	756	[37–44]	61	230	[54–67]	56	282	[50–62]	54	208	[47–61]	57	335	[51–62]
Lower white-collar worker	44	689	[40–47]	70	126	[62–79]	55	238	[49–62]	60	524	[55–64]	65	604	[61–69]
Higher white-collar worker	44	737	[40–48]	67	113	[58–76]	53	304	[48–59]	60	367	[55–65]	64	263	[58–70]
Public or private employment															
Public employed	44	830	[40–47]	65	229	[59–71]	51	368	[46–57]	56	627	[52–60]	60	826	[56–63]
Private employed	40	3 036	[38–42]	63	792	[60–67]	50	803	[47–54]	55	963	[52–58]	60	1 223	[57–63]
Voters identify themselves with a party															
No	58	1 731	[56–61]	72	485	[68–76]	62	796	[59–66]	71	915	[68–75]	74	1 379	[71–76]
Yes	27	2 130	[25–29]	56	536	[51–60]	39	745	[36–43]	39	880	[36–42]	31	670	[28–35]
Political awareness (pol. interest and media use)															
Low	44	1 274	[41–47]	65	263	[59–71]	59	498	[55–64]	59	395	[53–64]	65	543	[61–69]
Medium	41	1 457	[38–43]	66	369	[61–71]	53	558	[48–57]	55	500	[51–60]	61	761	[58–65]
High	38	1 135	[35–41]	61	389	[56–66]	42	485	[38–47]	54	900	[50–57]	47	354	[41–52]
Political knowledge															
Low	44	990	[41–48]	65	188	[58–72]	59	298	[53–65]	62	543	[57–66]	64	437	[60–69]
Medium	41	1 445	[39–44]	61	553	[57–65]	53	909	[50–56]	56	619	[52–60]	59	569	[55–63]
High	38	1 431	[36–41]	68	280	[62–74]	40	334	[35–46]	50	633	[46–53]	56	646	[53–60]

(Cont'd)

Table 7.5: (Cont'd)

	Denmark 2007			Finland 2003			Iceland 2007			Norway 2005			Sweden 2006		
	%	n	CI	%	n	CI	%	n	CI	%	n	CI	%	n	CI
Left-right self-placement															
Left (0–3)	41	1 130	[38–43]	64	145	[56–72]	47	210	[40–54]	45	413	[40–50]	44	442	[40–49]
Middle (4–6)	46	1 780	[44–48]	64	605	[60–68]	56	1 084	[53–59]	62	1 087	[59–65]	68	1 154	[65–70]
Right (7–10)	32	882	[28–35]	60	207	[53–68]	35	247	[29–41]	46	295	[40–52]	51	298	[46–57]
Distance from mean left-right self-placement															
Low	43	601	[40–47]	71	224	[65–76]	56	551	[51–60]	61	398	[56–67]	71	627	[68–75]
Medium	50	1 609	[46–54]	57	461	[51–64]	61	632	[56–66]	63	901	[58–68]	63	527	[59–67]
High	38	1 582	[36–40]	63	272	[58–67]	42	358	[38–46]	50	496	[46–53]	47	740	[44–51]
Civil status															
Single	43	1 220	[40–46]	63	418	[58–68]	53	497	[48–57]	55	505	[51–60]	60	880	[57–63]
Married/sambo	40	2 646	[38–42]	65	603	[61–69]	50	1 044	[47–54]	56	1 290	[53–58]	57	1 758	[54–59]
Degree of urbanisation															
Country side	41	684	[38–45]	67	221	[60–74]	51	636	[46–55]	53	570	[49–57]	55	427	[50–60]
– in between	40	2 487	[38–42]	62	589	[58–66]							58	1 842	[56–60]
Big city	44	664	[40–47]	66	211	[59–73]	51	905	[48–55]	56	1 223	[53–59]	61	369	[56–66]
Changed party															
No	29	2 674	[27–31]	56	685	[52–60]	41	734	[37–44]	39	952	[36–42]	39	1 296	[36–41]
Yes	68	1 189	[65–71]	79	336	[74–83]	62	807	[59–66]	76	821	[73–79]	77	1 342	[74–79]
Total (all voters)	41	3 866	[39–43]	64	1 021	[61–67]	51	1 541	[48–54]	55	1 795	[53–58]	58	2 638	[56–60]

Note: Only the Finnish data is weighted due to sampling procedure. The categories for political awareness and political knowledge are calculated so approximately 1/3 of voters are placed in each category for each of the two countries.

Finally, we can see that campaign deciders are the ones who, most often, tend to change party, i.e. decide during the campaign. For many of them, this also facilitates a change in party choice from the previous election.

However, it might be easier to look at the binomial regressions in Table 7.6 in order to identify similarities and differences, as many of the independent variables in the bivariate analyses in Table 7.5 correlate and might then cancel out the other variables that are controlled for.

Younger people are more likely to decide during the campaign whereas older voters are less likely to do so. If age increases by a standard deviation around the mean age, the probability that the voters decide during the campaign decreases by 11 percentage points. Late deciders are clustered around the middle of the political left-right where parties also tend to cluster and are a common feature in the five Nordic countries. Voters who do not change party choice in the election, compared to the previous election, decide much earlier than voters who end up changing party. Across the five countries the probability of deciding during the campaign increases with 31 percentage points if the voter actually changes party. This finding suggests that the campaign is quite important among floating voters, and that for many votes the final decision to change party is actually taken during the campaign.

Voters with higher education decide 14 percentage points more during the campaign than voters with compulsory schooling. On the other hand, increased political knowledge and political awareness has the opposite effect as the two factors decrease the number of late deciders in the general model. This shows that political knowledge and awareness help people make up their minds before the campaign starts whereas higher education seems to make moves open to information and input during the campaign and thus later decisions.

Summing up: The young ones, the higher educated, the least politically aware, the voters close to the middle of the left-right scale, and voters changing party from the previous election, are the most likely to decide how to vote during the campaign. These patterns are generally consistent in all the Nordic elections.

However gender in the multivariate regression also shows the opposite effect for Finland compared to the other countries, suggesting that specific elections in each country count for the difference with regard to gender.

Conclusion

Within the last twenty years we have seen an increased professionalisation of the campaigns in the Nordic countries where parties use opinion polls, hired staff and various other external professionals in planning and conducting their campaigns. This development came first in Finland and last in Denmark especially because there were less restrictions on media campaigns and more candidate focused campaigns in Finland.

When it comes to the number of voters following the campaign, the five Nordic countries are scattered between other developed countries so we see no exceptionalism here.

We have seen an increase in the number of voters deciding during the campaign in all five Nordic countries. Close to 60 per cent of the voters today decide during the campaign except in Denmark where around 40 per cent decide during the campaign. The increased number of late deciders correlates strongly with increased volatility in Sweden and Norway, but not in the other countries at all. This suggests that the campaigns in Sweden and Norway have facilitated increased volatility whereas this is not the case in the other countries. One reason that might contribute to this is that the Swedes and Norwegians show the least amount of participation in campaign activities compared to the other countries, i.e. the parties are less able to directly influence the voters in these countries.

Denmark seems to be left behind the rapid trend of massive, increasing voter volatility, and the increased number of campaign deciders, compared to the other Nordic countries. Even through Denmark has experienced an increased number of late deciders, the volatility seems rather stable as about one-third of voters change party from one election to the next (Stubager *et al.* 2013). This slow development in Denmark also causes the differences between the Nordic countries to be larger than before.

Across the five Nordic countries similar variables tend to explain whether or not individual voters make their decision during the campaign. A typical campaign decider is younger, higher educated, a white-collar worker, who does not identify with a party, who places herself on the middle of the left-right political scale, has a low level of knowledge and political awareness, and changes party in the elections.

Table 7.6: Modelling the probability of deciding late – marginal change (percentage point)

	Denmark 2007		Finland 2003		Iceland 2007		Norway 2005		Sweden 2006	
	Model 1	Model 2	Model 1	Model 2	Model 1	Model 2	Model 1	Model 2	Model 1	Model 2
Age in election year	-9***	-5***	-15***	-13***	-12***	-10***	-7***	-5**	-7***	-3*
Women	5***	3	-6*	-5	15***	11***	10***	8***	3	3
Lower secondary	7***	8***	6*	8*	4	6	3	7	14***	16***
Higher education	8**	9***	9*	11**	7	11**	6	15***	17***	21***
Not single	-2	2	2	3	2	5	6*	7**	0	2
Self-employed	-3	-1	-8	-5	7	10	0	2	5	6
Lower white-collar	-2	0	-1	-1	4	4	5	8*	1	4
Higher white-collar	0	2	-5	-3	3	4	6	9**	-2	-2
Blue-collar	-4*	-3	-12***	-12***	9	6	5	6	-7	-3
Degree of urbanisation	0	0	-7	-8	-4	-2	1	1	2	2
Public sector	-1	-2	-2	0	1	1	-2	0	2	3
Stable voter (party choice)		-37***		-16***		-17***		-35***		-38***
Left-right self-placement		-2		3		-8		11		15**
Left-right extremeness		-15***		-6		-19***		-27***		-38***
Political awareness		-6		-19*		-20**		-14		-21***
Political knowledge		-3		2		-5		-17***		5

(Cont'd)

Table 7.6: (Cont'd)

	Denmark 2007		Finland 2003		Iceland 2007		Norway 2005		Sweden 2006	
	Model 1	Model 2	Model 1	Model 2	Model 1	Model 2	Model 1	Model 2	Model 1	Model 2
No. respondents	3 816	3 816	1 002	1 002	1 07	1 07	1 489	1 489	1 558	1 558
McFadden pseudo R^2	0.02	0.12	0.08	0.10	0.06	0.11	0.03	0.14	0.05	0.19
Log likelihood	-2.52	-2,281	-605	-590	-699	-663	-993	-877	-1,005	-849
Chi^2	126.50	604.70	101.70	130.76	84.22	156.38	65.71	297.30	95.50	406.92

Note: *p<0.1, **p<0.05, ***p<0.01. Education (Ref category: compulsory schooling); Employment (Ref category: Outside the labour market). Individual weights are used for Finland 2003. Additional sample weights are used in the models including all five Nordic countries so each country has 1,000 respondents, Finland 2003 is the reference.

Chapter Eight

Voters and the Government

All political history shows that the standing of a Government and its ability to hold the confidence of the electorate at a General Election depends on the success of its economic policy. (Harold Wilson [1968], former British Prime Minister, in Mueller [2003: 429]).

Introduction

The ancient Norse sagas tell us that the Vikings rewarded their king in times of good harvest, and that they killed him in times of poor harvest. Transferred to the context of our modern democracies, this story would fit a widely recognised notion from the literature on economic voting: voters reward the government when economic conditions are good, but they punish the government in times of economic recession. This more or less universal 'truth' has been subject to an extensive amount of empirical research, in which students have attempted to define which types of conditions are most relevant for the economic vote. Much of this research indicates that there is a relationship between the economy and the vote, but the direction and the strength of this relationship is complex and less intuitive than the simple notion of economic voting would predict (*see* e.g. Lewis-Beck and Paldam 2000; van der Brug *et al.* 2007; Dutch and Stevenson 2008). Moreover, the electoral fortunes of incumbent parties are not conditioned by economic factors alone. Systematic research across countries reveals that electoral performance varies according to system-specific variables such as type of government, critical events and changes in the political environment of political parties (Bengtsson 2004; Narud and Valen 2008).

These observations form the point of departure for this chapter, in which we will explore the electoral rewards and punishments of incumbent parties in a Nordic context. First, to what extent are incumbent parties held to more severe standards than opposition parties? Second, to what extent is their electoral performance conditioned by economic factors? And third, under which conditions is the economy a constraint on incumbent parties? In the subsequent empirical analysis we analyse these questions on the basis of aggregate as well as individual data. We begin by reviewing the economic development of the Nordic countries in the postwar period, and then give an overview of the electoral performance of the governments. In so doing, we explore the possible effect of economic development on the electoral performance of governments. In the second part of the analyses we lean on survey data from the national election studies.

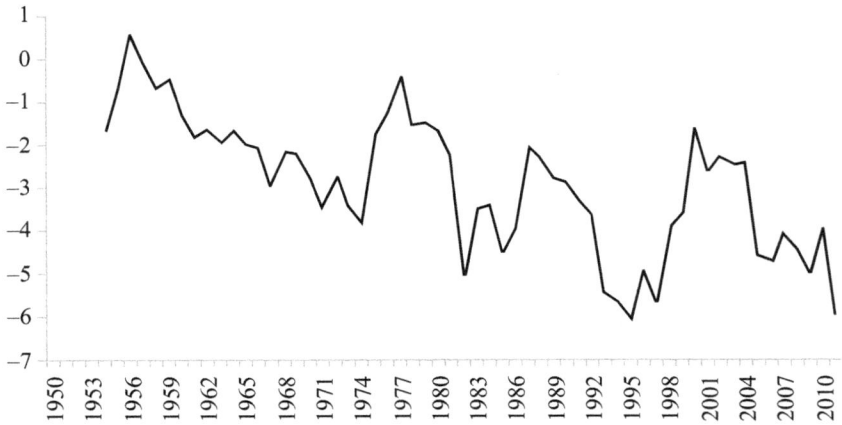

Figure 8.1: Average incumbency effects in 17 European countries 1950–2011 (five year moving average)

Note: Countries included in the graph are: Austria, Belgium, Denmark, Finland, France, Germany, Greece, Iceland, Ireland, Italy, Luxembourg, Netherlands, Norway, Portugal, Spain, Sweden, and U.K.

Incumbency effects revisited

The theoretical assumption behind the 'negative incumbency effect' hypothesis is based upon the notion that voters judge governing parties retrospectively upon their performance (Fiorina 1981; Söderlund 2008). Governing parties may be held to more severe standards than opposition parties, particularly concerning consistency between promise and performance. In terms of vote-seeking it may therefore be a disadvantage to hold office. The idea that there is a 'wear and tear' on parties in government has received fairly wide empirical support (*see* e.g. Rose and Mackie 1983; Narud and Valen 2008; Hansen 2009a). In Figure 8.1 the five year moving average incumbency effect is presented for seventeen European countries during the period 1950 until 2011. And as we can see, the average result for parties in government at the time of the election is indeed negative. Even though great variations may be observed among countries in the magnitude of the electoral losses (and gains), the average incumbency loss has increased since the 1950s. It also seems as if the level of volatility has increased and that the variation in the losses suffered by governments varies extensively from one period to another. The periods with the on average highest incumbency losses, appears to be found in economic hard times such as during the oil crisis at the beginning of the 1980s, the economic down turn in the 1990s and the financial crisis at the end of the first decade of the new millennium.

A number of scholars have made attempts to define the institutional conditions under which voters constitute a constraint on parties in government (e.g. Strøm 1990; Powell and Whitten 1993; Narud and Irwin 1994; Müller and Strøm 1999;

Anderson 2000; Bengtsson 2004; Narud and Valen 2008). The main argument has been that the performance of incumbents is conditioned by the clarity of responsibility of the parties involved. Clarity of responsibility is enhanced by party system characteristics; such as the number of parties, the cleavage system, and consequently, the dimensionality of the policy space. In addition, clarity of responsibility may be linked to the type of government, i.e. minority *vs.* majority, and coalition vs. single party government. The most fundamental difference is between two-party systems on the one hand and multi-party systems on the other, since they generate different types of government. According to the logic of retrospective voting, with only two parties competing, voters can more easily assign blame and punish the government for poor performance by voting against it. Voters in multi-party systems, on the other hand, are less likely to employ such retrospective penalties, since coalition governments are the norm rather than the exception. With a coalition government there is no indication as to which incumbent the voters should hold accountable – or as to which alternative party they should turn to.[1] The basic argument in the literature on party choice has been that coalition government, and particularly oversized ones, obscure accountability, thereby reducing the ability of the electorate to assign blame (Dahl 1966; Epstein 1967; Schattschneider 1942; Austen-Smith and Banks 1988; Laver and Shepsle 1990; Strøm 1990; Narud 1996). To a certain extent, the same logic applies to minority governments. Since these governments must rely on the support of opposition parties to enact legislation, they can always attempt to shift the blame for policy failures to other parties (Strøm 1990; Powell and Whitten 1993). Based on the above reasoning, we should expect different patterns of responsibility assignment in the Nordic countries. As was shown in Chapter Two, the tradition of government formation varies from one Nordic country to another. In all cases there are aspects which make it difficult for voters to assign responsibility, but of a different kind. While Norway, Denmark and Sweden have a tradition of single party minority government, Finland and Iceland have on most accounts formed majority coalitions, and in the Finnish case even oversized coalitions. If the argument that majority (and oversized) coalitions, in particular, deflect responsibility patterns, we would expect governments in Finland and Iceland to be less harshly judged for their actions by voters than governments in the other Nordic countries, dominated by single party minority governments. However, when looking at Figure 8.2, where the average incumbency effect during the period 1950 until 2011 is displayed per country, we find the opposite pattern. While incumbency effects are relatively modest in Denmark, Norway and Sweden, they are substantially higher in Finland and, in particular, in Iceland. Moreover the comparative outlook tells us that the Nordic countries are dissimilar on this account. While the first three are among the four countries with the lowest incumbency effects overall, Finland is further down the list and Iceland belongs to the countries where governments, on average, have suffered the most.

---

1. This argument is valid also in prospective terms. The proposition then would be that the effect of incumbency is related to the voters' perception of the parties' future achievements, and that they vote for those parties they believe would be best qualified for dealing with certain policies.

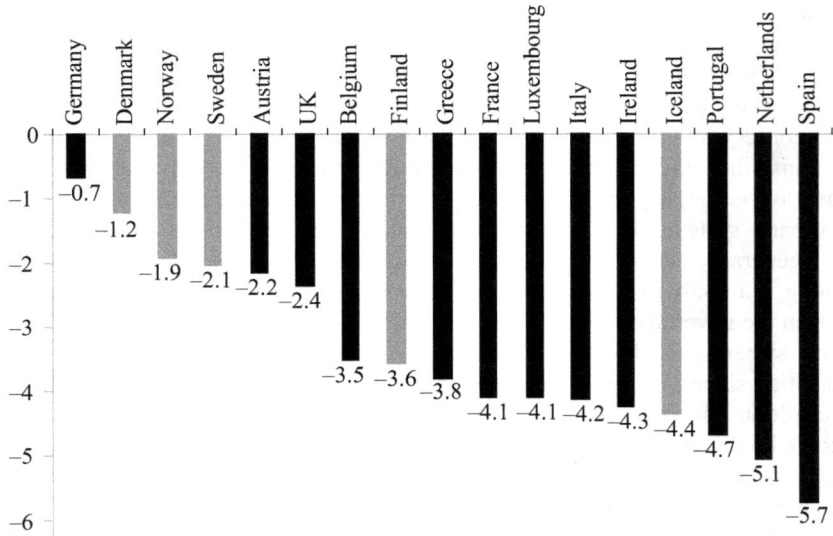

Figure 8.2: Average incumbency effects 1950–2011, comparative perspective

When comparing the average cost of ruling in the Nordic countries during the period displayed in Figure 8.2 with the cost of ruling during the last decade, we also find distinct differences among the countries (data not presented here). The cost of ruling has been substantially higher during the last decade in all of the Nordic countries except in Sweden. The overall pattern is hence, that cost of ruling has increased over time on most accounts, but the relative magnitude of the effect is stable: governments are more harshly punished in Iceland and Finland and less so in Sweden, Norway and Denmark.

Clearly analyses from previous research reveal that we are faced with some very complex relationships. In general, institutions and structural attributes matter less, whereas the strongest effects lie in the most proximate circumstances surrounding the election, that is, in terminal events and macro-economic conditions. Concerning the latter, it is evident that governments lose much more in poor economic times than they do when the economy is good, a fact that leads us to the next and most important issue to be discussed in this chapter: the impact of the economy on the popular support of the incumbents.

'It's the Economy, stupid …'

One of the most widely recognised assumptions-encapsulated in the above citation from campaign strategist James Carville during Bill Clinton's 1992 presidential election campaign – has been that the electoral fate of governments is linked to the country's economic performance (Fiorina 1981; Lewis-Beck 1988, 1991; Lewis-Beck and Paldam 2000; Dorussen and Taylor 2002; van der Brug *et al.* 2007; Dutch and Stevenson 2008). Voters will reward the government when economic conditions are good, but they will punish the incumbent when economic conditions are poor. Hence, clarity of responsibility refers to the government's control, or rather, the electorate's perceptions of the government's control, over economic development in a given country. By considering the national economic performance in the period before an election, voters assign blame or credit to the incumbent government, and the vote is shifted accordingly.[2]

Considerable research efforts have gone into specifying precisely how the economy influences elections and have found that the relative importance of economic factors varies between countries and over time, and with the level of analysis. There is some very strong evidence for economic voting in the US, for example, whereas the empirical evidence for other parts of the developed world is much weaker. The economic effect on the vote also seems to vary with the level of welfare state development, suggesting that the economy plays less of a role in states with high levels of spending (Pacek and Radcliff 1995; for evidence in the US, see Singer 2010). This in turn, would suggest weaker economic voting among the Nordic countries compared to many others (*see* Figure 2.1 in Chapter Two). Unemployment, real disposal income and inflation are the most consistent influences, whereas a country's balance of trade is generally not significant (Harrop and Miller 1987: 218). Furthermore, the various types of economic indicators seem to hit governments with a different policy platform differently (Narud and Valen 2008; Martinsson 2009), but also that the electoral result can vary for parties with different governmental responsibilities (Narud and Valen 2008).

Moreover it seems as if governments seldom are rewarded during good economic times; a result often called the 'grievance-asymmetry' hypothesis (or a negative bias in the electorate), stating that voters are particularly alert to economic troubles (*see* e.g. Dorussen and Palmer 2002: 10). In 'good' times voters may take the economy for granted, and this makes way for non-economic issues on the political agenda. In addition, there is the possibility that good economic development over a longer periods of time create expectations among the voters that are almost impossible to meet. By most objective economic measures, affluence has increased in the Western world over the last few decades and the standard of living has improved (Dalton 2004). It could be that the policy performance of the government is falling short of voters' expectations, simply because they demand governments to 'deliver' even more than they already do in terms of welfare, education, and other types of benefits when the economy is good, whereas these types of expectations are not salient in times of economic recession. Indeed, these are propositions that we will come back to when approaching the individual level data in our five Nordic cases.

---

2. In general, the various models of economic voting have received little empirical support (for an overview *see* Lewin 1991). Lewis-Beck (1986), for instance, found very limited evidence that personal retrospective economic considerations, whether simple or mediated, had any effect on the vote. However, when related to mediated retrospective evaluations of the *national* (as opposed to the personal) situation, economic factors have been found to correlate clearly with voting behaviour (*see* e.g. Butler and Stokes 1969).

Incumbency effects – individual data analysis

In the next section we turn to the main issues of interest in this chapter: to what extent does support for the incumbent parties vary with social and demographic characteristics of individual voters? Are there variations between different groups of voters according to their level of party identification, political awareness, knowledge, and ideological orientation? And finally, do voters' economic perceptions matter for their support of incumbent parties? We set out to explore these questions in the subsequent part of the chapter. In so doing, we first analyse the effect of our independent variables on the entire government. We then examine possible differences between individual parties in the cabinet (in the case of coalition governments), most importantly, the parties holding the Prime Ministry and the portfolio of the Minister of Finance. Unfortunately, the Icelandic voter surveys have no items on the economy, so this part of the analyses will be restricted to the other four countries. Observe that, for the purpose of this chapter, we will use the Finnish parliamentary election of 2003, not the 2007 election as is the case with the other chapters. The reason is simply that the quality of the data is better in the 2003 survey concerning the items on the economy and the vote.

As demonstrated by the table, there are considerable variations between the ideological composition, the size and the types of governments facing their respective voters in each country. In line with their long tradition for minority governments, the Norwegians had a center-right minority coalition at the time, whereas in the Swedish case it was a single party minority government of the Social Democrats. Denmark had an Agrarian-Conservative minority coalition government, but unique for a right-leading government in Denmark, the government had a majority with the popular right party – Danish People's Party. Finland, also in line with its tradition for broadly-based majority coalitions, had the oversized 'rainbow government' at the time of the 2003 election, even though the Greens had left the cabinet the year before due to disagreement over plans to build a new nuclear power plant. Iceland had a center-right majority coalition, which barely managed to save its majority status by one mandate after the poor result of the Progressive Party (Agrarian). This did not prevent the incumbent government from handing in its resignation, however, and Prime Minister, Geir Haarde, the head of the Independence Party (Conservative) formed a new government with the Social Democrats on the basis of forty-three out of sixty-three seats in the *Althingi*. Less than two years later Prime Minister Haarde would tender his resignation from the Cabinet after fierce popular protests due to the government's handling of the financial crisis. A virtual landslide election would follow, in which Haarde's party, the Independence Party, lost one-third of its votes and nine seats in the *Althingi*. That is, however, another story, which we will touch upon briefly in the end of this chapter when discussing the economic crisis that came up in the fall of 2008.

The Icelandic case illustrates an important point. In a coalition government it is quite unusual for coalition partners to suffer the same fate. Some lose, some gain, and most commonly, they jostle each other for votes (Rose and Mackie 1983). Indeed, this was the case for all the governments we see in the table, save of course

Table 8.1: An overview of the electoral fate of the incumbent governments at the time of election in each country

	Denmark 2007	Iceland 2007	Finland 2003	Norway 2005	Sweden 2006
Cabinet and party of PM and Min. of Finance	Fogh Rasmussen II (Ag., Cons.)	Haarde (Cons., Ag.)	Lipponen* (Sd, Left All., Sw PP, Cons.)	Bondevik II (Chr., Cons., Lib.)	Persson (Sd.)
	PM = Lib.	PM = Cons.	PM = Sd.	PM = Chr.	PM = Sd.
	Min. Fin. = Lib.	Min. Fin. = Cons.	Min. Fin. = Cons.	Min. Fin. = Cons.	Min. Fin. = Sd.
Type of government	Minority coalition	Majority coalition	Oversized majority coalition	Minority coalition	Single party minority
Gain/loss of votes individual cabinet parties	Ag. = -2.8	Cons. = +2.9	Sd. = +1.6	Christians = -5.6	Sd. = -4.7
	Cons = +0.1	Ag. = -6.0	Left Alliance = -1.0	Cons. = -7.1	
			Swedish PP = -0.5	Lib. = +2.0	
			Cons. = -2.4		
Tot. pct. gained/lost	-2.7	-3.1	-2.3	-11.7	-4.7

* The Greens departed from the so-called 'rainbow government' of Lipponen in 2002 and did not face the voters as an incumbent party in the following election year. Consequently, the party is excluded from the table.

the Swedish single party government, in which case the votes went in only one di-rection; to the opposition. In the Norwegian case the Christian People's Party and the Conservatives had their worst elections in decades, much to the benefit of the Liberal Party which increased its share of the votes by two percentage points. In Denmark the Conservatives and the Agrarians ensured marginal gains, but no ad-ditional seats, after an election campaign dominated by welfare, taxes, and immi-gration issues (Kosiara-Pedersen 2008: 1043). Prime Minister Fogh Rasmussens's Party, the Agrarians, suffered a setback of 2.8 percentage points and lost six seats. The party was still the largest in the *Folketing*, however, slightly ahead of the Social Democrats, and Fogh Rasmussen formed his third government shortly after the election. The minority coalition needed parliamentary support, however, from the Danish People's Party in order to secure a majority.

In Denmark there has been a clear cost of ruling regarding the Prime Minister's party, regardless of the nature of the economy. From 1975–2008 the Prime Minster's party, on average, lost 1 percentage point per year – much to the benefit of its coalition partners (Hansen 2009a). The reasons for these patterns are three-fold. First, the Prime Minister's party is the main exponent of unpopular laws while other parties easily can free ride and keep a low profile. Second, the Prime Minister's party is held responsible for possible crises while other parties can deflect responsibility. Finally the Prime Minister and his party are, to a large extent, exposed in the media at all times. Voters may simply grow tired of the same face and party (Hansen 2009a).

Table 8.1 reveals that three of the Finnish incumbent parties suffered a loss of votes, whereas the Social Democrats gained after an election campaign dominated by personal clashes between rival leaders and an issue agenda in which welfare issues played an important part. The deteriorating forecast for the economy, however, constrained party pledges in the campaign (Downs and Riutta 2005: 432). In Sweden, after 12 years in office, Göran Persson's social democratic government was defeated by the center-right Alliance in the 2006 election. The fate of the government puzzled many observers, as indeed had been the case also for its Norwegian counterpart the year before. In both countries economic development had been most rewarding, and should – according to the classical theory of economic voting – have been to the benefit of the incumbent governments. In this case the map did not match the terrain – an issue we shall return to shortly.

Table 8.2 gives an overview of the economic perceptions of the voters at the time of the general elections. It is quite clear that differences in voters' perceptions of the economic situation cannot explain the differences in government losses at the polls. In their evaluation of both the retrospective national and personal economy, the Norwegian voters were clearly the most positive ones. Nevertheless, the Norwegian government suffered the greatest losses by far. The Finnish voters were, on the other hand, most negative on both scores while the Finnish government only suffered minor losses compared to its Swedish and Norwegian counterparts. The perceptions of the Danish and Swedish voters were rather similar in those respects; more positive than among the Finnish voters and more negative than among the Norwegian ones.

Table 8.2: Voters' perception of the economy (Iceland not included due to lack of data) (per cent)

	Denmark 2007	Finland 2003	Norway 2005	Sweden 2006
National economy retrospective				
Worse	11	32	2	10
The same	54	43	51	50
Better	36	25	47	40
Personal economy retrospective				
Worse	14	21	9	14
The same	44	53	55	52
Better	42	27	36	34
Personal economy prospective				
Worse	30	10	11	10
The same	1	58	57	60
Better	69	32	32	30
No. of respondents	4 018	1 270	2 012	1 125*
Government losses	-1.3%	-2.3%	-11.7%	-4.7%

* missing cases excluded.

The prospective evaluation of their personal economy was remarkably similar among Finnish, Norwegian and Swedish voters; in all three countries only one out of every ten voters expected their economic situation to get worse – while this was the case for a third of the Danish voters. However, the Danish government fared better at the election than the other three! The subsequent empirical analyses will concentrate on possible differences between various groups of voters in their support (or lack of support) for incumbent parties. The analyses will concentrate on the impact of the economic variables compared to other types of indicators. We will start by presenting some descriptive information about voters' support in the five countries at hand, and then test the robustness of the results by way of binominal regression analyses for four of them.

Incumbency and voter support

Table 8.3 shows the bivariate relationship between voting for the incumbent government and demographic, attitudinal, and economic perception variables in the five Nordic countries. The effects of the demographic and regional variables (e.g. gender, age, degree of urbanisation etc.) are not justified theoretically in this chapter, but are consistent with the other chapters in this volume. It is nevertheless of interest to include them in a comprehensive model. As already mentioned, we lack the economic variables for Iceland, but include the country in the descriptive statistics to see the impact of the other types of variables, most importantly the ones dealing with the labour market and the ideological left-right scale.

Table 8.3: Voters who voted for the incumbent government by background, attitudes and perceptions (per cent with CI)

	Denmark 2007		Finland 2003		Iceland 2007		Norway 2005		Sweden 2006	
	%	[CI]	%	[CI]	%	[CI]	%	[CI]	%	[CI]
Gender										
Men	41	[39–43]	51	[46–55]	44	[41–48]	29	[26–32]	34	[32–37]
Women	31	[29–33]	53	[49–58]	33	[29–36]	26	[23–29]	33	[30–35]
Age in election year										
18–24	24	[18–30]	43	[34–53]	35	[28–41]	18	[12–25]	29	[24–35]
25–34	29	[25–33]	51	[42–59]	32	[26–38]	25	[20–31]	30	[25–34]
35–44	40	[37–44]	44	[36–51]	44	[38–49]	30	[25–34]	30	[26–34]
45–54	31	[28–35]	54	[47–62]	42	[36–48]	32	[27–37]	36	[32–40]
55–64	36	[32–39]	61	[54–68]	41	[35–47]	27	[22–32]	38	[34–42]
65–00	43	[40–46]	54	[47–62]	36	[30–42]	26	[21–32]	35	[31–40]
Civil status										
Single	30	[28–33]	50	[45–55]	33	[29–37]	25	[21–29]	33	[30–36]
Married/partner	39	[37–41]	54	[50–58]	41	[38–44]	29	[26–31]	34	[31–36]
Degree of urbanisation										
Country side	42	[38–46]	64	[56–72]	43	[39–47]	21	[17–24]	31	[26–35]
–	36	[34–38]	50	[45–54]	–	–	–	–	36	[34–38]
Big city	29	[25–32]	52	[45–59]	35	[32–39]	30	[28–33]	24	[20–28]

(Cont'd)

Table 8.3: (Cont'd)

	Denmark 2007		Finland 2003		Iceland 2007		Norway 2005		Sweden 2006	
	%	[CI]	%	[CI]	%	[CI]	%	[CI]	%	[CI]
Schooling										
Compulsory schooling	28	[25–31]	49	[43–55]	35	[31–39]	11	[7–15]	45	[41–49]
Lower secondary school (student)	38	[36–40]	52	[48–56]	43	[39–47]	24	[21–27]	39	[36–42]
Higher education (university, teachers, nurses)	36	[32–40]	56	[48–63]	37	[32–42]	36	[33–39]	21	[18–23]
Employment										
Outside the labour market	35	[33–38]	52	[47–56]	33	[29–37]	23	[20–27]	35	[32–39]
Self-employed	50	[44–57]	36	[25–46]	47	[40–55]	40	[31–49]	17	[10–24]
Lower white-collar worker	34	[31–38]	57	[48–67]	39	[33–46]	28	[24–32]	30	[26–34]
Higher white-collar worker	42	[38–45]	56	[46–65]	40	[34–45]	36	[31–41]	18	[13–22]
Blue-collar worker (incl. unskilled workers)	29	[26–32]	54	[47–61]	41	[35–47]	15	[10–20]	45	[40–51]
Party identification										
Weak Party ID	32	[30–34]	50	[46–55]	26	[23–29]	28	[25–31]	24	[21–26]
Strong Party ID	39	[37–41]	54	[49–58]	52	[49–56]	27	[24–30]	50	[46–54]
Political awareness										
Low	34	[32–37]	49	[42–55]	31	[27–35]	22	[18–26]	38	[34–42]
Medium	38	[36–41]	50	[44–55]	41	[37–45]	24	[20–28]	31	[28–34]
High	35	[32–38]	56	[51–61]	43	[39–48]	31	[28–34]	28	[23–33]

(Cont'd)

Table 8.3: (Cont'd)

	Denmark 2007		Finland 2003		Iceland 2007		Norway 2005		Sweden 2006	
	%	[CI]	%	[CI]	%	[CI]	%	[CI]	%	[CI]
Political knowledge										
Low	31	[28–33]	49	[41–56]	27	[21–32]	25	[21–29]	39	[34–43]
Medium	38	[36–41]	53	[49–58]	39	[36–43]	28	[25–32]	33	[30–37]
High	38	[35–40]	52	[46–58]	47	[42–52]	28	[25–32]	28	[24–31]
Left right self-placement										
Left	9	[7–10]	72	[65–80]	5	[2–8]	2	[0–3]	59	[55–64]
Middle	37	[35–39]	48	[44–52]	35	[32–38]	31	[28–34]	27	[25–30]
Right	69	[66–72]	55	[47–62]	83	[78–88]	51	[45–57]	4	[2–7]
Left right self-placement extreme										
Middle on left-right scale	24	[21–28]	39	[34–47]	26	[22–30]	18	[14–22]	29	[26–33]
Inbetween	34	[32–36]	57	[51–60]	38	[35–42]	30	[27–33]	25	[21–28]
Extreme on left-right scale	43	[41–46]	57	[54–67]	58	[53–63]	30	[26–34]	37	[34–41]
Personal economic (retrospectively)										
Much worse	21	[17–24]	55	[47–62]	–	–	23	[16–30]	24	[18–31]
Same	35	[32–37]	53	[48–57]	–	–	26	[23–29]	34	[30–38]
Much better	42	[40–45]	49	[43–55]	–	–	30	[27–34]	31	[26–36]

(Cont'd)

Table 8.3: (Cont'd)

	Denmark 2007		Finland 2003		Iceland 2007		Norway 2005		Sweden 2006	
	%	[CI]	%	[CI]	%	[CI]	%	[CI]	%	[CI]
Personal economic (prospectively)										
Much worse	24	[22–26]	52	[42–62]	–	–	36	[29–43]	32	[23–41]
Same	25	[10–40]	53	[49–57]	–	–	26	[23–29]	32	[29–36]
Much better	41	[40–43]	50	[44–55]	–	–	27	[23–31]	31	[26–36]
National economic (retrospectively)										
Much worse	22	[18–26]	49	[44–55]	–	–	7	[−2–16]	19	[11–26]
Same	24	[21–27]	53	[48–58]	–	–	19	[17–22]	32	[28–36]
Much better	43	[41–45]	54	[48–61]	–	–	36	[33–40]	34	[30–39]
Public sector										
No – private	39	[37–41]	52	[48–55]	42	[39–46]	32	[28–35]	31	[28–33]
Yes public	24	[22–27]	53	[46–59]	36	[31–41]	23	[19–26]	34	[31–37]
Voted for the same party this and the last election										
No	23	[20–25]	47	[42–53]	20	[17–22]	21	[18–24]	19	[17–21]
Yes	43	[41–45]	54	[50–58]	59	[56–63]	32	[29–35]	49	[46–51]
Total	36	[34–37]	52	[49–55]	39	[36–41]	27	[25–30]	33	[32–35]

Table 8.3 indicates that voters' support for the government is a reflection of the social and ideological profile of the incumbent parties. Hence, consistent with the electoral bases of social democratic parties, the Swedish labour government received more support from people with only compulsory schooling and blue-collar workers, than from the more highly educated and the white collar employees, particularly the ones with a higher status. The opposite tendency is evident for the Norwegian non-socialist government, and to a certain extent for the Agrarian-Conservative Danish government, which received more support from the higher educated groups, the self-employed, and the white collars. These governments also have their electoral strongholds among voters in the private sector. The broadly based Finnish government and the Icelandic centrist-conservative government express different patterns in relation to the background variables. In most cases (save the Norwegian one) party identification seems to favour the incumbent parties, whereas government support does not seem to be linked to the level of political awareness and knowledge among the voters (save for Iceland on political knowledge).

If we move to the two items dealing with ideology, left-right self-placement and extremeness, the connection between the ideological leaning of the voters and the policy profile of the government is clearer. Consequently, the support for the governments with a rightist or centrist-right profile (Iceland, Denmark and Norway) increases as we move from a leftist to a rightist self-placement on the left-right scale. The opposite is of course true for the Swedish labour government. The oversized Finnish government has its clearest stronghold among the left-leaning voters, which reflects the dominant position of the Social Democrats, but consistent with the 'rainbow' profile of this coalition, it also receives considerable support from rightist voters.

Finally, the three economic indicators express some interesting patterns, particularly for the Danish case. The support for the Agrarian-Conservative coalition of Fogh Rasmussen increases markedly with voters' positive perceptions of the economy. This is true for both the personal economic perceptions (retrospectively as well as prospectively) and for the retrospective evaluations of the national economy. The latter is the case also for the centrist-right Norwegian coalition, in which the support for the government increases with positive perceptions of the national economy. The results go in the same direction concerning the perceptions of past personal economic development, but the difference between the three groups is not significant (cf. the confidence interval). Neither are the results for voters' perceptions of future personal economic development. In the Swedish case we find a result in the expected direction concerning perceptions of the past national economic development. Voters who evaluate the development positively show significantly higher support for the Swedish single party labour government. Perceptions of the personal economic development (future and past) does however not seem to influence support for the government. Even though the results run in the expected direction for the Finnish voters concerning the national economy, the difference between the various groups is small and insignificant. The same is true for the two indicators tapping personal economic perceptions. Indeed, the Finnish results go hand in hand with the evidence shown by Lewis-Beck (1988) that the more parties included in the cabinet, the smaller the impact of the economy on the voters' decision to vote for or against the cabinet parties.

We discussed initially the impact of the economy on different parties in a coalition, most importantly the party of the Minister of Finance and the party of the Prime Minister. Do we find similar results in the present material? This question is relevant only in the Norwegian and Finnish cases, since these are the only governments in which the two portfolios are held by different parties. In the other three countries the same party holds both the PM and the Minister of Finance. If we look at the Norwegian case, there are indeed interesting differences between the two parties in the coalition, that is, the Christian Peoples' Party who had the Prime Minister, and the Conservatives who had the Minister of Finance (table not shown). There are significant differences between various voter groups in their support for the Conservatives; popular support increases markedly the more positive the perceptions of the national economy in the past. The same tendency is not present for the PM's party. Hence, economic perceptions do not seem to matter for the support of the Christians, whereas they do matter for the Conservatives. Since the economy does not make a difference in the Finnish case, there is no reason to expect any significant differences between the various voter groups here. This assumption receives empirical support in the material.

Multivariate analysis

So far, we have been preoccupied with differences between various voter groups in their support for the incumbent parties. In order to see the relative impact of the economic items in relations to other factors, we have run a bloc-wise binominal regression with the various types of background variables in bloc 1, the ideological variables, political awareness and knowledge plus voting stability in the second block, and the economic variables in bloc 3. What are the effects of the economic evaluations in relation to the other sets of variables on voters' support for the incumbent parties? As mentioned earlier, due to the lack of economic indicators, Iceland is not included in this part of the analysis.

Table 8.4 shows that great differences exist between the various countries in the significance of the variables in each bloc. Hence, many of the tendencies from Table 3.4 are evident also in the multivariate analysis. If we begin with Denmark, partly due to the size (large no. of respondents), most of the results are significant. All the background variables in bloc 1, save being a blue-collar worker, have significant effects on voter support for the incumbent government. The explained variance is very low, however, indicating that the relative importance of these variables is meager. Introducing bloc 2 to the model boosts the explained variance dramatically, from .04 to an impressive .25. The increased variance stems primarily from the effect of the left-right self-placement variable, even though stability of the vote (i.e. voted for the same party) also has a significant effect. Hence, the probability of supporting the incumbent government increases by 17 percentage points if your vote went to the same party in both elections (i.e. this

Table 8.4: Modelling the probability of voting for the incumbent government

	Denmark 2007			Finland 2003			Norway 2005			Sweden 2006		
	Model 1	Model 2	Model 3	Model 1	Model 2	Model 3	Model 1	Model 2	Model 3	Model 1	Model 2	Model 3
Age in election year	3***	2*	3***	6***	5***	5***	4***	2**	2*	-1	3	3
Women	-6***	-3*	2	4	1	1	-1	2	4*	-4	-5	-4
Lower secondary	9***	7***	7***	6	6	6	22***	14***	14***	6	5	5
Higher education	7**	7**	5*	9	7	8	37***	25***	24***	-30***	-12**	-13**
Not single	6***	7***	7***	4	4	4	-1	-3	-3	1	4	4
Self-employed	10***	10**	8**	-18***	-16**	-15**	16***	9*	8	-12	-2	-2
Lower white-collar	6**	6*	3	9	11*	12**	3	3	2	5	2	1
Higher white-collar	10***	9***	4	4	6	6	8*	5*	5	-3	2	1
Blue-collar	-3	-3	-5*	6	6	6	-8*	-6*	-6*	7	1	1
Degree of urbanisation	-11***	-8***	-8***	-7	-10*	-10*	7***	3	3	2	7	7
Public sector	-16***	-10***	-10***	-6	-7	-7	-14***	-5**	-4**	6*	-3	-3
Voted for the same party this election and at the last election	/	17***	16***	/	4	4	/	9***	9***	/	27***	27***
Left-right self-placement	/	77***	74***	/	-46***	-***	/	92***	91***	/	-90***	-90***
Left-right extremeness	/	2	2	/	35***	35***	/	-26***	-26***	/	-31***	-31***
Political awareness	/	3	-3	/	12	12	/	5	3	/	-5	-7
Political knowledge	/	5	4	/	-3	-4	/	6	5	/	-26***	-27***

(Cont'd)

Table 8.4: (Cont'd)

	Denmark 2007			Finland 2003			Norway 2005			Sweden 2006		
	Model 1	Model 2	Model 3	Model 1	Model 2	Model 3	Model 1	Model 2	Model 3	Model 1	Model 2	Model 3
Personal eco. (retrospectively)	/	/	15***	/	/	-7	/	/	1	/	/	5
Personal eco. (prospectively)	/	/	17***	/	/	1	/	/	-1	/	/	-2
National eco. (retrospectively)	/	/	34***	/	/	7	/	/	12***	/	/	5
No. respondents	3 965	3 965	3 965	1 002	1 002	1 002	1 489	1 489	1 489	835	835	835
McFadden pseudo R^2	0.04	0.25	0.27	0.02	0.06	0.06	0.07	0.29	0.29	0.08	0.33	0.34
Log likelihood	-2.480	-1.957	-1.892	-678	-654	-652	-821	-632	-624	-479	-345	-344
Chi^2	225.62	1 270.97	1 400.82	30.05	78.61	82.34	128.6	505.97	521.55	79.68	346.98	348.89

Note: *$p<0.1$, **$p<0.05$, ***$p<0.01$. Education (Ref category: compulsory schooling); Employment (Ref category: Outside the labour market). Finland 2003 election.

election and the former one). None of the other three variables in this block have any significant effect on the vote for the incumbent parties. Interestingly, most of the effects from the background variables hold up in the second model. The explained variance increases further (to 0.27) when the third block is introduced, and similar to the tendencies we saw from Table 8.3, all the economic variables are significant. The strongest effect on voters' support for the incumbents is from retrospective perceptions of the national economy. This is in line with comparative findings elsewhere, in which case voters' perceptions of the national economy have proven to be more important than personal economic considerations (*see* e.g. Lewis-Beck and Paldam 2000; Hansen and Bech 2007). The effects of the background variables are weakened somewhat as a result of introducing block 3 to the model, but some are still significant. This is most certainly the case with the left-right self-placement indicator from bloc 2 which still has a strong and significant effect on voters' support for the incumbents.

The results for the other three countries bear some similarities to the Danish case, particularly the effect of introducing bloc 2 to the model. Yet, there are quite a few differences concerning the effect of individual variables in this block. In Norway and Sweden there is a strong and significant effect of the left-right self-placement scale, but also the stability of the vote is significant. In both cases, and opposite to the Danish case, left-right extremeness has a strong and significant effect on support for the incumbents. Introducing bloc 3 and the economic indicators increases the explained variance by approximately 1 per cent in Norway, whereas it means next to nothing in Sweden. In the latter case, government support seems primarily to be influenced by left-right considerations, as the effect of the second block is larger here than in the other three countries. The effects of the economic variables are insignificant in Sweden. In the Norwegian case, voters' perceptions of the national economy have a positive and significant effect on the support for the center-right coalition, as the probability of voting for the incumbent government increases by 12 percentage points. By contrast, the effects of the personal economic indicators are insignificant. In all the Scandinavian countries the effect of education holds up in the final model, but consistent with the results in Table 8.3, the direction of the effects are linked to the policy profile of the incumbent parties. That is, the lower educated are likely to support the labour government (Sweden), whereas the higher educated prefer the liberal-conservative cabinets.

This is a valid conclusion also from examining individual parties (table not shown). Analysing the effect of the economic variables separately for the PM's party and the party of the Minister of Finance in Norway, reveals two interesting findings. The effect of the national economy is restricted to the party of the Minister of Finance, i.e. the conservatives, whereas the Christians are not affected by economic voting at all. The explained variance of the model is also much higher for the conservatives than for the Christians, the former expressing a much clearer profile on the left-right dimension and being the party responsible for economic affairs within the coalition.

Finland deviates from the other three countries as the effect of higher education is insignificant for the support of the incumbent cabinet. Lower education does have an effect, however, and in a positive direction. So does age and being a white-collar employee, whereas being self-employed decreases the probability of voting for the incumbent government. The left-right self-placement variable is significant and runs in a negative direction, but it is weaker in Finland than in the other three countries. There is also a strong and significant positive effect of left-right extremeness, whereas the stability of the vote is unimportant. As indicated already by the results of the descriptive table, the effects of the economic indicators are insignificant. Here, we could argue that the pattern for Finland is in line with the general reward-punishment argument for economic voting, that is, as coalition governments get larger (oversized) and more complex, voters find it difficult to attribute responsibility to specific incumbent parties. The overall impression is that our comprehensive model does not do very well in the Finnish case compared to the other three countries, as the explained variance is much weaker.

Across the four countries left-right placement has the largest effect on the probability of supporting the incumbent government, whereas stability of the vote and national economic perceptions come next.

The economy and the vote in the Nordic welfare democracies

Based on the above analyses we must conclude that economic voting was not a dominating factor in any of the four elections we have analysed here, even though we found significant effects in two of them, Denmark and Norway. But even here the overall impact of the economy was very modest compared to other factors, especially ideology and previous voting behaviour (voting stability). Of course, our material is limited and has its methodological imperfections, but our findings are nevertheless in line with other studies of multiparty systems similar to the Nordic ones. Some influential large-scale studies done by, for example, van der Brug et al. (2007) have not found any wide-spread evidence of economic voting, even though there are cross-national differences. These differences are mainly due to institutional variations and contexts which generate high clarity of responsibility, as we have discussed initially in this chapter. Voters are more likely to vote economically if the political institutions clarify who is responsible for what, and if there is a viable alternative to the incumbent government (Powell and Whitten 1993). Listhaug (2005), for example, claims that the weak and irregular effects of economic voting found for Norway may be explained by the dominance of minority governments, a weak opposition and political events that dominated over economic concerns in the elections studied. Similar arguments may be valid for the Finnish system which is dominated by oversized coalition governments.

All the Nordic countries are open economies in which the national economy is integrated into the global economy. Hence, the 'blame' or 'reward' for economic development will not necessarily be assigned to the national government. In a Norwegian context, studies made by Aardal and Listhaug (1986), Aardal and Valen (1995), as well as by Narud and Valen (2007) show that a considerable number of voters point to 'other reasons' than government policy when asked who is responsible for the development in the labour market. In times of high unemployment these kinds of perceptions could indeed mitigate the negative effect on the vote for the incumbent government. Moreover, evidence shows that the economic vote varies from election to election, and that the magnitude and direction of it varies with negative and positive economic developments. As we have touched upon previously, comparative research on the aggregate level points to some very clear negative effects of economic recession, whereas there is little indication of any positive effects of economic improvement (Narud and Valen 2008: 384). This kind of 'grievance-asymmetry' indicates that there is a negative bias in the electorate, making the voters more alert to economic troubles than to good news (Dorussen and Palmer 2002: 10). Nannestad and Paldam (1997) link this phenomenon to 'risk aversion' and to the social welfare functions of governments, e.g. the worries that voters have for unemployment as a problem in society. These arguments are interesting in connection with some of the Swedish studies, which indicate that personal unemployment influences the saliency of the issue (Martinsson 2009). Testing out the grievance asymmetry hypothesis based on a pooled cross-section model to micro-level data in Denmark from the period 1986–1992, Nannestad and Paldam (1997) find that the impact of the economic variables on the probability of supporting the government is asymmetric, and that the difference is in the direction expected, in other words there is a clear tendency towards grievance asymmetry. This is an important finding, because it indicates that there is an intrinsic cost of ruling, and that there are other aspects at hand when voters evaluate government performance at election time.

One such factor is welfare policies. The Nordic countries are highly developed welfare states, and this fact has at least two (presumably) important consequences. One is the generally weak impact of the economy on the vote. Pacek and Radcliff (1995: 58) claim that the level of welfare development affects voter sensitivity to economic conditions by altering voter decision calculi. In marginal welfare states the lack of a social 'safety net' will tend to increase citizen sensitivity to economic fluctuations, making them particularly alert to economic declines. By contrast, in true welfare states the general public seems to have created a system whereby they have removed short-term economic performance as the major electoral issue. 'In this way', Pacek and Radcliff (1995: 58) argue, 'the existence of the welfare state is itself a kind of standing accountability – a way of assuring material well being – which makes an American-style electoral obsession with the economy unnecessary'. The other consequence is the high saliency of welfare policies in the election campaigns. Based on cross-sections from the national elections studies in Sweden, Kumlin (2003) claims that economic voting has gradually been diminishing over time, especially since the mid-1990s. Instead, retrospective voting based on other issues has increased, such as welfare, health-care, education and child care. Similar conclusions may be drawn concerning the Norwegian system. If we take a look at the elections in 2001 and 2005, despite huge incomes from the oil industry, the economy, at least in terms of the traditional macroeconomic indicators, played a very modest role for voters' party choice. The single most important factor was the governments' performance on welfare issues, which was evaluated negatively by many voters (Narud and Valen 2007). The overall analyses of the 2001 election showed that Labour had lost its traditional ownership of welfare issues. Parallel to these results, dissatisfaction with government performance on welfare policies clearly contributed to the poor result of the center-right cabinet also in 2005. Voters' evaluations were particularly bad on education, health policy and old age care, three of the core areas of the Conservatives and the Christian People's Party (Narud and Valen 2007). In addition, voters' views on how to spend the revenues from the oil fund had a strong and negative effect on the incumbent parties' support, suggesting that the government's restricted oil policy did not go well with voters who held a more expansive view on this question.[3] Public opinion data from the 1997–2005 period show that citizens want to spend more of the money than the actual government policies allow for (Listhaug 2007; Narud and Valen 2007: 277). Hence, the conflicting views between government policies and the mass public on public spending have, over the years, created a so-called 'frustration gap' – and have triggered a debate about the 'curse of the oil purse' (e.g. Listhaug and Narud 2011). This gap more or less closed in the most recent election of 2009 as a result of the effects of the financial crisis, a topic that we shall briefly reflect upon in the subsequent part of this chapter.

The financial crisis of 2008

In the autumn months of 2008, around the world stock markets fell, large financial institutions collapsed, and governments had to come up with rescue packages to counteract the effects of the financial 'tsunami'. Regarding the Norwegian and Swedish governments, the crisis started to show its effects in the second half of 2008, and from this point on, the support for the incumbent governments increased markedly (Oscarsson 2010; Narud 2011). In Norway the positive effect was particularly evident for Labour, whereas in Sweden it was the Conservatives (*Moderaterna*) who gained the most votes. The surge for the incumbent parties was in line with similar trends for government parties in other European countries at the time. As the arrows for the banks and the stock markets pointed downwards, they pointed upwards for Gordon Brown in the UK, for Merkel in Germany, Sarkozy in France and Berlusconi in Italy. In other words, the economic crisis seemed to favour the parties in office. Some commentators related these trends to the phenomenon of 'risk aversion', and people's general preference for certainty over uncertainty in times of emergency (*see* e.g. Colomer 2008, for this line of argument). When subject to serious shocks people seek refuge in the arms of the sitting government under the maxim: 'you know what you've got, but not what you'll get'.

Indeed, the success of the Norwegian and Swedish governments in 2009 and 2010 indicates that these types of mechanisms may have played a role. If

---

3. Norway has developed strong state institutions to handle the management of oil revenues. A key institution is the oil fund or, using the official name, the Government Pension Fund, which invests the income from oil abroad, and sets a rule for spending per year – four per cent.

we have a look at the Norwegian government first, the financial means available to it through the oil fund must have been a tremendous asset for the incumbent government. It gave the incumbent parties the opportunity to show 'muscles' in a situation where the economic recession created insecurity among many voters. In so doing, the government was able to meet a long-standing demand among many voters to use more of the oil money to solve domestic problems. Hence, analyses of the election show that the great majority of the voters were very pleased with the government's handling of the crisis (Narud 2011). A second factor of great relevance was the lack of clear-cut government alternatives in 2009. The parties to the centre and right were not able to bridge the distances between them, and this weakened their position as a viable alternative to the red-green coalition. No doubt, the rifts between the opposition parties gave the incumbent government an important weapon in the election campaign and strengthened its position as the most capable alternative for government office. The victory of the red-green coalition in 2009 was unprecedented in Norwegian politics, as the only coalition which had previously regained it majority after an election was the centre-right coalition of Mr. Borten in 1969.

Similar factors were at play in Sweden (Oscarsson and Holmberg 2013). Before the crisis the Swedish opposition parties had an immense lead – as much as 22 per cent according to the opinion polls. However, Labour did not succeed in finding a common platform with its potential allies, the Greens and the Left Socialists. As the crisis kept rolling, the opposition parties gradually lost ground – much to the benefit of the the centre-right Alliance. In addition, the political agenda changed dramatically and focus switched from welfare issues to economic matters and issues dealing with the labour market. The government's job was to find countermeasures to dampen the negative effects of the crisis. Due to the success of these measures (e.g. support given to domestic demands and public finances) Sweden did not experience such a severe recession as many other countries. The recession did, however, trigger an increase in unemployment, particularly among the young people. Prime Minister Reinfeldt nevertheless succeeded in convincing the voters that the international market, and not the government, was to blame. The polls showed that the government's handling of the crisis was highly appreciated, and that the Alliance – not Labour – had gained ownership of the unemployment issue. Hence, in the general election of 2010 the incumbent parties jointly gained 1.2 per cent and ended up with 173 seats in parliament. This result was 2 seats short of a majority – mainly because the nationalist Sweden Democrats entered parliament for the first time. The centre-right Alliance, nevertheless, continued as a minority government, and this was the first time in almost a century that a Swedish centre-right government, that had served a full term, was re-elected.

We do not yet know the effect of the recession on all incumbent governments, for instance the Danish one, and the development of the crisis from a 'financial' to 'labour market' crisis may have quite different effects than the reactions we observed initially. Like all other countries, the global financial crisis hit Denmark in late 2008, and in the period 2008–2009, GDP dropped by 5.9 per cent and unemployment increased from 4.4 to 7.4 in the same period. Danish analysts have identified the drop in the Danish GDP as the largest since 1820 and thus struck the country even harder than the one in the 1930s (Goul Andersen 2013). Consequently, the number of Danes who feared unemployment increased markedly after 2008, and according to the opinion polls, more and more people expressed a fear of economic insecurity (Goul Andersen and Hansen 2013). Consequently, it would be strange if such a development did not have any negative consequences for the support of the incumbent government in the election to come. Gallup's Poll, 15 May 2011 (and other polls show same tendency) shows that the Government would lose up to 5.6 percentage points and also lose power to the opposition.

The crisis certainly did have negative effects in the UK and in Ireland where the incumbent parties (Labour and Fianna Fáil, respectively) suffered severe losses in the elections of 2010 and 2011. Much the same tendency was evident in Finland which was hit hard by the financial crisis. The recession was one of the deepest ever in Finnish economic history, even though the country did enter the recession with strong public finances and stable banks. The strategy of the Finnish government was to avoid cut downs in order to keep the Finnish economy rolling, to promote private spending at high levels, and to avoid the levels of mass unemployment from the 1990s. The government's policy was seen as successful – but it came at the price of a large increase in public debt. In general the ruling four party coalition – the Conservative party, the Centre party, the Green party and the Swedish People's Party – were appraised for their handling of the financial crisis. The Minister of Finance, Jyrki Katainen, party leader for the Conservatives, was considered as a responsible actor and received positive international attention for his work. His party also managed to keep and even increase its popularity throughout the crisis. In the general election of 2011 the Conservatives did however lose six seats but still managed to become the largest party in the Finnish parliament, and Jyrki Katainen took the position as prime minister in the following government. The Centre Party, previously the largest party in parliament, was hit most severely and lost 16 seats from the previous election in 2007. Three of the four incumbent governing parties lost a combined 27 seats. The big winner was the anti-immigration and anti-euro True Finns who won 39 of the 200 seats in parliament. No doubt, the party's rejection of accepting rescue funds for individual EU countries was an important prerequisite for its success at the polls.

Of all the Nordic countries, the international financial crisis had, by far, the most dramatic impact in Iceland. In October 2008, its three major banks collapsed. These collapses (*hrun*) and the following economic crisis (*kreppa*) are generally considered the most serious disaster suffered by the country for a very long time. The collapse of the Icelandic financial system had dramatic political consequences, and led to the most massive and violent protest demonstrations ever seen in Reykjavik. This led to the fall of the government coalition, and the removal of the directors of the Central Bank (Mr. Oddson, a former conservative prime minister) and the Financial Supervisory Authority (FSA). The neoliberal era in Icelandic politics – which had started with a conservative-led government coalition in 1991 – came to an end as public opinion moved dramatically to the left (Harðarson and Kristinsson 2009).

The roots of the Icelandic financial crisis can be traced to the privatisation of the banks in 1998–2003, followed by an enormous growth in the size of the

Icelandic banking sector abroad – made possible by Icelandic membership in the European Economic Area (EEA) in 1994. The size of the banks had grown to more than tenfold that of the national economy. In those circumstances it was obvious that the Central Bank would not be able to fulfil its role as a lender in the last resort.

As later revealed in an extensive and extremely critical 'truth report', published in 2010 by an independent investigative committee (set up by the *Althingi*), serious mistakes were made during the privatisation of the banks: instead of opting for a distributed ownership, including participation of some experienced foreign financiers, the banks were sold to a handful of Icelandic businessmen with political connections – but no experience of banking. Those businessmen proved to be ready to take adverse risks, and created complex networks of cross ownerships between the banks and their own firms (*see* Danielsson and Zoega 2009). This irresponsible (and sometimes illegal) behaviour was possible as the Icelandic regulatory frameworks and institutions proved too weak and incompetent – and both the government of the Independence Party (IP) and the Progressives (before the 2007 election) and the coalition of the IP and the Social Democrats (SDA) (after the 2007 election) completely failed to face the problem and take some appropriate action.

In the aftermath of the 2008 crash the government sought the assistance of the IMF and several foreign governments, including the Nordic ones. The state took over (temporarily) the banks – and consequently, financial services for the public never broke down. However, in the first months following the crash, no politician or any public official resigned or accepted responsibility for the disaster. Massive protests took place in Reykjavik during the last months of 2008, culminating in the 'pots and pans revolution' in January 2009 (so called as protesters banged their pots and pans in front of the *Althingi* building). The protests led to the downfall of the IP-SDA government, and a minority government of the SDA and the Left Greens was formed on the of February – promising new elections.

The April elections of 2009 was historic indeed. The Icelandic election study of 2009 shows that voters put most of the blame for the crisis on the IP-SDP government, the Independence Party, the Central Bank and the FSA – and of course the commercial banks. IP's coalition partners, the PP (1995–2007) and the SDA (2007) were, to a less degree than the IP, blamed by the voters – but much more so than the opposition parties, the Left Greens and the Liberals. The IP, SDA and the PP responded to criticism by changes in leadership, candidates and policies (Harðarson and Kristinsson 2010b).

The results were a disaster for the Independence Party, which obtained 23.7 per cent (its worst result ever) – losing 12.9 per cent compared to 2007. The major winner was the environmentalist left-socialist party, the Left Greens – almost topping the IP by its 21.7 per cent, a gain of 7.9 per cent from 2007. Both the Social Democrats and the PP gained slightly, SDA with 29.8 per cent (+3 per cent), the PP with 14.8 per cent (+3.1 per cent). One new party, the Citizens' Movement (mainly based on protesters from the 'pots and pans revolution'), got four MPs elected (7.2 per cent of the vote) – thus replacing the Liberals as the fifth actor in the *Althingi* (Harðarson and Kristinsson 2010a). The election resulted in the first overall majority in Icelandic history for the two socialist parties, the Social Democrats and the Left Greens, who consequently continued their government coalition – this time as a majority government.

The Icelandic case is a clear example of voters harshly punishing a government party considered responsible for economic hardship – in this case, one of the worst disasters in Icelandic history. By hindsight, the shortcomings and failures of the Icelandic governments prior to the crash are probably also more obvious and clear-cut than most often is the case.

Conclusion

We started this chapter with the citation of former Prime Minister Harold Wilson, who asserted the importance of the economy for voters' support for incumbent parties. Evidence from a number of comparative studies suggests that there is an effect of the economy on the vote, but that these effects are moderated by political institutions, contextual factors, and by different aspects of the economy. The importance and direction of economic factors vary between countries, between elections, over time, and with the level of analysis. In this chapter we have explored the electoral rewards and punishments of incumbent parties in a Nordic context, and analysed to what extent their electoral performance is conditioned by economic factors. We have also attempted to define under which conditions the economy is a constraint on incumbent parties.

The analyses show that in the context of the Nordic systems, the wear and tear on incumbent governments has increased over the decades, but also that the average cost of ruling varies from one country to another. From a comparative perspective the Nordic context does not constitute a sphere of its own. On the individual level, the most important factor for government support is the voters' ideological left-right position. Economic factors related to the national level have some effects in two of the four countries, but the overall impact of the economy is meager. Our study is limited to one election in each country, and it is important to stress that previous studies have shown some variations between elections with varying economic contexts. However, the main conclusion from the body of Nordic studies is that the pure theory of economic voting has received little support. How can we explain this tendency?

One reason may have to do with the countries' positions as small nations with open economies. The influence of the national government on economic development is limited, and voters are thus less likely to hold the government accountable for the economy and it is easier for the incumbent in a small country to blame bad international economic developments. Furthermore, the broad coalition governments and broad support in parliaments for economic legislation also makes it more difficult for voters to blame just the government for any wrong doings (Hansen and Stubager 2013).

Another, but by no means incompatible, explanation has to do with the generous welfare provisions in the Nordic countries. Economic and social safety-nets lower the saliency of economic issues and make voters less alert to economic fluctuations. Instead, they are preoccupied with the preservation and the quality of welfare goods. In the context of the Norwegian petrol economy, for instance, it is likely that the strong government involvement in the oil sector has strengthened citizens' expectations of all the benefits they may get from the oil income. These expectations are on many parts linked to welfare policies. Hence, a key aspect of voters' decision to reward or punish the incumbent government seems to be linked to their *expectations* of government performance rather than actual government performance. Moreover, voters' expectations are linked to their perceptions of the resources available to the government to solve current issues.

The contrasting cases analysed in this chapter show that the relationship between economic voting and the state of the economy is more complex than the conventional models would predict. One example is the contrasting patterns of blame and reward centred towards the Nordic governments in the aftermath of the financial crisis. Variations in such factors as the political context, the economic resources, and the issue agenda can alter the direction and the weight of the economic vote. These observations suggest that economic voting should be assessed within in a broader model of voting behaviour.

Chapter Nine

Voters and Party Choice

> Electoral competition involves two very different but complementary groups, individual voters and political parties. An election result is not just the product of organized party efforts, nor is it produced solely by the choices of individuals. It is produced by the interaction between parties and voters (Rose and McAllister 1986: 7).

Party choice is the key dependent variable in electoral research. In this chapter we will perform comparative analyses of the determinants of party choice in the five Nordic countries. The analyses rest on the conclusions made from earlier chapters in this book. We start off with an assessment of the strength of the historically most important factor in analyses of political change in the Nordic countries: the class cleavage and the strong relationship between occupational status and party choice. In subsequent analyses we make an intentional simplification of the party choice variable by dichotomising into left-right or red-blue voting. In the final section of the chapter we estimate a more complete explanatory multinomial model of party choice that, aside from the SES-variables, political knowledge and political awareness, also include the issue dimensions recently introduced in Chapter Five.

In the 1950s and 1960s, the Nordic countries (except Iceland) experienced the strongest class voting in the world (Knutsen 2006), partly explained by the high degree of unionisation and partly explained by the dominance of the traditional left-right cleavage. To us, the development of class voting in the Nordic countries stands out as an excellent illustration of the general evolution of voting behaviour in the post war period. Today, however, the exceptionalism of the Nordic Countries when it comes to class voting is far from clear. In Figure 9.1, we present the Alford's index of class voting based on the CSES for a number of selected countries. The well-known Alford index is commonly used for comparative analyses of class voting (Knutsen 2006; Nieuwbeerta 1995) and is calculated as the difference between the vote share for the parties on the left (in this case the Left (various socialist parties) and Social Democratic Parties (including Green parties) among the working class (measured by occupation) and the vote share for the same parties among the middle class (Alford 1963; Borre and Goul Andersen 1997: 121; Sainsbury 1987).

Figure 9.1 illustrates that Sweden and New Zealand have the strongest class voting among the selected countries whereas South Korea and Norway have the weakest. The Nordic countries are mixed in between the other countries and do not stand out as a special group, thus when it come class voting the Nordic countries do not aggregate into one group.

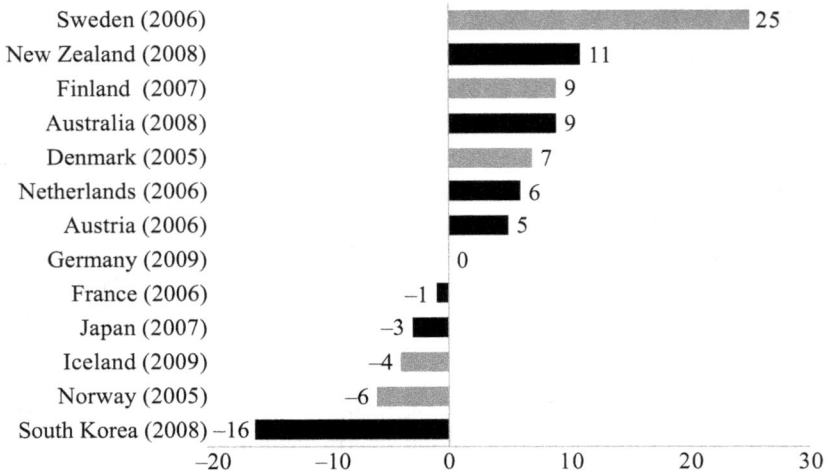

Figure 9.1: Alford's index for selected countries

Source: CSES Module 3: Alford's index operationalised as percentages of workers voting for the parties on the left (various socialist parties, Social Democratic Parties, and Green parties) minus white-collar employees voting for the same parties.

Class voting in the Nordic countries

If we zoom in on the five Nordic countries over time we see a dramatic decline in class voting. In Figure 9.2, we present the Alford's index of class voting for the Nordic countries 1950–2009.

The decline of class voting measured by Alford's class voting index (AI) is strong in all five Nordic countries (Figure 9.2). However, while four of the countries display a robust continuous trend throughout the post war period, in Sweden class voting has actually stopped declining and stabilised during the past two decades (AI=25). Today, class voting is most pronounced in Sweden (AI=25) and Finland (AI=19) whereas both Norway and Iceland have negative index values, which means that the proportion of votes for socialist parties is *higher* among the middle class than in the working class. There are some discrepancies between Figures 9.1 and Figure 9.2, due to different calculations. In Figure 9.1 we apply the CSES Module 3, which has fewer variables, but allows comparing the index to a wider set of countries. Figure 9.2, which is directly calculated from the Nordic National Election Studies, has more variables and allows e.g., more accurate coding of workers and non-workers.

There are at least five different explanations of the decline of class voting in the Nordic countries (Borre and Goul Andersen 1997; Oskarson 1994; Listhaug 1989). Firstly, the voters have, during the last 60 years, experienced major changes when it comes to the social divisions of society, e.g. women have been integrated into the labour market, an increasing number of non-manual jobs have evolved in the private sector, and the number of jobs (and their variety) in the public sector have increased dramatically. Thus the measure of 'occupational status' upon which the Alford index

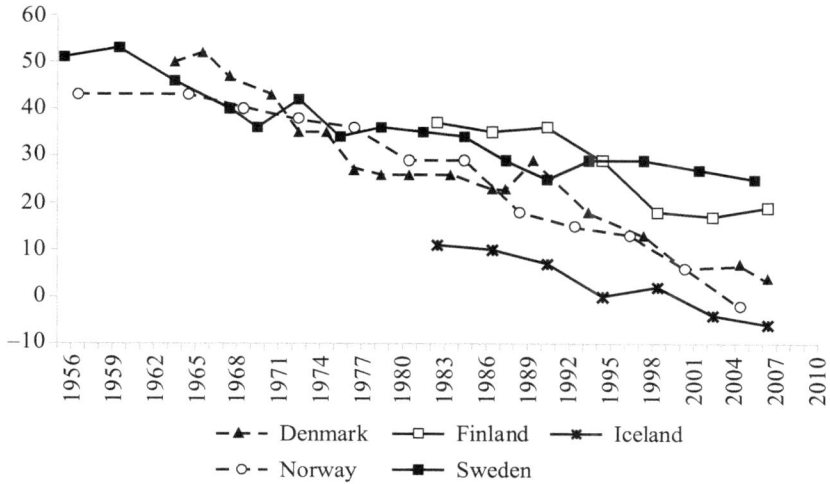

Figure 9.2: The strength of class voting in the Nordic countries 1950–2009 (Alford's index)

is based has been challenged by the increasing complexity. Together with these changes, a stronger and more complex middle class has evolved – modernisation processes have produced an *atomisation* and individualisation of social hierarchies. As a consequence, many scholars have challenged Alford's index arguing that it is an obsolete measure of class voting (*see* e.g. Heath *et al.* 1985). Still, in its simplicity, Alford's index effectively summarises the general trend of class voting.

Secondly we have seen a decreasing unionisation as fewer voters are members of labour unions today than previously. Furthermore membership of a union is not identical with a special attachment or support to a particular party and members can, in some cases, choose to decline that any money from their member fees should be passed along to a political party. Moreover, voters are not in the same way as before limited to a particular union, i.e. there is more competition among unions. We have also seen a general weakening class identity – also in the work place itself as e.g., fewer discussions about politics take place with colleagues than previously. This weakening class identity has gone hand in hand with a decline of party identification (*see* Chapter Five).

Thirdly, the increasing level of education (and through education's socialisation capabilities) has partly provided a new cleavage structure challenging traditional forms of class voting (Stubager 2008, 2010). Studies have also shown how the level of political knowledge in the early 1970s, to a large extent helped voters follow traditional class voting whereas today political knowledge helps voters to break out of traditional class voting (Hansen 2009b). Increasingly individualised voters are not as dependent on taking cues from collectives (e.g. family, unions or other organisations) today as they were a couple of decades ago.

Fourth, we have seen a rise of issue voting over the last sixty years where voters, to a larger extent, tend to follow parties accordingly to their views on specific issues rather than follow a deterministic, class voting chain of reasoning (Borre 1997; Oscarsson and Holmberg 2008a).

Fifth and finally, the emerging of strong populist parties on the right, which have attracted many *working class conservative* voters, also tend to break down the original idea behind class voting and, not at least, the main justification for Alford's classic operationalisation of the class voting index. The explanation may help to understand why Sweden with the weakest populist right party (*Sverigedemokraterna*) still has the highest level of class voting measured by Alford's index.

Generally speaking you might say that the voters of today have moved further into the Michigan funnel of causality (Campbell *et al.* 1960: 24–37; Bartels 2010). In all the Nordic countries, we have experienced eroding social cleavages where socio-economic factors simply do not structure party choice as effectively today as they did in the 1950s and 1960s (Stubager 2003; Holmberg and Gilljam 1987). Socio-demographics have been left aside to more short term and somewhat ever changing elements of issue positions, candidate sympathy mediated by political awareness, interest, and knowledge.

Bloc voting in the Nordic countries

The socio-political cleavage structure in the Nordic countries has historically produced a five parties-system (a communist, social democratic, conservative, agrarians and liberal party), which have been later supplemented with popular right parties and, in some cases also green environmentalist parties (*see* Chapter Three for a more detailed account of the development of the Nordic party systems). With the exception of Finland, in this multiparty context coalition formation has generally taken place along the traditional economic left-right dimension, i.e. parties have chosen to support an either left-leaning or right-leaning Prime Ministerial candidate forming two blocs of parties – a socialist and a non-socialist/bourgeois bloc. Furthermore it is often the case that parties run on a platform which clearly stipulates which bloc they will support after the election.

Over time there are, of course, many exceptions to this rule, e.g. the Danish Social Liberals usually support a left-leaning government, but in 1988–1990 the party was part of a right-leaning government with Poul Schlüter from the conservatives as Prime Minister. Most often the parties' coalition preferences are well known to the voters beforehand, but again there are exceptions, for example, Finland stands out as an exception from the general rule. Finnish coalition formation has over the years been very pragmatic and the country lacks a tradition of bloc building as parties are reluctant to declare their preferred coalition partners in advance. Since the 1980s, governments have been oversized coalitions, regularly including parties from both the left and the right of the ideological spectra. An exception from the general pattern happened after the election in 2007 when a four-party, right-leaning coalition government was formed (Borg and Paloheimo

2009). The tradition of an ideologically motley government does not, however, indicate that ideology is unimportant for Finnish voters when deciding on how to vote (Paloheimo and Sundberg 2005; Papageorgiou 2010). Also in Iceland the specific government coalition alternatives are seldom known before the election, nevertheless voters have some idea whether a party would support a right or left-leaning government before an election.

Bottom line is that in all the Nordic countries left-right leaning of parties act as a very important cue for voters. This tendency is also more and more supported by the media that increasingly focuses on each coalitions' candidate for Prime Minister, for instance when setting up special debates with only the two prime ministerial candidates present. Particularly in Denmark and Sweden, recent election campaigns have shown strong tendencies of presidentialisation in this respect.

Yet another argument for focusing on the categories of left and right-leaning votes are that if a voter changes party it happens to a very large degree within one of these blocs of parties. That is, party change between the two blocs is quite rare (Hansen et al. 2007; Stubager et al. 2013). For instance, in the case of Sweden, about two-thirds of total voter volatility consists of within bloc party switching (Oscarsson and Holmberg 2011).

Table 9.1: Overview of the dependent variable: party choice (left-leaning/right-leaning) in the Nordic countries 2005–2007 – sample/actual (per cent)

Party	Denmark 2007	Finland 2007	Iceland 2007	Norway 2005	Sweden 2006
Left-leaning (subtotal)	51/49	42/39	47/44	46/43	48/46
Social Democrats	23/26	23/21	28/27	34/33	36/35
Left-Socialist	16/13	9/9	16/14	11/9	6/6
Greens	–	10/9	3/3	–	6/5
Far Left	3/2	–	–	1/1	–
Social Liberals	9/8	–	–	–	–
Right-leaning (subtotal)	49/51	58/59	53/56	54/56	52/52
Conservatives	11/10	20/22	38/37	16/14	27/26
Liberals	–	5/5	5/7	6/6	8/8
Agrarian	27/26	23/23	10/12	8/7	8/8
Christian Democrats	1/1	6/5	–	5/7	7/7
Populist	10/14	4/4	–	19/22	2/3
Total	100/100	100/98	100/100	100/99	100/98
n	3 862	1 085	1 216	1 661	2 570

Note: For details of which parties are included in each category, see Appendix. Total differs from 100 due to votes for other parties.

In this part of the chapter, we will perform the simplest analysis possible of the determinants of party choice in the Nordic multiparty systems. The dependent variable, party choice, has been reduced to a left/right dichotomy (*see* Table 9.1) where 'left voting' is defined as voting for left parties such as the social democrats, left socialist and green parties, and where 'right voting' is defined as voting for conservative, liberal (except Denmark where the Social Liberals are included with the left), agrarian, Christian democratic and populist parties. We use the labels left-leaning and right-leaning in order to signal that we are actually conceptualising a broader category than just left votes and bourgeois votes.

Table 9.1 shows that we had a right-leaning majority in all five Nordic countries also resulting in blue governments in the following term, in all countries except Iceland. The social democrats enjoy strongest support in Sweden and Norway and weakest in Finland and Denmark. The conservative parties are very strong in Iceland compared to Denmark and Norway. The greens have established themselves in Finland and Sweden but are not represented by a particular party in Denmark and Norway. Iceland's only attempt to establish a green party, failed in 2007. Thus, as also argued in Chapter Three, there are substantial differences among the five Nordic countries when it comes to the party system.

In Table 9.2 we applied the red/blue party variable from Table 9.1 as a dependent variable in a descriptive analysis of the various socio-demographics, in order to highlight the differences within and between the five Nordic countries. Table 9.2 presents the proportion of votes for a right-leaning party among different voting groups. A striking result when analysing Nordic voting behaviour in the late 2000s is that the differences in the proportion of right-leaning voters in different socio-economic groups are so small, and that the tendencies are surprisingly dissimilar across the Nordic countries. That means socio-demographics can only explain a few differences in whether or not the voters vote for a left or right-leaning party. A few examples will illustrate these findings.

Gender: With the exception of Finland where there is no difference between men and women, men tend to vote more for the right-leaning parties than women. In Finland, there are, however, relatively distinct differences in terms of party vote inside each of the blocs (Paloheimo and Sundberg 2005). A potential interpretation of this finding is that the strong candidate-focused elections in Finland may provide other cues than left-right-leaning of parties (Holli and Wass 2009). The gender gap in bloc voting is largest in Iceland where 62 per cent of all men vote for a right-leaning party compared to only 45 per cent of women.

Age: In Denmark there is a clear age division where young people are much less likely to vote for a right-leaning party than the elderly. The same tendency is found in Finland among the youngest group of voters, but not in any of the other countries. Mobilisation of the young at the left has occurred in both Denmark and Finland which might account for some of the variations regarding age.

Education: In the Nordic countries, there are only small differences between voters with different education levels when it comes to the propensity for right-leaning voting. In Finland and Sweden, the tendency for the higher educated to vote for right-leaning parties are more pronounced. However, in Iceland, the higher educated are more left-leaning (46 per cent) than voters with less education.

Employment: The class conflict is still evident in Denmark, Norway, Sweden and Finland, but not in Iceland. In these four countries, unemployed and blue-collar voters have the lowest propensity for rightist-voting. Furthermore, the self-employed are more likely to vote for a right-leaning party in these four countries than other employment groups. Iceland stands out here as the right have the least support among white-collar workers, according to the table.

Public/Private sector: Private sector employees are also more likely, in general, to vote for the right-leaning parties compared to public employees.

PartyID: In Iceland: the party identified tends to vote right; while in Sweden the party identified tend to vote left. One interpretation is that the Swedish Social Democrats and the Icelandic Conservatives have historically had a more dominant position in their respective party systems than has been the case for any party in the other three countries.

Political awareness: Small effects across the board. In Denmark, the politically aware tend to vote for left parties, and in Sweden the politically aware tend to vote for right parties.

Left-right: As expected, there is a very strong relationship in all countries.

Civil Status: Married people/people living together are more right-wing than singles in all Nordic countries. This suggests that the more established tend to be somewhat more liberal or conservative in their party choice. In Table 9.3, where we control for age and other variables we see that even after these controls, married voters still vote more to the right in Denmark and Finland.

Degree of Urbanisation: In Denmark, Finland and Iceland, countryside voters are clearly more right-wing than urban voters. In Norway and Sweden the tendency is in the same direction but insignificant.

Political knowledge: Also in this respect, the patterns are dissimilar between the Nordic countries. The knowledgeable voters have a tendency for right-leaning voting in Sweden but not in Denmark, Finland, Iceland or Norway. In Norway, it is close to being the other way around; the proportion of right-leaning voters is higher among voters with low- and medium political knowledge (57 per cent) than among the most knowledgeable voters (50 per cent).

Table 9.2 gives us three similar and consistent patterns across the Nordic countries. Right-leaning voters are more likely to be married, live in urban areas and are employed in the private sector. But it also gives us a rather scattered picture of the socio-demographics effect of voting for either left or right. In order to explore this further, the next stage of the analyses is to perform a multivariate analysis (Table 9.3). Following the same routine from all the other chapters of this book, we have estimated two models for each country separately: the first model includes the socio-economic variables and in the second model we add ideological predispositions (left/right-ideology) and political knowledge/awareness variables (the same way as in the other chapters).

Table 9.2: Proportion of voters voting for a right-leaning party (per cent, confidence intervals) in the Nordic countries 2005–2007

	Denmark 2007			Finland 2007			Iceland 2007			Norway 2005			Sweden 2006		
	%	n	CI	%	n	CI	%	n	CI	%	n	CI	%	n	CI
Gender															
Men	54	1938	[52–57]	58	550	[53–62]	62	612	[59–66]	59	876	[56–63]	54	1285	[51–57]
Women	42	1913	[40–44]	58	535	[53–62]	45	604	[41–49]	48	785	[45–52]	50	1285	[48–53]
Age in election year															
18–24 years	31	214	[25–37]	47	80	[35–59]	53	163	[45–60]	55	146	[47–63]	50	270	[44–56]
25–34 years	41	493	[37–46]	63	162	[55–71]	48	199	[41–55]	47	253	[41–53]	52	407	[47–57]
35–44 years	52	646	[49–56]	59	134	[50–68]	55	255	[49–61]	57	362	[52–62]	56	466	[52–61]
45–54 years	44	701	[40–47]	60	182	[52–67]	56	233	[49–62]	55	344	[50–60]	47	466	[42–51]
55–64 years	47	829	[44–50]	55	237	[48–62]	55	197	[48–62]	54	293	[49–60]	50	486	[46–55]
65+	58	958	[55–61]	59	290	[53–65]	53	169	[46–61]	56	259	[50–62]	57	475	[52–61]
Civil status															
Single	43	1218	[40–46]	52	427	[47–57]	50	359	[45–55]	49	455	[45–54]	49	865	[46–52]
Married/living with partner	51	2644	[49–53]	61	658	[57–66]	55	857	[52–58]	56	1206	[53–59]	54	1705	[51–56]
Degree of urbanisation															
Country side	55	683	[52–59]	80	126	[72–88]	61	493	[57–65]	57	521	[53–61]	58	415	[53–63]
Mid-sized town	49	2485	[47–51]	51	689	[47–55]	–	–	–	–	–	–	50	1786	[48–52]
Big city	39	663	[35–42]	68	270	[61–75]	49	723	[45–52]	53	1138	[50–56]	57	369	[52–62]

(Cont'd)

Table 9.2: (Cont'd)

	Denmark 2007			Finland 2007			Iceland 2007			Norway 2005			Sweden 2006		
	%	n	CI	%	n	CI	%	n	CI	%	n	CI	%	n	CI
Schooling															
Compulsory schooling	46	731	[42–49]	48	270	[42–55]	54	414	[49–59]	48	216	[41–54]	42	531	[38–46]
Lower secondary school (student)	50	2671	[48–52]	60	546	[56–65]	58	464	[54–63]	57	721	[54–61]	48	1005	[45–52]
Higher education (university, teachers, nurses)	42	460	[38–47]	62	269	[56–69]	46	338	[41–51]	53	724	[50–57]	62	996	[59–65]
Employment															
Outside the labour market	49	1449	[46–51]	56	400	[51–62]	50	418	[45–55]	52	512	[47–56]	51	708	[47–54]
Self-employed	63	233	[57–69]	75	103	[65–84]	60	139	[52–69]	75	120	[67–83]	72	105	[64–81]
Lower white-collar worker	44	689	[41–48]	52	143	[43–61]	53	184	[46–60]	49	490	[45–53]	53	591	[49–57]
Higher white-collar worker	49	737	[45–53]	67	171	[60–75]	48	262	[42–55]	57	346	[51–62]	70	262	[65–76]
Blue-collar worker (incl. unskilled workers)	47	754	[43–50]	51	268	[45–58]	62	213	[56–69]	57	193	[50–64]	38	324	[33–43]
Public or private employment															
Public employed	32	828	[29–35]	47	170	[41–52]	45	303	[40–49]	47	585	[44–51]	57	794	[54–61]
Private employed	53	3034	[51–55]	59	915	[55–63]	61	625	[58–65]	57	889	[54–60]	60	1204	[52–68]
Party identification															
No	46	1725	[44–48]	56	415	[51–61]	43	544	[39–47]	58	826	[55–62]	60	1325	[58–63]
Yes	50	2131	[48–52]	59	670	[55–63]	62	672	[58–66]	50	835	[47–53]	39	673	[35–42]

(Cont'd)

Table 9.2: (Contd.)

	Denmark 2007			Finland 2007			Iceland 2007			Norway 2005			Sweden 2006		
	%	n	CI	%	n	CI	%	n	CI	%	n	CI	%	n	CI
Political awareness															
Low	51	1270	[48–54]	61	284	[54–67]	53	317	[48–58]	56	346	[51–61]	49	524	[44–53]
Medium	50	1457	[47–52]	55	355	[50–61]	55	466	[50–59]	53	346	[48–57]	54	752	[51–58]
High	44	1135	[41–46]	58	427	[53–63]	52	433	[48–57]	54	854	[51–58]	56	344	[51–61]
Political knowledge															
Low	49	987	[46–52]	55	186	[47–63]	52	172	[45–60]	57	484	[52–61]	43	424	[38–48]
Medium	50	1444	[48–53]	58	320	[53–64]	52	758	[48–56]	57	578	[53–61]	54	566	[50–58]
High	46	1431	[44–49]	58	579	[54–63]	58	286	[53–64]	50	599	[46–54]	59	625	[55–63]
Left-right self-placement															
Left	13	1131	[11–15]	12	162	[7–17]	8	177	[4–12]	11	395	[8–14]	4	434	[2–6]
Centre	51	1778	[48–53]	57	636	[53–61]	52	816	[49–56]	60	987	[57–63]	62	1119	[60–65]
Right	89	883	[87–91]	95	253	[92–98]	94	223	[91–97]	95	279	[92–98]	95	299	[93–98]
Changed party															
No	57	2700	[56–59]	42	482	[37–46]	54	710	[50–58]	64	1 242	[62–67]	57	358	[52–63]
Yes	27	1 162	[25–30]	61	734	[58–65]	54	950	[51–57]	41	1 328	[38–43]	58	727	[54–62]
Total (all voters)	48	3 862	[47–50]	54	1 216	[51–56]	54	1 660	[52–57]	52	2 570	[50–54]	58	1 085	[55–61]

Note: The data is weighted for Finland. The categories for political awareness and political knowledge are calculated so approximately 1/3 of voters are placed in each category for each of the five countries.

Notably, the explained variances (pseudo McFadden R^2) for the first model in each country (only SES-variables) are surprisingly weak (0.03–0.06). Although our set of SES-variables can be said to be incomplete – at least in comparison with most nation-specific analyses of social cleavages – the general conclusion is that belonging to a socio-economic group offers quite limited explanatory power in the twenty-first century models of party choice in the Nordic countries. This shows how SES-variables seem to count for less of the variation in party choice than previously (Stubager 2003).

As expected, voters' left-right self-placement has a very strong effect on bloc voting in all the Nordic countries. According to the results, the estimated marginal effect of moving from the most left to the most right position along the left-right dimension on the propensity to vote right-leaning is 100 percentage points (!) in the Swedish case. This once again shows the very strong effect of left-right self-placement as the central heuristic shortcut for deciding what party to vote for.

Surprisingly, there are strong negative effects of political awareness in Denmark and Norway (and in Denmark also a strong negative effect of political knowledge). This is partly explained by the fact that the strong populist parties (Danish People's Party and the Norwegian Progress Party) are included among the right-leaning parties. Many of their supporters have relatively low political awareness.

The urbanisation variable survives and even gets stronger in Norway when including the controls for left-right, political awareness and political knowledge in all five countries. Urbanisation shows robust negative effects on the probability of voting for parties on the right. The effect is negative (more urban means less to the right), which follows the traditional understanding that the agrarians have strong support in rural areas.

Also being private or self-employed is associated with voting for right-leaning parties in all countries except Iceland where no relationship is found. This very much follows the traditional cleavages established along with the parties when they were first created (*see* Chapters Two and Three).

In Denmark, Norway and Finland education has no effect when controlling for left-right self-placement, etc. (model 2). One explanation is that it is the populist parties, that are included among the right-leaning parties, which tend to depress the effect of education. Many of these voters have less formal education compared to other voters. In Finland, also, the agrarian party has strong support among the least educated, which again would depress any educational effect across the left and right divide. In the two countries where the populist right is weak (Sweden) or non-existing (Iceland) we see an interesting effect. In Iceland the higher educated are 16 percentage points less likely to vote for a right-leaning party whereas in Sweden they are 24 percentage points more likely to vote for a right-leaning party.

In Iceland and Denmark women significantly tend to vote more for the left before the control of left-right position (model 1). This can partly be understood as a consequence of their employment not only in the public sector but also in public employment – in the 'caring professions', in health care and education – which are overrepresented by women. In Iceland we see that when controlling for left-right

Table 9.3: Modelling the probability of voting for a right-leaning party – marginal change (percentage point)

	Denmark 2007		Finland 2007		Iceland 2007		Norway 2007		Sweden 2006	
	Model 1	Model 2	Model 1	Model 2	Model 1	Model 2	Model 1	Model 2	Model 1	Model 2
Age in election year	4***	4***	0	-3	8	2	1	0	6***	1
Women	-9***	-8***	-3	-3	-18***	-8	-6**	-5	0	1
Lower secondary	4	1	12***	6	3	-2	12***	8	12***	2
Higher education	-2	-4	10**	5	-8	-16**	11**	6	24***	23***
Not single	5***	7***	7**	7*	6	6	3	-2	4	-3
Self employed	11***	12**	15**	11	5	-10	20***	16**	12**	11
Lower white-collar	7**	6*	-9	-8	9	-2	-4	-8	0	5
Higher white-collar	8***	8**	7	-1	7	2	0	-3	9**	0
Blue-collar	3	1	-8*	3	5	4	-4	-6	-8*	-3
Degree of urbanisation	-15***	-14***	-11**	-12*	-13***	-22***	-3	-12***	-2	-8
Public sector	-21***	-16***	2	7	-6	0	-16***	-5	-13***	0
Left-right self-placement	/	91***	/	95***	/	98***	/	98***	/	100***
Left-right extremeness	/	25***	/	0	/	15	/	19**	/	-4
Political awareness	/	-17***	/	-2	/	-7	/	-22**	/	5
Political knowledge	/	-13***	/	3	/	2	/	2	/	-4
No. respondents	3 815	3 815	1 039	1 039	928	928	1 471	1 471	1 522	1 522
McFadden pseudo R²	0.05	0.33	0.03	0.28	0.06	0.35	0.04	0.39	0.05	0.52
Log likelihood	-2,512	-1,778	-685	-508	-603	-418	-975	-619	-1,001	-507
Chi²	261.40	1,728.51	45.03	398.92	71.06	440.42	75.80	787.55	99.28	1,086.68

Note: *p<0.1,**p<0.05,***p<0.01. Education (Ref category: compulsory schooling); Employment (Ref category: Outside the labour market) Individual weights are used for Finland 2007. The marginal change in percentage points on the dependent variable when the independent variable changes from 0 to 1 with other variables held at their mean. The marginal change for age is the change from ½ standard deviation below the mean to ½ above the mean on age with all other variables held at their mean.

position, the gender variable becomes insignificant, suggesting that in Iceland it is an attitudinal dimension rather that a gender issue when it comes to voting left or right. In Denmark it remains significant to suggest that gender still plays a role after controlling for employment and left-right position.

In order to explore the specific characteristics of each party voter we will, in the next section, apply a multinomial logistical regression analysis where the dependent variable is not simply left or right, but includes all parties. For clarification we have a model for each country: Tables 9.4a to 9.4e.

Nordic voting behaviour: the multinomial story

Nordic voters' support for socialist/non-socialist parties has had a tremendous impact on the actual outcome of elections; i.e. what types of government are formed on the basis of general elections. When analysing political change in the Nordic countries in the post war era, using a left-right dichotomy for party choice may well suffice, at least as long as the ambition stays at giving a broad picture.

Admittedly, the use of a simple left-right dichotomy in an analysis of party choice will eventually obscure many important nuances of party competition in the Nordic countries – especially because of the populist right. Of course, each party in the Nordic party space has a *raison d'être*: there is a reason why they are represented, and there is a reason behind their individual gains and losses at general elections. In the following analyses we will simultaneously analyse all party choices available to Nordic voters in one single model, separately for each country. In Tables 9.4a-e below, we will present results from multinomial regression analyses that also include ideology, more specifically individual voter's positioning along the left-right dimension, and five complementary issue dimensions: size of public sector, immigration, moral, environment, and the European Union (*see* Chapter Three for details). The issue dimensions are selected to represent the most important political dimensions in the Nordic party space, and the ones that have been shown to have the strongest explanatory power in analyses of party choice in nation-specific studies of voting behaviour. The positive and negative effects of the different issue dimensions on the probability of voting for a specific party, will give us a clear picture of the party's ideological fundamentals in the electorate.

Once again, the models in Table 9.4a-e present the marginal change in percentage points. These percentage points represent the effect on the probabilities of voting for each of the parties included in the model when each of the independent variables changes and all the other variables are held constant at their means. All changes on the independent variables are from a minimum value to a maximum value except age, where it is a change from a half standard deviation below the age-mean to a half standard deviation above the age-mean (otherwise there would be a tendency to compare the effect of an eighteen year old with only a few people in the old age group sample, thus strongly exaggerating the effect of age). First we will comment on the country-specific findings and then address the findings compared across the five Nordic countries.

Denmark 2007 election

In the first model in Table 9.4a we see that women are two percentage points less likely than men to vote for the conservatives and women are four percentage points less likely to vote for the social liberals. These differences are even present when controlling for the variable that more women are likely to work in the public sector.

Age has some effect, as age increases voters tend to vote more for the social democrats and are less likely to vote conservative when controlling for the other variables. This tells us that voters do not necessary become more conservative with age when taking other variables into account. The findings here, in the Danish election of 2007, actually support the opposite.

Public sectors employees are six percentage points less likely to vote for the agrarian party compared to the variable of being a private sector employee.

Self-placement on the left-right has the strongest and expected effect across the parties. The average absolute change is 18 percentage points (last column in Table 9.4a). The effect follows the traditional left-right economic conceptualisation of Danish parties where the parties are placed on a one dimensional scale from left to right as Far Left (*Enhedslisten*), Left Socialist (*SF*), Social Democrats, Social Liberal, Populist Right, Conservative and Agrarian i.e. we find a positive effect of the left-right self-placement to the right of Social Democrats on the political spectrum and negative to the left of Social Democrats. Also attitudes to public sector size and environment tend to follow the traditional economic left-right scale.

Immigration and EU issues cross cut the traditional left-right economic dimension. EU-sceptical voters are most likely to vote for the Left Socialist or the Populist Right whereas the most pro-European voters are more likely to vote for the Agrarian party. Pro-immigration voters are most likely to vote for the Social Liberals and the least likely voters for the Populist Right.

The more knowledgeable voters tend to vote more for the Conservative, Social Liberal and Agrarian parties. This is even so when controlling for age and educational level, which tells us that political sophistication adds an additional dimension of understanding to party choice (*see also* Hansen 2009b; Oscarsson 2007).

Attitudinal items including self-placement on the left-right have a much larger impact than socio-demographics. This tells us again that socio-demographics have lost most of their previous relevance when understanding party choice.

The least politically aware tend to vote blank and provide 'other' votes much more than any other group.

Finland 2007 election

There is no significant effect of gender on party choice in the 2007 Finnish election.

Sixty year old voters are 7 percentage points more likely to vote for the Social Democrats compared to a forty-one year old, when other variables are held at their mean. This finding is equivalent to those in Denmark and Norway but opposite to the findings in Sweden. This suggests that the Swedish Social Democrats have mobilised the younger voter much more than is the case in Denmark, Finland and Norway.

The model in Table 9.4b shows very few significant effects for education. The only significant findings show that the probability for voting for the Social Democrats drops with 9 percentage points, going from the variables of compulsory schooling to higher education, whereas the Greens have the opposite trend. The effects are due to the strong support for the Social Democrats among the traditional working-class population and the Green party's stronghold among younger generations with a university degree. This very weak effect of education is equivalent to that found in Denmark and Iceland, both countries showing a very weak effect of education on party choice, but is in sharp contrast to Sweden and Norway with very strong educational cleavages.

Changing from 'outside the labour market' to lower white-collar or blue-collar worker means it becomes 10 percentage points less likely for votes to be given to the Conservatives. Previous analyses clearly show that the Conservative party finds its traditionally strongest support among higher white-collar and self employed voters (Paloheimo and Sundberg 2005). The widening of the party's support in the 2007 election and its profile as the new 'workers party' did, however, imply that the profile of the party's supporters became slightly less distinct.

The probability for voting for the Agrarian party increases with 30 percentage points if the voter lives in a rural area and by 15 per cent if the voter is self employed (including farmers). This shows that the agrarian party in Finland still has a very strong base in rural areas and among farmers, findings which contradict those of the Danish Agrarian party who today have a much broader base than just in agriculture. The Finnish Agrarian party has another interesting base: voters working in the public sector tend to vote 14 percentage points more for the Agrarian party than if working in the private sector and the party also has a strong positive effect if voters believe in an increasing public sector. The result is in line with the Agrarian party's strong defence of the current Finnish municipality structure, which involves many small municipalities functioning as important employers, in particular in the less populated parts of Finland. The Finnish Agrarian party is thus composed of two overlapping, but different groups.

Iceland 2007 election

In the Icelandic election of 2007, men are four percentage points more likely than women to vote for the liberals, when the other variables in the model are held constant.

There is a large impact of urbanisation on the Agrarian party where people living in a rural area have a 19 percentage point higher probability to vote for the Agrarians compared to people living in an urban area. Nevertheless, it is interesting that the self-employed do not have a higher probability to vote for the Agrarians as we would except if the electoral support consisted of farmers. But there is no significant effect of employment status at all among the Icelandic

Table 9.4a: Modelling party choice in the Nordic countries: Denmark 2007 (multinomial logistic regression, marginal change in percentage points)

	Socdem	Con	Social Lib	LeftSoc	PopR	Agr	ChrDem	FarLeft	Other	Average absolute change
Women	-6	-2**	-4***	0	1	-2*	-0*	0**	0	2
Age in election year	6	-3***	-1***	0**	0	-2***	0***	0	0	1
Lower secondary	-5	6***	-2	-2	0	3	0	0	0	2
Higher education	-13	12***	6***	1**	-1	-5	0**	0	0	4
Self-employed	-10	6**	2	-2	0	3	0*	0	0	3
Lower white-collar	-1	-1	-3	-1	0	6	0*	0	0	1
Higher white-collar	-5	1	0	-2	-1	9**	0	0	-1	2
Blue-collar	10	-4***	-5***	-0*	0	-1	0	0	0	2
Degree of urbanisation	9	2	1	3	0	-12***	-0**	0**	-2***	3
Public sector	3	0	0	4*	-2**	-6**	0	0	1	2
Ideology: Left-right self-placement	-38	30***	2***	-37***	5***	44***	0***	-4***	-1*	18
Ideology: European Union	-12	10***	4***	-23***	-6***	30***	-1***	-1***	-2	10
Ideology: Environment	35	-6***	11	20***	-7***	-57***	-0**	1***	3	15
Ideology: Immigration	16	-3***	40***	15***	-53***	-19***	4***	1***	-0*	17
Ideology: Public sector	54	-22***	-5***	14	-0***	-41***	-0**	1**	-1***	15

(Cont'd)

Table 9.4a: (Cont'd)

	Socdem	Con	Social Lib	LeftSoc	PopR	Agr	ChrDem	FarLeft	Other	Average absolute change
Ideology: Moral	17	-5***	5	7	1	-10***	-16***	0**	0	7
Political knowledge	-10	6***	7***	-4	0	1	0	0	-1	3
Political awareness	6	3	2	-2	2	9	0	0	-20***	5
Number of respondents	3 859									
McFadden pseudo R²	0.31									
Log likelihood	-5,051									
Chi²	4,497.01									

Note: SocDem is the reference category for the dependent variable (party choice). The level of significance is based on the logit coefficients, thus there is no test of significance related to the Social Democrats as this party is the reference. Marginal change in percentage points change from min to max on the independent variable when other variables are held at their mean, except age where it is a change from a ½ standard deviation below the age-mean to ½ standard deviation above the age-mean (In the Danish election 2007 the change is from 43 to 60 years old). The other category is other votes and blank votes. Abstentions are excluded from the model. Constant not shown. Education (Ref category: compulsory schooling); Employment (Ref category: Outside the labour market).

166 | The Nordic Voter

Table 9.4b: Modelling party choice in the Nordic countries: Finland 2007 (multinomial logistic regression, marginal change in percentage points)

	SocDem	Con	Lib	LeftSoc	PopR	Agr	ChrDem	Greens	Other	Average absolute change
Women	1	-1	-1	1	0	-1	0	-1	2	1
Age in election year	7	-2*	-1**	1	-1***	-5**	-0**	-3***	3	2
Lower secondary	-1	-3	-1	0	-1	0	0	3	2	1
Higher education	-7	2	3	2	-2**	3	0	7**	-7	4
Self-employed	-15	-3	-4	-2	9**	15**	-5***	7**	-1	7
Lower white-collar	10	-10**	-6***	-2	1	1	0	-1	8	4
Higher white-collar	-2	1	-4	-2	8*	-4	0	1	3	3
Blue-collar	0	-10	-5*	1	8**	10	0	-4	0	4
Degree of urbanisation	9	5	1	3	1	-30***	0	1	11	7
Public sector	-18	-1	3**	1*	0	14***	0*	2**	-2	5
Ideology: Left-right self-placement	-29	77***	4***	-65***	0***	16***	0***	-3	-0***	22
Ideology: European Union	23	13	13*	-4**	-10***	-9**	-1***	-13***	-12**	11
Ideology: Environment	-12	5	-13	1	2	7	0	23***	-13	8
Ideology: Immigration	-16	-11	7**	0	-1	13	1**	10**	-4	7
Ideology: Public sector	24	-4	1	0	2	24	0	-58***	10	14

(Cont'd)

Table 9.4b: (Cont'd)

	SocDem	Con	Lib	LeftSoc	PopR	Agr	ChrDem	Greens	Other	Average absolute change
Ideology: Moral	5	0	-2	1	-1	-18	-1***	4	12	5
Political knowledge	-3	7	6	2	-1	-3	0	-10	2	4
Political awareness	2	-4	-14**	-3	2	15	0	5	-3	5
Number of respondents	701									
McFadden pseudo R^2	0.29									
Log likelihood	-1,012									
Chi^2	16,914.71									

Note: The data is weighted in order to adjust for the oversampling of Swedish speaking Finns. SocDem is the reference category for dependent variable (party choice). The level of significance is based on the logit coefficients, thus there is no test of significance related to the Social Democrats as this party is the reference. Marginal change in percentage points change from min to max on the independent variable when other variables are held at their mean except age where it is a change from a ½ standard deviation below the age-mean to ½ standard deviation above the age-mean (In the Finish election 2007 the change is from 41 to 60 years old).The other category is other votes and blank votes. Abstentions are excluded from the model. Constant not shown. Education (Ref category: compulsory schooling); Employment (Ref category: Outside the labour market).

Table 9.4c: Modelling party choice in the Nordic countries: Iceland 2007 (multinomial logistic regression, marginal change in percentage points)

	SocDem	Con	Lib	LeftSoc	Agr	Greens	Other	Average absolute change
Women	6	-2	-4**	0	5	-1	-5*	3
Age in election year	-1	2	0	-2*	-1	0	3	1
Lower secondary	3	1	-1	1	-1	-1*	0	1
Higher education	9	-6	-3	1	-1	-1	0	3
Self-employed	-4	0	-4	2	-3	2	7	3
Lower white-collar	-2	12	-4	0	-5	0	-1	4
Higher white-collar	-7	10	-3	1	-3	0	2	4
Blue-collar	1	2	-2	-1	1	-1	-1	1
Degree of urbanisation	10	4	0	1	-19***	3**	1	5
Public sector	0	1	-1	0	0	1	0	1
Ideology: Left-right self-placement	-24	97***	-0**	-71***	-0***	-0**	-2**	28
Ideology: European Union	39	-24***	-3***	-5***	-8***	-2***	2**	12
Ideology: Environment	31	-40***	2	19**	-29***	12***	5	19
Ideology: Immigration	5	-3	-5**	6**	2	0	-5	4
Ideology: Public sector	20	-35***	-2	5	12	-1	2	11
Ideology: Moral	4	-4	-4	3	2	-1	-2	3

(Cont'd)

Table 9.4c: (Cont'd)

	SocDem	Con	Lib	LeftSoc	Agr	Greens	Other	Average absolute change
Political knowledge	6	-11	-1	-1	14***	-2	-5	6
Political awareness	5	17	5	0	-3	1	-24***	8
Number of respondents	1 015							
McFadden pseudo R²	0.29							
Log likelihood	-1,181							
Chi²	974.02							

Note: SocDem is the reference category for dependent variable (party choice). The level of significance is based on the logit coefficients, thus there is no test of significance related to the Social Democrats as this party is the reference. Marginal change in percentage points change from min to max on the independent variable when other variables are held at their mean except age where it is a change from a ½ standard deviation below the age-mean to ½ standard deviation above the age-mean (In the Iceland election 2007 the change is from 37 to 53 years old). The other category is other votes and blank votes. Abstentions are excluded from the model. Constant not shown. Education (Ref category: compulsory schooling); Employment (Ref category: Outside the labour market).

Table 9.4d: Modelling party choice in the Nordic countries: Norway 2005 (multinomial logistic regression, marginal change in percentage points)

	SocDem	Con	Lib	LeftSoc	PopR	Agr	ChrDem	FarLeft	Other	Average absolute change
Women	4	2	-1	0	-2	-2	0	0	-1**	1
Age in election year	0	1	3**	0	-3	0	0	0	1	1
Lower secondary	-29	2**	1	0	-5	-1	2***	30	-1	8
Higher education	-26	3*	7**	1*	-10	1	2**	23	-1	8
Self-employed	-7	5	-1	1	-5	9*	0	0	-1	3
Lower white-collar	7	1	-2	2	-6*	-1	-1	0	0	2
Higher white-collar	5	3	-2	2	-6	0	-1**	0	0	2
Blue - collar	7	-4	1	-1	-4	0	0	0	-1*	2
Degree of urbanisation	3	4*	1	0	3	-9***	-1	0	0	2
Public sector	0	-2	1	1**	-2	2	-1	0	0	1
Ideology: Left-right self-placement	-61	47***	7***	-34***	42***	-2**	2***	-1***	0**	22
Ideology: European Union	22	11***	-2*	-2***	7	-29***	-5***	-0***	-1***	9
Ideology: Environment	-32	-9	28***	10***	2	-3	3***	0	0	10
Ideology: Immigration	-7	8**	20***	1	-42***	3	17***	0***	-1	11
Ideology: Public sector	82	-38***	-24***	3	-24***	4	-2***	0	0*	20
Ideology: Moral	54	0**	3	6***	-1***	0**	-62***	0	0	14

(Cont'd)

Table 9.4d: (Cont'd)

	SocDem	Con	Lib	LeftSoc	PopR	Agr	ChrDem	FarLeft	Other	Average absolute change
Political knowledge	-3	1	6	1	-9	7**	-2*	0	0	3
Political awareness	27	-10**	2	-1	-14**	-4	1	0	0	7
Number of respondents	1 490									
McFadden pseudo R²	0.41									
Log likelihood	-1,601									

Note: SocDem is the reference category for dependent variable (party choice). The level of significance is based on the logit coefficients; thus there is no test of significance related to the Social Democrats as this party is the reference. Marginal change in percentage points change from min to max on the independent variable when other variables are held at their mean except age where it is a change from a ½ standard deviation below the age-mean to ½ standard deviation above the age-mean (In the Norwegian election 2005 the change is from 38 to 54 years old).The other category is other votes and blank votes. Abstentions are excluded from the model. Constant not shown. Education (Ref category: compulsory schooling); Employment (Ref category: Outside the labour market).

Table 9.4e: Modelling party choice in the Nordic countries: Sweden 2006 (multinomial logistic regression, marginal change in percentage points)

	SocDem	Con	Lib	LeftSoc	PopR	Agr	ChrDem	Greens	Other	Average absolute change
Women	-8	4	1	-1	-0**	4	1	0	-2	2
Age in election year	3	-3	1	0	0	2	-2	-0***	-2*	1
Lower secondary	-35	-20	-10	-1	0	-18	-7	98	-6	22
Higher education	-40	-10**	0***	-1	0	-10*	-2**	66	-3	15
Self-employed	-23	8*	-6	0	0	25***	1	0	-3	7
Lower white-collar	-2	3	4	0	0	3	-1	0	-7***	2
Higher white-collar	-6	-1	-3	1	-1	18**	-3	0	-5*	4
Blue-collar	1	-3	4	0	0	4	-3	0	-4	2
Degree of urbanisation	1	5	6	0	0*	-14*	-1	0*	3	3
Public sector	-1	3	2	0	0	-1	-1	0	-2	1
Ideology: Left-right self-placement	-83	71***	12***	-15***	-0***	9***	7***	-0***	-1***	22
Ideology: European Union	19	10	-4	-2***	0	-3	-6**	-0***	-13***	6
Ideology: Environment	6	31**	-1	-1	-0**	-23**	-1	-1***	-9**	8
Ideology: Immigration	12	-29**	-10	2	-3***	14	12	0	2	9
Ideology: Public sector	68	-44***	-16***	7**	0*	-4***	-18***	-0***	7	18
Ideology: Moral	-6	32**	8	3**	0	6	-48***	0	5	12

(Cont'd)

Table 9.4e: (Cont'd)

	SocDem	Con	Lib	LeftSoc	PopR	Agr	ChrDem	Greens	Other	Average absolute change
Political knowledge	-4	-4	15	-2	-0**	-8	-2	0	4	4
Political awareness	5	-11	11	-1	0	3	-2	0	-6	4
Number of respondents	974									
McFadden pseudo R^2	0.36									
Log likelihood	-1,173									
Chi^2	1,303.60									

Note: SocDem is the reference category for dependent variable (party choice). The level of significance is based on the logit coefficients, thus there is no test of significance related to the Social Democrats as this party is the reference. Marginal change in percentage points change from min to max on the independent variable when other variables are held at their mean, except age where it is a change from a ½ standard deviation below the age-mean to ½ standard deviation above the age-mean (In the Swedish 2006 the change is from 39 to 56 years old).The other category is other votes and blank votes. Abstentions are excluded from the model. Constant not shown. Education (Ref category: compulsory schooling); Employment (Ref category: Outside the labour market).

voters and the aggregated socio-demographics carries the weakest impact on party choice across all five Nordic countries, i.e. suggesting a very weak class cleavage structure among Icelandic voters.

The attitudinal items have a very strong effect on party choice. It is 97 per cent more likely for the vote to be conservative if voters are further to the right on the left-right scale compared to being further to the left. On the other hand there is a 71 per cent higher probability to vote for the Left Socialists if voters are further to the left on the left-right scale compared to being further to the right. Self-placement on the one dimensional left-right economic scale has once again proven to be the strongest predictor of party choice and an extremely important cue for voters when making their choice.

As in Denmark, the less politically aware the voters are, the more likely it is that they will vote 'blank' or for a candidate outside the established parties.

Moral and the immigration issues do not play a role in Icelandic party politics, as the changes in probabilities are very small and mostly insignificant. This goes along with the fact that there is no Christian party or populist right, established in Iceland.

Norway 2005 election

Social Democrats have a very strong base among voters who have compulsory schooling as their final level of education, for example, voters are 26 percentage points less likely to vote for the Social Democrats if they have higher education compared to voters whose final education was compulsory schooling.

As in the other five Nordic countries age and gender only play a very minor independent role explaining party choice.

The Agrarians have a strong base among the self-employed and in rural areas (e.g. farmers) and also among those voters who are very sceptical of the EU. The Agrarian party is actually the most pro-EU in Denmark, so once again we find very different effects between parties across countries.

The populist right and the conservatives have a strong base among the least politically aware, that is, when political awareness decreases the likelihood to vote for these two parties increases. When it comes to the popular right, the findings replicate those in the other countries, but the conservatives show a unique pattern and even in direct opposition to the findings in Iceland.

Urbanisation also plays a role when it comes to the conservatives, i.e. voters living in cities are 4 percentage points more like to vote conservative than if they live in rural areas. The Agrarian party has the opposite tendency. If voters live in rural areas they are 9 percentage points more likely to vote for the Agrarian party. These two findings illustrate nicely the traditional cleavage between industrial city areas and agricultural rural areas.

Left-right self-placement and attitudes to the size of the public sector show the most effect with the full variables on party choice in the Norwegian 2005 election, by having an absolute average effect of respectively 22 and 20 percentage points. The results echo the results from Chapter Three by showing that the probability for voting for a party on the left increases if a voter moves to the left on this scale and it decreases if the voter moves to the right.

Conservative voters are very positive about the EU and believe in a small public sector. The popular right has a strong base among voters with anti-immigration views but also has a strong impact of being on the right on the left-right self-placement. This last part contradicts the findings from the popularist right parties in Denmark, Sweden and Finland where we found very little effect of left-right self-placement on popular right voters. This tells us that the Norwegian popular right shows itself to be a stronger brand of the political right than in the other four Nordic countries.

The Christian Democrats have their stronghold among voters with strong moral views and are positive to immigration, but otherwise the other independent variables have a limited effect on their votes.

Sweden 2006 election

We can see from Table 9.4e that education plays a very strong role in explaining party choice in the Swedish 2006 election. The Green party has many highly educated voters and very few voters with only compulsory schooling whereas the other parties, which have significant results, have the opposite effect, i.e., voting for Social Democratic, Conservative and Agrarian parties is more likely if the level of education is lower. The strong role of education shows, along with Norway, that there are only two Nordic countries which stand out with a clear educational cleavage. Interestingly, in the multivariate analysis, the effects of education on party choice in Norway and Sweden cannot be explained by the fact that physical age is correlated with educational level.

As in Norway the probability for voting for the Agrarians increases when the voters are self-employed or live in the rural areas. That is, in Norway and Sweden, the Agrarians can still be understood as a party with a strong rural and agricultural base, whereas in the other three countries, their social base is much broader.

If the employee is a white-collar worker there is an 18 percentage point higher chance that this person would vote for the Agrarian party compared to those outside the labour market. Also, the self-employed in Sweden tend to vote more for the Agrarians.

The conservatives and the populist right both increase their votes if voters support strict immigration laws, which suggests that both types of party have an established base on strict immigration among the voters.

Christian Democrats, as in all the Nordic countries (except Iceland which does not have a Christian party), increase their support by holding more moral conservative values.

Similarities and differences across the five Nordic countries on party choice

Traditional left-right self-placement is still the most important party cue when voters make up their mind in the Nordic countries. But we have seen that other issues, especially EU issues and immigration, tend to matter more and cross cut the traditional left-right scale. This is most profound in Denmark and is also due to a very established popular right party, which is on the right on immigration but more pragmatic on the economic left-right scale, along with a sceptical EU position.

The classic one-dimensionality is still profound in Sweden, but also here there is an emerging popular right – the Sweden Democrats which challenge this picture.

Sweden and Norway have a clear educational cleavage when it comes to party choice, whereas the other countries have a much weaker educational cleavage.

Across all the five Nordic countries we find that the overall explanatory power of socio-demographics is weak.

The Social Democrats still have a base among blue-collar workers in Denmark and Norway, but not in the other countries. Being left on the classic economic left-right dimension along with supporting a large public sector is, across all five countries, associated with voting for the Social Democrats – the Social Democrats are still in the eyes of the voters the caretaker of a strong welfare state.

The Conservatives in Iceland are associated with sceptical EU-attitudes whereas this is the opposite in the other countries where the Conservatives represent a strong pro EU-view. That is, with Iceland not being member of the EU and lacking a Populist Right to represent anti-EU attitudes, the Conservatives seem to cover these views.

Agrarian parties still have a stronghold in more rural areas in all five countries. Even the traditional base of many self-employed farmers has today been challenged and has forced the party to broaden its electoral base.

The Christian Democrats still have a stronghold on moral issues in the four countries in which they are present. In Iceland, where the Christian Democrats do not run, the moral issues seem to cross cut the present parties and are not monopolised by any party.

One lesson to draw from the similarities and differences across the countries is the presence or absence of a Populist Right and a Green party. This seems to affect the other parties and how they take on those issues which these types of parties otherwise would have covered. That is, the party system seems to have a clear effect on the issues each of the parties within the system emphasise in order to gain votes.

Conclusion: a dominating left-right dimension, but a fragmented issue space

Alford's index, that measures the difference between working class and middle class shares of votes for parties on the left, shows that Sweden is among those countries in the world with the highest index value of 25. The other four Nordic countries have lower values and Norway and Iceland even had negative values in the 2009 and 2005 elections. These four countries do not stand out when comparing the level of Alford's index of class voting to other developed countries nor do they stand out when it comes to the development over time, where there has been a trend of steady decline. Across all five countries there has been a continuous decline on the index since the 1960s. If this trend continues, all countries will have an Alford index close to zero or even negative within a few elections. The low and declining trend of the index tells us that the time when being a blue-collar worker automatically meant voting for the left has passed. Many of these voters now vote for Agrarian or populist right parties, as in the Danish case. Particularly, the Social Democrats have lost voters to the populist right in Norway and Denmark, countries which have strong populist right parties. Sweden, where, the blue-collar voter still remains loyal to the left and with only a weak populist right party, seems to be the country that needs to fully catch up with the general development among the four other Nordic countries. When it comes to the similarities between the Nordic countries, our analysis over time has shown that in applying the Alford index, the countries stand out as more different than ever before.

Today socio-demographics variables are weak when it comes to predicting party choice in the Nordic countries. This means that there is little in the way of an automatic response or habit left when it comes to party choice in the Nordic countries. Party choice is a reflective choosing of politics, weakly associated with demographics. The equal opportunity established by the strong welfare state has caused voters to leave their socio-demographic heritage behind and vote according to attitude rather than entrenched, social heritage.

Even through the significance of socio-demographic variables is relatively weak in all Nordic countries, Sweden and Norway stand out with particularly strong educational cleavages in their electoral behaviour, compared to Iceland and Finland with non-existing or weak educational cleavages.

One strong similarity between the Nordic countries is the clear effect of a left-right dimension in electoral behaviour. The Nordic voters use left-right self-placement as a very strong cue for deciding how to vote. In all countries the left-right dimension is the strongest single predictor for party choice. Sweden stands out with the most uni-dimensional party space compared to the other Nordic countries where left-right dimensionality partly seems to dominate other issues. Denmark closely follows by experiencing a slightly more multi-dimensional party space.

When it comes to party choice the immigration issue matters the most in Denmark and the least in Iceland. EU-issues matter the most in Iceland and the least in Sweden. The environment issue matters the most in Iceland and the least in Sweden. Moral/ethical dilemmas matter the most in Norway and the least in Iceland. This fragmented electoral behaviour emphasises again the many and apparent differences between the Nordic countries.

Chapter Ten

The Not-So-Exceptional Nordic Voter

From the Wikipedia 'Exceptionalism' entry: Exceptionalism is the perception that a country, society, institution, movement, or time period is 'exceptional' (i.e. unusual or extraordinary) in some way and thus does not need to conform to normal rules or general principles (http://www.wikipedia.org/Exceptionalism).

Introduction

One general finding of this book is, as always, that the devil is hidden in the details. This project started out from a general understanding that the Nordic countries are remarkable similar. However, we feel our work with this book has opened a Pandora's box of unique features about each one of the Nordic countries. Today, even on basic features such as the size of the welfare state, the Nordic countries are more different than they have been for the previous 20 years. The large variation between the countries has made comparison difficult, but it has also helped us arrive at initially quite unexpected conclusions.

The overall aim of this research collaboration has been to present the first book-length comparative analysis of voting behaviour in the Nordic countries. We have provided a detailed account of key indicators that are present in most analyses of voting behaviour – such as voter turnout, party identification, satisfaction with democracy, time of vote decision, preferential vote, government support, and the classic determinants of party choice – as well as an account of the institutional settings that explain the differences between the Nordic countries.

In comparative analyses, the five Nordic countries are routinely lumped together under the parole of 'Nordic exceptionalism'. Indeed, there are still many reasons to treat the five Nordic countries as 'most similar systems'. However, in this book, we have highlighted the surprisingly large variations in electoral behaviour between these five countries. *The Nordic Voter* challenges a widespread practice to group Denmark, Finland, Iceland, Norway and Sweden together in analyses of comparative research. Our general claim, substantiated by a unique and extensive empirical analysis of voter behaviour, is that the dissimilarities between the Nordic countries are in fact so large – both in terms of institutional settings and micro level voting behaviour – that it is not justified to make general claims of a Nordic voter. In other words, the old story of 'remarkable similarities' has now been substituted with numerous examples of 'remarkable dissimilarities' between the Nordic countries.

The main insight from this research is, hence, that we have found and described large dissimilarities in electoral behaviour in the Nordic sphere. In most of our analyses throughout the book, one or two of the countries deviate quite substantially from the others in terms of level estimates and/or micro level relationships. And more often than not, the Nordic countries appear neither exceptional nor similar in a broader comparative perspective, severely weakening arguments to treat the Nordic countries as a distinct group of systems. As regards many aspects of electoral behaviour, we conclude that the variation *within* the Nordic countries tends to be larger than the variation *between* the Nordic countries and other established multiparty democracies in the world.

The starting point for our analyses has been the general decline story of withering democratic ties, also described as the decline of the 'party-in-the-electorate', that we have seen across the developed world, e.g. declining party membership, declining trust, increased volatility, increased number of late deciders and withering socio-demographic ties with parties. As we have been able to show in this book this development is also generally present in the Nordic countries, but again one country stands out compared to the others. In this case it is Sweden which (still) has the strongest elements of class voting among other developed democracies in the world.

In each chapter throughout this book, we have highlighted the similarities and differences between the countries and have used the variation between countries in our quest to increase our understanding of the Nordic voters. Among the five Nordic countries, the amount of between-country variation is today, on many variables, sufficient to provide bases for a careful selection of cases to be used in a comparative design.

The chapters from Three to Nine have concluded on different aspects of the Nordic voter. Table 10.1 serves as a heuristics tool or analytic framework that will help us structure the conclusion in each chapter related to the conclusion here. Each chapter's conclusion is on the horizontal – the rows – in Table 10.1. That is, for example, the conclusions in Chapter Three are a) Nordic exceptionalism compared to other developed countries, b) showing the similarity of aggregate levels between the Nordic countries, c) and how the development has occurred differently over time and, d) finally, using individual level election data to compare the electoral behaviour.

In this concluding chapter we use Table 10.1 and conclude vertically by structuring our discussion from the columns. This gives us four concluding sections.

The Nordic voter – No Nordic exceptionality

We have compared the five Nordic countries on a number of factors with other developed nations in order to investigate if the five Nordic countries can be characterised as distinct from other nations. The answer here is no – the five Nordic countries are not exceptional compared to most countries on most factors. On almost any factor some other countries outside the Nordic region have more in common and other nations less than what we have observed within the Nordic countries. This is the case on factors such as the effective number of parties in

Table 10.1: Analytic framework

Chapter	Exceptionality (Compared to Non-Nordic countries) — The five Nordic countries standout from other countries?	Similarity (aggregate levels) (Between Nordic Countries) — The five countries are grouped together in a comparison with other countries?	Similarity (trajectory) (Time series compared between Nordic Countries) — The five Nordic countries have experienced a similar time trend?	Similarity (micro level correlates) (Between Nordic Countries) — The same variables explain voting/political behaviour in the five Nordic countries?
	(a)	(b)	(c)	(d)
3 Party system characteristics	No	Yes	(n.a.)	Yes
4 Voter turnout	No	No	Partly	Yes
4 Satisfaction with democracy	Partly	Partly	Partly	Yes
5 Party identification	No	Yes	No	Yes
6 Preferential voting	No	No	No	No
7 Time of voting decision	No	No	Yes	Yes
8 Government performance	No	No	Partly	No
9 Party choice	No	No	Yes	Yes

Note: 'Partly' means there is a pattern for some of the Nordic countries, but not for all five.

parliaments, party competition and dimensionality, party attachment, voters' capability to recall candidates in their constituency and the number of voters who indicate that they follow the campaign. On these factors none of the Nordic countries stand out.

When it comes to class voting, Sweden is the only Nordic country that still stands out with the strongest class voting among all the countries we have been able to compare. In other Nordic countries such as Iceland and Norway, the strength of class voting is quite weak. There is no clustering of Nordic countries when it comes to class voting today.

Comparing the average incumbent effect across the Nordic countries, we see relatively weak negative effects in Sweden, Denmark and Norway and somewhat stronger negative effects in Finland and Iceland. But again, we see even weaker effects in Germany and stronger negative effects in e.g. Spain and the Netherlands, than in any of the five Nordic countries.

The Nordic countries voters are polarised as party voters and are quite diffused over the left-right self-placement scale compared with many other counties – except Finland which is substantially less polarised. But again, for example, Canada and Spain are even more polarised in left-right terms and Australia much less so. This is also the case of ideological congruence, where the Nordic countries have less ideological congruence, but this time the Netherlands has even less than them.

The closest we get to Nordic exceptionalism is on features related to the general wellbeing of democracy. When it comes to indicators such as high trust in politicians, high turnout and high satisfaction with democracy, the five Nordic countries do, in general, stand out compared to other established democracies. However, here there are exceptions from the rule: for instance, Iceland has had low trust in parliament and less satisfaction with democracy since the financial crises from 2008 onwards. And Finland is yet another exception when it comes to voter turnout, which is considerably lower than in the other four Nordic countries.

So overall, we conclude that Nordic voters are not exceptional compared to other nations, but that voters in the three Scandinavian countries of Denmark, Norway and Sweden are exceptionally satisfied with their democracy, have high levels of trust in politicians and they tend to turn out in high numbers in order to confirm their support for representative democracy, compared to voters in other nations. So on these few and limited variables we might be able to conclude that some *Scandinavian* exceptionalism is still present, but it is definitely not a Nordic one.

The Nordic voter – The five Nordic countries cannot be characterised as a single system

After having concluded that the Nordic countries are not exceptional, we now turn to the question of whether the five Nordic countries should be considered as a uniform group of states when compared to a wider selection of advanced democracies.

Starting out with the electoral system this seems not to be the case. On the contrary, we find strong differences between the five Nordic countries where in Finland it is mandatory to vote for a candidate and Norway only allows voting for a party, and the other three countries are found in between. The historical Stein Rokkan cleavage model still comes into its right in all five Nordic countries as all the countries have parties that traditionally follow this cleavage structure. However, new parties have emerged in all the countries, but not necessarily the same ones. The popular right have a strong base in Denmark and Norway, and in Finland and Sweden we see increased support for populist parties (although with a slightly different profile) as well. However, in Iceland no populist party has emerged nor a green party, parties which have been established in Finland, Sweden and Norway, but not in Denmark. That is, even though the five Nordic countries have a PR-system and party system rooted in the Stein Rokkan cleavage model, it would be a strong oversimplification to characterise or group them as a single system.

On the effective number of parties in parliament, Denmark, Sweden and Norway are quite similar, but Finland with more, and Iceland with substantially fewer parties, deviates from this pattern. When it comes to voter opinion on the necessity for parties, party competition and dimensionality party attachments, voters' capability to recall candidates in their constituency and the number of voters indicating that they follow the campaign, then the five Nordic countries are dispersed along with many other nations.

In the previous section, when dealing with Nordic exceptionalism, there appears to be a pattern for the Scandinavian (Denmark, Norway and Sweden) voter when it comes to turnout and satisfaction with democracy. Here we can add the negative effect on incumbency to this pattern of Scandinavian similarities, since governments in these three countries, on average, are substantially less punished by voters than governments in Iceland and Finland.

The Nordic voter – Similar time-trends, but more different than before

So the Nordic countries are not exceptional and our detailed investigation reveals more differences than similarities. But have the Nordic countries experienced similar time trends? The overall answer is yes. The five Nordic countries have indeed experienced the same development over time on a number of key factors. Class voting has gone down in all countries and fewer voters than before have a clear party attachment. At the same time more voters decide what (or whom) to vote for late in the campaign and electoral volatility has increased over time in all five countries. We also see a tendency towards an increasing negative incumbency effect in all five countries over time. When it comes to electoral turnout the five countries, except Denmark, have all experienced decreasing turnout over time. Also when it comes to total government expenditure per capita we have seen an increasing trend in the Nordic countries, except in Iceland where a very substantial drop after the financial breakdown in 2008 was experienced.

So with a few exceptions, the Nordic countries have experienced the same trends over time and these trends correspond to the trends in most other developed countries. But remarkably, these similar trends have not produced more similar countries. On the contrary, comparing the deviation in the beginning of the time period with the end of our time period, the five Nordic countries are today more different than ever before. This is the case with factors such as government expenditure, turnout, party ID, volatility, class voting and time of decision. On all these variables the five Nordic countries are more different than previously. Increasing Europeanisation, globalisation and Americanisation, might be elements that have diffused the once similar nations in somewhat different directions, and have also changed citizens' centre of attention. As an example, twenty to thirty years ago it was quite likely that Nordic voters could and would watch TV from neighbouring Nordic countries. Today it is seldom possible, and even less likely, due to the structuring of the TV markets. This also means that it is less common today that Nordic citizens hear Nordic languages that are different to their own and many turn to English when communicating with other Nordic citizens – especially among the young generations.

The Nordic voter – A similar story with significant deviations

The fourth column in our analytic framework in Table 10.1(d) highlights our conclusion on the question: do the same variables explain political behaviour and, in particular, voting behaviour in the five Nordic countries? As the fourth column shows, we have answered yes and no to this question depending on the particular issue. It is actually in this final column that our comparative design really shows its strengths as the differences (often institutional) between the Nordic countries can help explain and aid the understanding of the different outcome in the five Nordic countries. Two sets of variables can contribute to our understanding here. First of all there is the macro/institutional variable i.e. the difference between the countries on party system and electoral system. Secondly, we have the micro/ individual variables such as the particular voter's age, gender, education etc. In this concluding section we will try to apply both sets of variables.

We find many differences when it comes to the party system between the Nordic countries (*see* above), however the issue space still, to a large extent, reflects the same general left-right ordering of the parties. General left-right self-placement is still the most influential variable when explaining party choice in all countries. Furthermore, with few exceptions, the left-right placement of the parties also tends to go hand in hand with many other issues such as the EU, immigration, environment and moral issues. That is, including these issues in the Nordic party space has increased the complexity of vote choice, but much realignment along the traditional left-right dimension has occurred rather than dealignment. There is no doubt that the green parties and, in particular, the populist parties have challenged the traditional cleavage structure in Nordic society. Especially by introducing a strict view on immigration and a sceptical view on EU integration, along with a generous support for the welfare state, the traditional left-right cleavage has been challenged. But if picturing the parties in this two-dimensional space (traditional left-right/size of public sector and EU/immigration) the realignment occurs along the diagonal and a continuous dimension which thus still prevails in the Nordic countries.

When it comes to voter turnout we see that Denmark stands out with highest turnout (88 per cent) and Finland with the lowest (71 per cent) with the other countries in between. To understand this pattern we must rely on institutional variables. Two institutional elements stand out. First the mobilisation of the least engaged voters through populist parties. In Denmark, the Danish People's Party has been able to mobilise the least educated, least politically interested and politically aware and thus, has actually prevented the general turnout from dropping. Furthermore the elections in Denmark have traditionally been close races, also encouraging parties to make an extra effort to mobilise the electorate. In Finland the populist party, the True Finns, is a rather 'young' and less established party which is still only starting to exploit this electoral base. Furthermore, the traditional oversized coalition government in Finland makes the electoral choice appear as less important for many Finns – our analysis shows that the Danes find it the most important who to vote for and the Finns the least important. Together this suggests that the institutional variable of party system (established populist party) and competition between parties can provide some understanding of the differences between the Nordic countries. The strengths of the institutional variables are also supported by the fact that the individual variables such as age, gender, education, etc., follow the same patterns – a pattern that actually resembles much of the rest of the developed world, regardless of the level of turnout.

The Nordic countries, except Iceland, are exceptional when it comes to trust in politicians and satisfaction with democracy. The decrease in trust in Iceland follows the strong economic set back and especially, the collapse of many Icelandic banks. Similarly in Denmark, we have seen a substantial drop after the financial crisis, which also hit the country hard. Along with clear negative incumbency effects in all countries, our analysis of the Nordic countries provides evidence of an electorate that punishes not only the government, but also politicians in general, with declining trust due to the economic set back. The individual analyses of satisfaction with democracy show similar correlations in all five Nordic countries as we find a positive correlation between satisfaction and party ID, political knowledge and awareness and voting for a winner – relationships which are confirmed by numerable studies across the developed world. The strength of the correlation when it comes to 'voting for a winner' is quite remarkable. Voting for a winner is operationalised as voting for the parties that form or supported the government after the election. This suggests that the question of being satisfied with democracy is not just a general indicator of the well-being of democracy, but to some extent, also a political statement whether or not voters see them as a winner of the election. This, in turn, challenges the common use of this question as a general health indicator of democracy.

Men, the least educated, and the older voters, place themselves at the extremes of the left-right scale, and the more politically aware tend to identify with parties more than other voters in all Nordic countries. We thus have the same pattern at the individual level in the Nordic countries.

Turning to preferential voting, we have already been able to demonstrate that the electoral systems in the Nordic sphere show a maximal degree of variation.

In Finland it is only possible to vote for a person (although votes are pooled at the party level) and in Norway only vote for a party are accepted. Denmark, Sweden and Iceland are in between, with Denmark having the strongest effect of preferential voting and Iceland the weakest, closely followed by Sweden. In Denmark, Sweden and Iceland we see how political awareness is strongly positively related to casting a personal vote, which tells us the larger information costs involved in voting for a person compared to voting for a party. In Finland where preferential voting is mandatory the pattern is the opposite. Here the less resourceful tend to emphasise the importance of candidates over parties, since its parties, due to personalised campaigns, appear as less distinct. On the individual level we find many similarities between Denmark and Sweden as stable voters (voting for the same party across time), voters with a party ID and voters with strong political awareness all tend to cast a vote more often for a specific candidate rather than party. On the other hand, we see that while in Denmark especially, it is the older generation that votes for a person, in Sweden, where the system of preferential voting is relatively new, it is the younger generation who seem to have picked up on the opportunity to vote personally.

The stronger differences between the Nordic countries on the option to cast a preferential vote and the effect of it, makes the individual level analysis hard to compare, thus concluding that Nordics live in a very different electoral system when it comes to preferential voting.

The professionalism in the Nordic election campaigns has increased in all the five countries and the media laws are still quite strict when it comes to particular television commercials. Over time there is a strong correlation between electoral volatility and the number of campaign deciders in Norway and Sweden, but not in the other three countries. The suggested explanation is that the nature of the campaigns are different. In Norway and Sweden fewer voters are actually reached by the campaign, whereas the campaigns in the other three countries reach more voters. This corresponds to the 'minimal effect' thesis from the campaign literature that suggests that campaigns, to a large extent, actually keep voters stable and reinforce initial voting preferences. Campaigns help voters vote as they usually do, thus reinforcing previous party choice. This seems to happen less in Norway and Sweden, partly explaining the strong correlation of increased volatility and number of late deciders. A typical Nordic campaign decider is younger, highly educated, a white-collar worker, who does not identify with a party, places herself in the middle of the left-right political scale, has a low level of knowledge and political awareness and changes party in the election. This pattern is profound in all five Nordic countries.

We have seen the negative incumbency effect in all five Nordic countries from a few percentage points in three Scandinavian countries to more than four percentage points in Iceland. Iceland was also the country hit the hardest by the economic crises, suggesting some relation between negative national economic performance and negative incumbency effect. As the economic voting literature suggests, retrospective egotropic voting has the clearest effect on vote choice, that is, voters perceiving the last years of national economic performance as good are much more likely to vote for a governing party. However, only in Norway and Denmark is this effect significant and substantial. In Sweden and Finland this effect is insignificant. So we conclude that we do not find a clear substantial voting pattern when it comes to economic voting. Our findings suggest that researchers within the area of economic voting need to include individual variables along with national macro economical indicators to comprehend economic voting behaviour in more detail.

As we have concluded, Nordic party space today still reflects the historical cleavage structures suggested by Lipset and Rokkan in the late 60s with some notable exceptions (green and populist parties in particular). This is also reflected in the explanation for why Nordic voters vote as they do. Left-right is still the strongest variable in all the countries when we try to explain party choice. However, the Nordic voter is less habitual when it comes to party choice than previously. As social and demographic ties with parties are weak and have been weakening for decades, for example today, social democrat and left parties in general across the Nordic countries no longer have a monopoly on the votes of the working class. When it comes to specific issues we do see some differences (e.g. moral-elements most important in Norway and Sweden and least in Denmark, Iceland and Finland), but once again, these are often reflected in differences in the party system (e.g. the presence of a significant Christian Democratic party). That is, we can see that the institutional variables (e.g. party system) and individual variables (e.g. age, gender, education) tend to go hand in hand in shaping party choice across the Nordic countries.

Concluding remarks

Nordic voting behaviour is a fascinating research object, not for its lack of exceptionalism compared to most other nations, nor for its lack of similar features, but because it allows a meaningful and genuine comparative research design. The Nordic countries have it all for that. The countries are truly different, but not so different that it does not make sense to compare them and identify factors that explain within country variation. We have tried this in this book on the Nordic voter.

Our main contribution is, to a large extent, descriptive with simple comparisons between the five Nordic countries and on key aspects with other developed nations. This is the first book-length analysis of Nordic voting behaviour which has enabled us to identify similarities and differences between the countries and point to factors that, to some extent, can explain these country differences. Furthermore, the comparison has also induced more perspective into our understanding of each of our own countries – contraction of unique features, which we previously took for granted.

It has proven more difficult than we ever imaged, but also more fruitful given the large variation between our countries. We hope our work will encourage others to go even deeper into these country differences and, in this endeavour, provide an even more nuanced and deeper understanding of the Nordic voter and Nordic democracy.

Appendix

National election studies in the Nordic countries

The national election programs in Sweden and Norway have longstanding traditions. They were established in the middle of the 1950s and are of the oldest in the world after the pioneer country, USA (1948). Denmark has performed regular election studies since the beginning of the 1970s and Iceland in every election since 1983. Finland can be described as the latecomer among the five Nordic countries. The first large scale election study in Finland was performed in 1991 and since then, three studies have been performed.

In Sweden, Professor Jörgen Westerstål started the election program in 1956. Since the introduction of the election program, more than 70,000 Swedes have been interviewed by the election program in conjunction with all national elections 1956–2010, referendums (1957, 1980, 1994, 2003) and European Parliamentary elections (1995, 1999, 2004, 2009). Today, Professor Sören Holmberg and Henrik Oscarsson are co-principal investigators. The SNES program is run by the political science department at the University of Gothenburg in collaboration with Statistics Sweden (SCB). For more information about the Swedish election program *see* http://www.valforskning.pol.gu.se.

The Norwegian election program was established in 1957 by Professor Stein Rokkan and Henry Valen. Professor Valen chaired the program until the year 1985 when Professor Bernt Aardal took over. The program is coordinated by the Institute of Social Research in Oslo and is deposited at the Social Science archive, NSD and open for public use. For more information about the Norwegian election program *see*: http://www.samfunnsforskning.no/valg.

In Denmark the first election study was performed in 1971. Today, the election program is coordinated by Rune Stubager, Department of Political Science, Århus University; Jørgen Goul Andersen, Department of Political Science, Aalborg University; and Kasper M. Hansen, Department of Political Science, University of Copenhagen. For more information about the Danish election program, *see*: http://www.valgprojektet.dk.

The Icelandic election program was established in 1983 by Professor Ólafur Th. Harðarson, who has chaired the program ever since. The Icelandic election studies are in open access *see* http://www.fel.hi.is/en/icelandic_national_election_study_icenes.

In Finland the first large scale election study was performed in 1991 by Professor Pertti Pesonen, Risto Sänkiaho and Sami Borg. However, Professor Pesonen had already, in the 1960s and 1970s, performed less extensive studies. A broader program of collaboration, and the establishment of the Finnish election program, did not take place until 2003 when a consortium of ten Finnish political scientists, headed by Heikki Paloheimo, joined the CSES project. Since then, two more studies have been performed (2007 and 2011). The program is coordinated and data is deposited in the Finnish Social Science Data Archive (FSD) and is run as an open consortium with participating researchers from five different universities. For more information about the Finnish election program *see* http://www.fsd4.uta.fi/en/.

Since 2003 all of the Nordic countries are members of the Comparative Study of Electoral Systems-cooperation (CSES) (www.cses.org) and in 2004 the Nordic Election and Democracy research consortium (NED) was established *see* http://www.nored.dk/default.asp.

Denmark 2007

The Danish National Election survey 2007 (principal investigator Professor Jørgen Goul Andersen) is a post-election survey conducted by a combination of face-to-face (n=735), postal (n=526), CAWI (n=181) and respondents from TNS GALLUP's online panel (n=2,576). A total of 4,018 respondents participated in the survey. The data was collected from November 2007 to June 2008. By the end of March, 72 % of all respondents had completed the questionnaire. The response rate in the TNS Gallup online panel was 43 and the combined response rate in the other parts of the study was 32. All analyses in this book are on the combined data file with 4,018 respondents.

Data was collected by TNS Gallup Denmark and is deposited at the Danish Data Archives (*see also* http://www.valgprojektet.dk).

Finland 2003

A post-election study was conducted after the parliamentary elections were held on the 16 of March 2003. The data was collected in two stages. The first stage involved face-to-face interviews with a total of 1,270 respondents based on multistage stratified sampling. The second part was collected via a self-administrated questionnaire, to be returned by mail, answered by 753 of the respondents interviewed in the first stage. The survey includes an oversample of the Swedish-speaking population, which is controlled for by using appropriate weights.

Face-to-face interviews were conducted from the 17 March to the 30 April 2003. The supplementary, self-administered questionnaires were returned before the 15 May 2003.

Data was collected by TNS Gallup Finland and is deposited at http://www.fsd.uta.fi (FSD1260).

Finland 2007

A post-election study was conducted after the parliamentary elections held on the 18 of March 2007. The data was collected in two stages. The first stage involved face-to-face interviews with a total of 1,422 respondents based on quota sampling (based on age, gender, and province of residence). The second part was collected via a self-administered questionnaire, to be returned by mail, answered by 1,033 of the respondents interviewed in the first stage. The survey includes an oversample of the Swedish-speaking population, which is controlled for by using appropriate weights.

Face-to-face interviews for the Finnish-speaking respondents were conducted from the 20 March to 23 April 2007 and face-to-face interviews for the Swedish-speaking respondents were conducted on 1 April to 20 May 2007. The supplementary, self-administered questionnaires were returned before 22nd May 2007.

Data was collected by Taloustutkimus OY and is deposited at http://www.fsd. uta.fi (FSD2269).

Iceland 2007

The Icelandic post-election survey of 2007 was carried out after the *Althingi* election of May 12 2007, and was the seventh since the series started in 1983. The study was designed by Professor Ólafur Th. Harðarson (the principal investigator), Eva Heiða Önnudóttir and Einar Mar Þórðarson. The Social Science Research Institute at the University of Iceland took care of data management. A national random sample of 2,600 eligible voters (18–80 years old) was drawn from the national register. Telephone interviews were carried out (by Midlun) with 1,595 individuals, or 61.3% of the gross sample. The interviews were conducted from June 2 to August 22. The study was funded by the Icelandic Research Fund (Rannis), and the University of Iceland Research Fund (*see* http://www.fel.hi.is/en/icelandic_national_election_study_icenes).

Norway 2005

The Norwegian post-election study of 2005 was conducted after the parliamentary election of 12 September 2005, and was the twelfth since the series were started in 1957. Central coordinators in 2005 were Professor Bernt Aardal and Professor Henry Valen at the Institute for Social Research (ISR), Oslo. ISR prepared the questionnaires, while Statistics Norway drew the sample, completed the collection of data and organised the data files. The gross sample consisted of 2,965 respondents, and the survey was answered by 2,012 persons. The response rate was thus 68 %. The face-to-face interviews lasted for about one hour and were conducted in the period of 13 September to 20 December. The election study is available at the Norwegian Social Science Data Services (NSD): http://www.nsd. uib.no/nsddata/serier/norske_valgundersokelser.html.

Sweden 2006

Since 1979, the Swedish National Election Studies are designed as two-wave rolling panel studies. SNES 2006 was collected as a pre- and post-election face-to-face interview study with a large, simple random sample of Swedish citizens 18–85 years eligible to vote (n=3,976). The response rate was 78%. Half of the respondents were interviewed before the election day, 19th September and subsequently received a short questionnaire after the election (election campaign-panel). Half of the sample in the SNES 2006 was interviewed in conjunction with the 2002 election (between elections-panel). Voter turnout is census controlled. The SNES 2006 is available at the Swedish National Data Archive (http://www. snd.gu.se).

Variables

Age: 18 +

Gender: 0 = male, 1 = female, Missing = missing

Education: 1 = Compulsory schooling (Lower education, no education, missing), 2 = Lower secondary school (student, all skilled labour), 3 = Higher education (university, teachers, nurses)

Marital status: 0 = single, missing, 1 = married, living together

Employed in public sector: 0 = no (and not in working life), 1 = yes, Missing = not working

Employment: 1 = Outside the labour marked (students, retired, unemployed, housewife/man), missing, 2 = Self-employed, 3 = Lower white-collar worker, 4 = Higher white-collar worker, 5 = Skilled and unskilled worker

Degree of urbanisation: 0 = Country side, missing, 1 = big city

Degree of believing in God (or church attendance): 0 = not believing in god/no church attendance, 1 = believing in god/regular church attendance. Note: Denmark is missing

Trust in politicians: 0 = no trust, 1 = much trust, 0.5= missing. Note: Finland missing

Interest in politics: 0 = no interest, 1= much interest, 0.5 = missing

Party identification: 0 = no, missing, 1 = yes

Left-right self-placement: 0 = most left, 1 = most right, 0.5 = missing

Left-right self-placement extremism: 0 = not extreme (middle, missing) 1 = most extreme (right or left)

Voted for the same party this election and at the last election: 0 = no/did not vote, 1 = yes

Decide during the campaign: 0 = no/did not vote, 1 = yes

Voted for a person (or party or candidate most important for Finland): 0 = no/ party more important, 1 = yes/candidate more important. Note: Norway missing

Did vote in this election: 0 = no, 1 = yes (incl. blanks)

Did vote in the previous election: 0 = no/not eligible to vote), 1 = yes (incl. blanks)

Party choice:

1. Social Democrats (Norway = *Arbeiderpartiet*, Finland = *Suomen Sosialidemokraattinen Puolue* [*Finlands Socialdemokratiska Parti*], Sweden = *SAP*, Iceland = *Samfylkingin* and Denmark = *Socialdemokraterne*)

2. Conservatives (Denmark = *Konservative*, Norge = *Höyre*, Finland = *Kansallinen Kokoomus* [Samlingspartiet], Sweden = *Moderaterna*, Iceland = *Sjálfstæðisflokkur*)

3. Liberals (Finland = *Svenska folkpartiet i Finland* [Suomen ruotsalainen kansanpuolue], Iceland = *Frjálslyndi flokkurinn*, Sweden = *Folkpartiet*, Norway = *Venstre*, Denmark = *Radikale Venstre* and *Ny Alliance*)

4. Left-Socialist (Denmark = *SF*, Sweden = *Vänsterpartiet*, Iceland = *Vinstrihreyfingin – grænt framboð*, Finland = *Vasemmistoliitto* [*Vänsterförbundet*], Norway = *Sosialistisk Venstreparti*)

5. Popular Right (Norway = *Fremskridtpartiet*, Denmark = *Dansk Folkeparti*, Sweden = *Sverigedemokraterna*, Finland = *Perussuomalaiset* [*Sannfinländarna*], Iceland not used)

6. Agrarian (Finland = *Suomen Keskusta* [*Centern i Finland*], Sweden = *Centerpartiet*, Norway = *Senterpartiet*, Iceland = *Framsóknarflokkurinn*, Denmark = *Venstre*)

7. Christian Democrats (Norway = *Kristlig Folkeparti*, Finland = *Suomen Kristillisdemokraatit* [*Kristdemokraterna i Finland*], Denmark = *Kristendemokraterne*, Sweden = *Kristdemokraterna*, Iceland = not used)

8. Greens (Finland = *Vihreä liitto* [*Gröna förbundet*] Sweden = *Miljöpartiet*, Iceland = *Íslandshreyfingin*, Denmark = not used, Norway = not used)

9. Far Left (*Enhedslisten, Rödt*)

10. Other votes (blanks, other parties, candidates outside parties)

11. Did not vote

Economic voting:

Egotropic retrospective perceptions: 0 = much worse, 1 = much better, 0.5 = missing
Egotropic prospective perceptions: 0 = much worse, 1 = much better, 0.5 = missing
Sociotropic retrospective perceptions: 0 = much worse, 1 = much better, 0.5 = missing
Sociotropic prospective perceptions: 0 = much worse, 1 = much better, 0.5 = missing
Vote for the incumbent Government?: 0 = no, 1 = yes, non-voters/blanks = missing
Vote for the incumbent party with PM?: 0=no, 1=yes, non-voters/blanks = missing
Vote for the incumbent party with Minister of Finance?: 0= no, 1 = yes, non-voters/blanks = missing
Vote for the incumbent party with Minister of Foreign Affairs?: 0 = no, 1 = yes, non-voters/blanks = missing

Power matters: 0 = it does not make a difference who is in power, 1 = it makes a difference who is in power, missing = 0.5

Vote matters: 0 = voting won't make a difference, 1 = voting can make a difference, missing = 0.5

Satisfied with democracy: 0 = not at all satisfied, 1= very satisfied, missing = 0.5

Indexes

Political awareness:

Includes: Political interest, talk to others about politics and media use. Each of these three variables contribute the same to the index (0-1)

Political knowledge:

0 points: all wrong, don't know, missing, 1: all correct
Knowledge item included in all five countries:
Correct ordering of the parties on the left-right scale (correct=the mean order of all respondents)

Denmark:

1. Which parties are members of the present Government?
2. How many members does the Danish Parliament have, not incl. the four from Greenland and the Faroe Islands?
3. How many countries are today members of EU?
4. Which of the following government expenditures are the highest?
   a) Expenditure for public schools
   b) Expenditure for pension
   c) Expenditure for defense
5. Which party does Mette Frederiksen belong to?
6. Which party does Troels Lund Poulsen belong to?
7. Which party does Kristian Thulesen Dahl belong to?

Finland 2003:

1. Which political party does Paavo Lipponen represent?
2. Which of the following countries is a permanent member of the United Nations (UN) Security Council?
3. Wages earned by employees are taxable income in Finland. We would like to ask you about state taxation. Let us presume that Virtanen earns 2,000 euros a month and Herranen 5,000. Which one of the following statements is closest to the truth?
4. Do you know which party has the most seats in the parliament? (Centre Party)

Finland 2007:

1. Who of the following was the Finnish Foreign Minister in 2006?
2. Which of the following parties has the second largest number of seats in the newly elected Parliament?
3. Which of the following countries is a permanent member in the United Nation (UN) Security Council?
4. Who is entitled to vote in Finnish parliamentary elections?
5. What do you think is meant by a parliamentary system?

Iceland:

1. Do you know which party Jónína Bjartmarz belongs to?
2. Can you tell me who is the deputy leader of the Independence Party?
3. And can you tell me how many constituencies there are in Iceland?

Norway:

1. Do you happen to know how many members there are in Parliament now after the election?
2. Do you remember who has been Minister of Modernisation in the last year before the elections?
3. There have been six nationwide referendums conducted in this country. Do you remember when the last of these was, and what it applied to?

Sweden 2006:

1. Open unemployment in Sweden is today less than 5%
2. Spain is a member of EU
3. The sickness benefit is today 90 % of the wage/salary from the first day of sick leave
4. Swedish foreign aid to developing countries is today 1% of the gross national income (GNI)
5. The tax on real estate property (houses) is today 2%
6. The Swedish Riksdag has 349 members
7. During the period 1998–2002/2002–2006, Sweden had a Social Democratic one party government
8. Do you know which party Bosse Ringholms belongs to?
9. Do you know which party Inger Davidsson belongs to?
10. Do you know which party Karin Pilsäter belongs to?
11. Do you know which party Gunilla Carlsson belongs to?
12. Do you know which party Fredrik Federley belongs to?
13. Do you know which party Yvonne Ruwaida belongs to?
14. Do you know which party Alice Åström belongs to?
15. Do you know which party Carin Jämtin belongs to?
16. Do you know which party Jan Eliasson belongs to?

Issue dimensions

Index: 0 (most negative) – 1 (most positive)

Attitudes towards the EU

Denmark:

1. What is your general attitude towards the EU?
2. Will you vote for or against the new EU treaty if there is a Danish referendum on it?

Finland:

1. How important are the following issues to you: Promoting European Union integration
2. EU membership is a good thing for Finland

Iceland:

1. Do you think that it is desirable or undesirable, that Iceland applies for membership in the European Union?

Norway:
1. Where would you place yourself on a scale of 0 to 10 where 0 means that Norway should absolutely not be a member of the EU, while 10 means Norway should absolutely join the European Union?

Sweden:
1. Are you in favour of or against Swedish membership in the EU or have you no definite opinion on the matter?
2. Do you think it is positive or negative for the EU to develop into a federation, a kind of United States of Europe?
3. What is your opinion on the proposal that Sweden should leave the EU?
4. What is your opinion on the proposal that Sweden should introduce the euro as its currency?

Attitudes toward the environment

Denmark:
1. Focus on an environment-friendly society, even if it involves low or no growth
2. Do you think the government is spending too much money, appropriate, or too little money on: Environmental problems
3. Efforts to improve the environment must not go so far as to damage business
4. We sometimes talk about a green dimension where some parties make tremendous emphasis on environmental concerns, while others say that environmental concerns will gradually start to take over. On the following scale 1 is the least green policy, while 5 is the most green. Where would you place yourself on such a scale?

Finland:
1. How important are the following issues to you: Fighting climate change
2. How important are the following issues to you: Other environmental protection issues

Iceland:
1. Do you agree or disagree that in the next year, action on environmental issues should be prioritised over attempts to increase economic growth – or do you think this makes no difference?
2. Do you think that the government should put strong emphasis, some emphasis or little emphasis on the development of power intensive industry?
3. I would be willing to give part of my income if I would be sure that the money would be used to prevent environmental pollution
4. I would agree to tax increases if the money would be used to prevent environmental pollution

5. If we want to take measures against unemployment in this country we will have to accept (compromise on) environmental problems

6. Environmental protection and fighting against pollution is not as urgent as often believed

7. Do you consider yourself to be very much interested in environmental issues, much interested, somewhat interested, little interested or are you not interested in environmental issues at all?

Norway:

1. Where would you place yourself on this scale? Value 0 expresses that environmental protection should not be carried so far that it goes beyond our standard of living, while the value 10 expresses the desire that we should focus more on the environment, even if it means a significantly lower standard of living for everyone, including yourself

2. We should allow oil and gas exploration in the Barents Sea

3. To secure economic growth, we need continued industrial development, although this would conflict with nature conservation interests

4. We should be building gas power plants even if CO_2 removal is not possible with current technology

5. There is far too little emphasis on environmental protection in today's Norway

Sweden:

1. What do you think of the proposal that Sweden should in the long term phase out nuclear power?

2. There are different views on nuclear power as an energy source. What is your attitude? Are you mainly for or against nuclear power, or do you have no definite opinion on the matter?

3. What do you think of the proposal to invest in an environmentally friendly society even if it means low or no economic growth?

4. What is your opinion on the proposal to stop private cars in inner cities?

Attitudes toward the immigration

Denmark:

1. Accept fewer refugees in Denmark

2. Should initial help for immigrants be preserved as now, should it be raised, so it gives the immigrant more help with cash, or should it be completely abolished, in order to give immigrants a normal financial situation?

3. The Fogh government has implemented a series of austerity measures to the refugee policy/immigration policy. Do you think that these restrictions have been appropriate, they have gone too far, or they have not been radical enough?

4. Immigration poses a serious threat to our national character

5. The Muslim countries, in the longer term, pose a dangerous threat to Denmark's security

6. Refugees and immigrants should have the same right to social assistance as Danes, even if they are not Danish citizens

7. If there are too few jobs, employers should prefer Danes rather than immigrants

8. Do you think the government is spending too much money, appropriate, or too little money on: Refugees and immigrants

9. The parties disagree on how many refugees we can accept. Some believe we accept too many. Others say we can easily take on more refugees. Here is a scale regarding attitudes towards refugee policy. Where do you place yourself on such a scale?

Finland:

1. How important are the following issues to you: Improving the circumstances of ethnic minorities

Iceland:

1. Do you agree or disagree that immigrants are a serious threat to our national characteristics?

Norway:

1. Some believe that Norway's aid to poor countries, the so-called developing countries, should be cut down, while others believe that it should be maintained as now or possibly increased. What is your opinion?

2. Where would you place yourself on this scale? A value of 0 on the scale expresses the standpoint that we should make it easier for immigrants to gain access to Norway, while the value 10 expresses the opinion that the number of immigrants to Norway should be restricted even more strongly than today

3. In bad times, we should first of all make sure there is work for Norwegians

4. If immigrants without Norwegian citizenship commit a crime, they shall be deported

Sweden:

1. What is your opinion on the proposal to accept fewer refugees?

2. What is your opinion on the proposal to increase financial support for immigrants so that they can preserve their own culture?

3. What is your opinion on the proposal to increase labour immigration to Sweden?

4. What is your opinion on the proposal to introduce a language test in order to become a Swedish citizen?

5. What do you think of the proposal to invest in a diverse society with great tolerance towards people from other countries with other religions and ways of life?

Attitudes toward the size of the public sector

Denmark:

1. Reduce the public sector
2. The parties disagree on how big the public sector should be. Some parties say we must cut down on government revenue and expenditure. Others say that we must expect increasing government expenditure and revenue in the future. Here is a scale regarding attitudes towards public expenditure. Where do you place yourself on such a scale?

Finland:

1. How important are the following issues to you: Improving the circumstances of the poor
2. How important are the following issues to you: Increasing health care resources
3. How important are the following issues to you: Diminishing unemployment
4. How important are the following issues to you: Improving the circumstances of the elderly

Iceland:

1. Do you agree or disagree that the government should use its power to increase the equality of income distribution in society? Or do you think this makes no difference?
2. Do you agree or disagree that taxes should be reduced, even though it means that public services will have to be reduced, e.g. in health care, education, or social security – or do you think this makes no difference?
3. Do you agree or disagree to increased privatisation of the health care system?

Norway:

1. Many government activities could be done better and cheaper, if they were left to the private sector
2. We should allow private commercial schools
3. It is more important to develop public services than to reduce taxes
4. Full employment could easily be secured if the state took more leverage over banks and corporate operations
5. High income should be taxed harder than it is today

Sweden:
1. What is your opinion on the proposal to reduce the public sector?
2. What is your opinion on the proposal to sell state enterprises and utilities to private interests?
3. What is your opinion on the proposal to let the private sector take over the practice of health care?
4. What is your opinion on the proposal to increase the number of private schools?

Attitudes toward moral issues (gay marriages, doctor-assisted suicides, abortions etc.)

Denmark:
1. We should aim for a society where Christian values play a larger role
2. The same opportunity to adopt children should be given to homosexuals as for heterosexuals

Finland:
1. How important are the following issues to you: Improving the circumstances of sexual minorities

Iceland:
1. Do you agree or disagree that homosexuals should have the same right as others to adopt children?

Norway:
1. Where would you place yourself on a scale of 0 to 10 where 0 means that Christian teaching should be compulsory in primary schools, while 10 means that Christian teaching should be voluntary in elementary school?
2. Homosexuals should be given the same opportunity to adopt children as heterosexuals
3. The church should be seperated from the state
4. We should aim for a society where Christian values play a larger role

Sweden:
1. What do you think of the proposal to invest in a society in which lesbian, gay, bisexual and transgender people's rights are strengthened?
2. What is your opinion on the proposal to prohibit all forms of pornography?
3. What is your opinion on the proposal to restrict the right to abortion?
4. What is your opinion on the proposal to allow gay couples to adopt children?
5. What is your opinion on the proposal to increase the penalty for buying sex?

Information on parties in the Nordic countries

Table A.1: Coding of party families (abbreviations used in Chapter Three)

	Denmark	Finland	Iceland	Norway	Sweden
Left Socialist parties (LeftSoc)	Socialist Peoples Party – *Socialistisk Folkeparti* (F)	Left-Wing Alliance – *Vasemmistoliitto* (f) *Vänsterförbundet* (s)	Left Greens – *Vinstrihreyfingin – grænt framboð*	Socialist Left Party SV – *Sosialistisk Venstreparti*	Left Party – *Vänsterpartiet*
Social Democratic parties (SocDem)	Social Democrats – *Socialdemokraterne* (A)	Finnish Social Democratic Party *Suomen Sosialidemokraattinen Puolue* (f), *Finlands Socialdemokratiska Parti* (s)	Social Democratic Alliance *Samfylkingin – jafnaðarmannaflokkur Íslands*	Labour Party DNA – *Det norske arbeiderparti*	Social democrats – *Socialdemokratiska Arbetarepartiet* (SAP)
Conservative parties (Con)	The Conservatives *De Konservative* (C)	National Coalition *Kansallinen Kokoomus* (f), *Samlingspartiet* (s)	Independence Party – *Sjálfstæðisflokkurinn*	Conservative Party H – *Høyre*	Conservative Party – *Moderaterna*
Liberal parties (Lib)	The New Alliance – *Ny Alliance* (Y) and the Social Liberals – *Det Radikale Venstre* (B) is joined to this category	Swedish People's Party *Suomen ruotsalainen kansanpuolue* (f) *Svenska folkpartiet i Finland* (s)	Liberal Party *Frjálslyndi flokkurinn*	Liberal Party V – *Venstre*	Liberal People's Party – *Folkpartiet liberalerna*

(Cont'd)

Table A.1: (Cont'd)

	Denmark	Finland	Iceland	Norway	Sweden
Populist parties (Pop)	Danish Peoples Party *Dansk Folkeparti* (O)	True Finns *Perussuomalaiset* (f), *Samnfinländarna* (s)		The Progress Party – FRP – *Fremskrittspartiet*	Sweden Democrats – *Sverigedemokraterna*
Agrarian parties (Ag)	Liberal Party – Venstre (V)	Finnish Centre, *Suomen Keskusta* (f), *Centern i Finland* (s)	Progressive Party *Framsóknarflokkurinn*	Centre Party *SP – Senterpartiet*	Centre Party – *Centerpartiet*
Christian Democratic parties (ChrDem)	Christian Democrats – *Kristendemokraterne* (K)	Christian League, *Suomen Kristillisdemokraatit* (f), *Kristdemokraterna i Finland* (s)		Christian Democrats – (Christian Peoples' Party) KRF – *Kristelig Folkeparti*	Christian Democrats – *Kristdemokraterna*
Green parties (G)		Green League, *Vihreä liitto* (f), *Gröna förbundet* (s)	Iceland Movement *Íslandshreyfingin*	The Greens MG – *Miljøpartiet de Grønne*	The Greens – *Miljöpartiet de gröna*
Far-Left parties (Far Left)	Red-green Alliance / *Enhedslisten* (Ø)			Red Party R – *Rødt*	

Brief description of each party included in the study:

DENMARK

Socialist People's Party, *SF – Socialistisk Folkeparti* (F)

A left-wing party founded in 1959 by the former communist Aksel Larsen focusing on introducing socialism through democratic means. Initially the party focused on the economy, disarmament, later feminism, environment and human rights. Historically the party had a sceptical stand on European integration through the EU, but since 2005 where Villy Søvndal became party leader we have seen a gradual change toward a more positive stand.

Party leaders: Aksel Larsen (1959–1968), Sigurd Ømann (1968–1974), Gert Petersen (1974–1991), Holger K. Nielsen (1991–2005), Villy Søvndal (2005–2012) and Annette Vilhelmsen (2012–): Latest election results: 2005: 6.0% (11/179), 2007: 13.0% (23/179), 2011: 9.2% (16/179).

Social Democrats, *Socialdemokraterne* (A)

Founded in 1871 as a branch of the first Socialist International by Pio, Brix and Geleff and by 1878, the Social Democratic Party was constituted separately from the trade unions, but was still very dominated by the unions. In 1913 it became the biggest party in parliament. This party has been a major player in securing workers rights and establishing the Danish welfare state. With a few exceptions, the Social Democrats held power throughout the years 1945–1982.

Recent party leaders: Mogens Lykketoft (2002–2005), Helle Thorning-Schmidt (2005–): Latest election results: 2005: 25.8% (47/179), 2007: 25.5% (45/179), 2011: 24.8% (44/179) (worst result ever in the party's history).

Red-green Alliance, *Enhedslisten* (Ø)

Founded in 1989 as a unity of three left-wing parties: the Left Socialist Party (VS), the Communist Party of Denmark (DKP) and the Socialist Workers Party (SAP), as well as some independent socialists. In the beginning it was an electoral collaboration but evolved into a membership organisation. The Red-green Alliance is the most extreme left-wing party and focuses on anti-privatisation, anti-capitalism and emphasises climate and environmental policies. Since 1994 the party has been represented in the Danish Parliament.

Historically, the party has had a flat structure with no official leader. However, since 2009, Johanne Schmidt-Nielsen has functioned as the political spokesman. Election results: 1994: 3.1% (6/179), 1998: 2.7% (5/179), 2001: 2.4% (4/179), 2005: 3.4% (6/179), 2007: 2.2% (4/179), 2011: 6.7% (12/179).

Social Liberal Party, *Det Radikale Venstre* (B)

The Danish Social Liberal Party was founded in 1905 as a result of a prolonged disagreement in *Venstre*; thirteen MPs from *Venstre* founded a new parliamentary party. One of the most prominent of the expelled MPs was C. Th. Zahle. He took the role as leader of the newly established party, *Det Radikale Venstre*. Historically the party is referred to as a centre party with a focus on reduced military spending.

Since 1929, the Danish Social Liberal Party has, with a few exceptions, functioned as a coalition partner with different governmental partners.

Recent party leaders: Niels Helveg Petersen (1978–1990), Marianne Jelved (1990–2007), Magrethe Vestager (2007–). Latest election results: 2001: 5.2% (9/179), 2005: 9.2% (17/179), 2007: 5.1% (9/179), 2011: 9.5% (17/179).

New Alliance, *Ny Alliance* (Y)

Founded in 2007 by two politicians from *Det Radikale Venstre:* MP Naser Khader and MEP Anders Samuelsen along with Gitte Seeberg from *De Konservative*. It was established as a liberal party that wanted a government with *Venstre* and *De Konservative,* which was independent of the Danish People's Party. In 2007 they entered the Parliament. But due to internal turbulence Gitte Seeberg (in 2008) and Naser Khader (in 2009) left the party. Hence the party changed its name to Liberal Alliance and emphasised a focus on economic liberalism with the new leader Anders Samuelsen.

Party leaders: Naser Khader (2007–2009), Anders Samuelsen (2009–). Election results: 2007: 2.8% (5/179), 2011: 'Liberal Alliance' 5.0% (9/179).

Conservative People's Party, *Det Konservative Folkeparti* (C)

Det Konservative Folkeparti was founded in 1915. Primarily its predecessor was the then main political faction in the Parliament, *Højre*. Historically, the party represented the landed aristocracy against the peasants. Ideologically, the party follows a conservative focus on the centre-right. The party has functioned in different coalition governments. From 1982–1993 the conservative leader Poul Schlüter served as the Prime Minister.

Party leaders: Per Stig Møller (1997–98), Pia Christmas Møller (1998–1999), Bendt Bendtsen (1999–2008), Lene Espersen (2008–2011), Lars Barfoed (2011–). Latest election results: 2001: 9.1% (16/179), 2005: 10.3% (18/179), 2007: 10.4% (18/179), 2011: 4.9% (8/179).

Left, *Venstre* (V)

Traditionally, the party served as the opposition to the aristocracy, representing the farmers' interests. The United Left (later renamed *Venstre*) was founded in 1870 by already existing liberal groups in parliament. *Venstre* is a centre-right party where the focus is on economic liberalism and pro-free market ideology. In 1905 *Venstre* took office but J. C. Christensen refused to cut military expenditure, which ended in the expulsion of 13 MPs who then founded *Det Radikale Venstre*.

Since 1918, the leader of *Venstre* has a couple of times served in the role of Prime Minister. The longest continuous period of service is from 2001–2011.

Recent party leaders: Uffe Ellemann-Jensen (1984–1998), Anders Fogh Rasmussen (1998–2009), Lars Løkke Rasmussen (2009–). Latest election results: 2001: 31.2% (56/179), 2005: 29% (52/179), 2007: 26.2% (46/179), 2011: 26.7% (47/179).

Danish People's Party, *Dansk Folkeparti* (O)

In 1995 prominent members of the Progress Party, including Pia Kjærsgaard and Kristian Thuelsen Dahl, broke out and founded *Dansk Folkeparti*. Pia Kjærsgaard was elected as the leader of the newly established party. The party is often referred to as following an ideology of right-wing populism, demanding a more critical approach to the EU and immigration. From 2001 to the 2011 election the Danish People's Party functioned as parliamentary cooperation liberal-conservative coalition government.

Recent party leaders: Pia Kjærsgaard (1995–2012) Kristian Thulesen Dahl (2012–). Latest election results: 1998: 7.4% (13/179), 2001: 12% (22/179), 2005: 13.3% (24/179), 2007: 13.9% (25/179), 2011: 12.3% (22/179).

Christian Democrats, *Kristendemokraterne* (K)

Unlike other Danish parties, the Christian Democrats, did not form as an outbreak from other parties. In 1970 ecclesiastical Danes, who believed that the youth revolt, the liberalisation of pornography and abortion legislation showed diminishing Christian values in the Parliament, founded the party. Historically, the party has been a centre party with a religious conservative focus. It has served as part of coalition governments from 1982–1988 and 1993–1994. It did not, however, receive any seats at the election in 2007 or 2011.

Recent party leaders: Jann Sjursen (1990–2002), Marianne Karlsmose (2002–2005), Bodil Kornbæk (2005–2008), Bjarne Hartung (2008–2011), Per Ørum Jørgensen (2011–). Latest election results: 2001: 2.3% (4/179), 2005: 1.7% (0/179), 2007: 0.9% (0/179), 2011: 0.8% (0/179).

FINLAND

Left-Wing Alliance, *Vasemmistoliitto* (f) *Vänsterförbundet* (s)

A left-wing socialist party founded in 1990 based on two former parties: Finnish People's Democratic League and Finland's Communist Party. Was a member of Prime Minister Paavo Lipponen's (SDP) oversized rainbow coalitions during the years 1995–1999 and 1999–2003.

Recent party leaders: Suvi-Anne Siimes (1999–2006), Martti Korhonen (2006–2009), Paavo Arhimäki (2009–). Election results: in 2003: 9.9% (19/200), 2007: 8.8% (17/200), 2011: 8.1% (14/200).

Finnish Social Democratic Party, *Suomen Sosialidemokraattinen Puolue* (f), *Finlands Socialdemokratiska Parti* (s)

A traditional Social Democratic Party founded in 1899 and one of the three main parties in Finnish politics. Often part of the government (since 1995): 1995–1999 (Prime Minister), 1999–2003 (Prime Minister), 2003–2007, 2011–.

Recent party leaders: Paavo Lipponen (1993–2005), Eero Heinäluoma (2005–2008), Jutta Urpilainen (2009–). Latest election results: 2003: 24.5% (53/200), 2007: 21.4% (45/200), 2011: 19.1% (42/200).

National Coalition, *Kansallinen Kokoomus* (f), *Samlingspartiet* (s)

A conservative party founded in 1918 and one of the three main parties in Finnish politics. For the first time in history it succeeded in becoming the largest party in the 2011 general election. Has participated in the government (since 1995): 1995–1999, 1999–2003, 2007–2011, 2011– (Prime Minister).

Recent party leaders: Sauli Niinistö (1994–2001), Ville Itälä (2001–2004), Jyrki Katainen (2004–). Latest election results: 2003: 18.6% (40/200), 2007: 22.3% (50/200), 2011: 20.4% (44/200).

Swedish People's Party, *Suomen ruotsalainen kansanpuolue* (f), *Svenska folkpartiet i Finland* (s)

A liberal party founded in 1906. The party's primary interest is to defend the interests of the Swedish speaking minority (5.5%) mainly living in the west and southern parts of Finland. Around 70 % of the Swedish speaking population votes for the party. The party has been included in every government since 1975.

Recent party leaders: Jan-Erik Enestam (1998–2006), Stefan Wallin (2006–2012), Carl Haglund (2012–). Latest election results: 2003: 4.6% (8/200), 2007: 4.6% (9/200), 2011: 4.3% (9/200).

True Finns, *Perussuomalaiset* (f), *Sannfinländarna* (s)

A populist and nationalist party founded in 1995 when its predecessor Suomen Maalaisliitto, went bankrupt. The party's program combines EU-criticism, conservative values and a left-wing economic policy and its popularity rests on the rhetoric skills of the party leader Timo Soini.

Party leader: Timo Soini (1995–). Latest election results: 2003: 1.6% (3/200), 2007: 4.1% (5/200), 2011: 19.1% (39/200).

Finnish Center, *Suomen Keskusta* (f), *Centern i Finland* (s)

An Agrarian party founded in 1906 and one of the three main parties in Finnish politics. It is the dominant party in the rural areas of Finland and it held the position of prime minister during the years 2003–2011.

Recent party leaders: Anneli Jäätteenmäki (2002–2003), Matti Vanhanen (2003–2010), Mari Kiviniemi (2010–2011), Juha Sipilä (2011–). Latest election results: 2003: 24.7% (55/200), 2007: 23.1% (51/200), 2011: 15.8% (35/200).

Christian League, *Suomen Kristillisdemokraatit* (f), *Kristdemokraterna i Finland* (s)

A Christian democratic party founded in 1958 that emphasises conservative and Christian values as well as social policy. The party succeeded in getting represented in the *Eduskunta* for the first time in the 1970 general election.

Recent party leaders: Bjarne Kallis (1995–2004), Päivi Räsänen (2004–). Latest election results: 2003: 5.3% (7/200), 2007: 4.9% (7/200) 2011: 4.0% (6/200).

Green League, *Vihreä liitto* (f), *Gröna förbundet* (s)

An environmentalist party founded in 1987, with two of its founding members in the green movement already elected to the Finnish parliament in 1983. The party is difficult to position on the left-right scale and can be described as a relatively urban party. It has been included in several governments since the first time in 1995 (1995–1999, 1999–2002, 2007–2011).

Recent party leaders: Osmo Soinivaara (2001–2005), Tarja Cronberg (2005–2009), Anni Sinnemäki (2009–2011), Ville Niinistö (2011–). Latest election results: 2003: 8.0% (14/200), 2007: 8.5% (15/200), 2011: 7.3% (10/200).

ICELAND

Left Greens, *Vinstrihreyfingin – grænt framboð*

A left-socialist party with strong environmental emphasis, founded in 1999, when the former left-socialist party The People's Alliance joined the Social Democrats in a new Social Democratic Alliance. Won a major victory in the 2009 elections, and consequently joined the first socialist majority government in Icelandic history, led by the Social Democrats.

Party leader: Steingrímur J. Sigfússon (1999–). Latest election results: 2003: 8.8% (5/63), 2007: 14.3% (9/63), 2009: 21.7% (14/63).

Social Democratic Alliance, *Samfylkingin – jafnaðarmannaflokkur Íslands*

A social democratic party, founded in 1999 as an electoral alliance of the old Social Democratic Party, the left-socialist People's Alliance, and the Women's Alliance. Became a formal party in 2000. The old Social Democratic Party (founded 1916) had usually been the smallest of the four major Icelandic parties since 1942, smaller than the left-socialists (Communist Party 1930–38, Socialist Party 1938–56, People's Alliance 1956–99). The old Social Democratic Party had frequently been a member of government coalitions, and the Socialist Party and the People's Alliance also participated in government at times. The Social Democratic Alliance has been in government since 2007, first with the Conservatives (until 2009), and then with the Left Greens.

Recent party leaders: Margrét Frímannsdóttir (1999–2000), Össur Skarphéðinsson (2000–2005), Ingibjörg Sólrún Gísladóttir (2005–2009), Jóhanna Sigurðardóttir (2009–). Latest election results: 2003: 31% (20/63), 2007: 26.8% (18/63), 2009: 29.8% (20/63).

Icelandic Movement, *Íslandshreyfingin*

An environmental (green) party, founded before the 2007 election. The party did not obtain any parliamentary representation, and subsequently passed away.

Party Leader: Ómar Ragnarsson. Election result: 2007: 3.3% (0/63).

Liberal Party, *Frjálslyndi flokkurinn*

Founded in 1998, slightly right of centre, with some populist (e.g. anti-immigration) tendencies. Major issue is opposition to the Icelandic quota system of fisheries. Had MPs elected in 1999, 2003, and 2007.

Recent party leaders: Sverrir Hermannsson (1998–2003), Guðjón Arnar Kristjánsson (2003–2010), Sigurjón Þórðarson (2010–). Latest election results: 2003: 7.4% (4/63), 2007: 7.3% (4/63), 2009: 2.2% (0/63).

Progressive Party, *Framsóknarflokkurinn*

Founded as a farmers' party in 1916 and is still much stronger in the regions than in the Reykjavík area. For decades, the PP was the second largest party in Iceland, usually polling around 25% of the votes, and frequently taking part in coalition governments, both with the conservatives and the left parties. The party's electoral strength has declined in the last 30 years.

Recent party leaders: Halldór Ásgrímsson (1994–2006), Jón Sigurðsson (2006–2007), Guðni Ágústsson (2007–2008), Valgerður Sverrisdóttir (2008–2009), Sigmundur Davíð Gunnlaugsson (2009–). Recent election results: 2003: 17.7% (12/63), 2007: 11.7% (7/63), 2009: 14.8% (9/63).

Independence Party, *Sjálfstæðisflokkurinn*

A conservative party, founded in 1929. Electorally largest in all elections until 2009, often polling around 40%. The party has from the beginning enjoyed a considerable share of the working-class vote (often around one-third). The 'natural party of government' in Iceland. Since 1946, the party has been out of government only in 1956–59, 1971–74, 1978–83, 1988–1991, and since 2009, when the party suffered an electoral disaster in the aftermath of the Icelandic bank crash of 2008.

Recent party leaders: Davíð Oddsson (1991–2005), Geir H. Haarde (2005–2009), Bjarni Benediktsson (2009–). Recent election results: 2003: 33.7% (22/63), 2007: 36.6% (25/63), 2009: 23.7% (16/63).

NORWAY

Centre Party, *Senterpartiet*

The party was founded in 1920 as the Agrarian League. Later it changed its name to Farmers' Party and the Centre Party name was not adopted until 1959. It could be described as an agrarian-interest party, and the organisation was very closed, attached to different farmer's organisations. In the postwar period, the party has joined government coalitions with nonsocialist parties in 1963, 1965 to 1971, 1972–1973 and between 1983–2000. In 2005 the party changed its allegiance and instead joined the Red-Green Coalition. The party has also through the years adopted and maintained a principled opposition against a Norwegian membership in the European Union. The party has seen a decline in vote share since it reached a record – when it received a total of 16.7% of the vote share in the 1993 election.

Recent party leaders: Anna Enger Lahnstein (1991–1999), Odd Roger Enoksen (1999–2003), Åslaug Haga (2003–2008), Lars Peder Brekk (2008), Liv Signe Navarsete (2008–). Recent election results: 2001: 5.6% (10/165), 2005: 6.5% (11/169), 2009 6.2% (11/169).

Christian People's Party, *Kristelig Folkeparti*

The party was founded in 1933. The first main leader of the party was dropped down from the liberal party list for the *Storting* election. The party attracts support mainly from religious activists both within and outside the state church. The Christian People's Party joined a government coalition with the other nonsocialist parties in 1963, 1965 to 1971, 1972–1973, and 1986–1989. During 1972–1973, the party also provided the government with their leader (Lars Korvald as Prime Minister). After the election in 1989, the party ruled in a coalition together with the conservative and centre parties and with the centre and liberal parties in 1997–2005. Their leader from 1983–1995, Kjell Magne Bondevik, known as one of the most prominent political figures in Norway, served as Prime Minister from 1997–2005.

Recent party leaders: Kjell Magne Bondevik (1983–1995), Valgerd Svarstad Haugland (1995–2004), Dagfinn Høybråten (2004–2011), Knut Arild Hareide (2011–). Recent election results: 2001: 12.4% (22/165), 2005: 6.8% (11/169), 2009: 5.5% (10/169).

Conservative Party, *Høyre*

The party came into life in 1884, mainly in order to oppose demand from the liberal's that the royal veto should be abolished, changing the political system in Norway in order to adopt the rules of parliamentarism. For most of the twentieth century, the Conservative Party was known for being the most critical voice towards socialism in the Norwegian parliament. In the postwar era it joined a government coalition with the other nonsocialist parties in 1963 and 1965 to 1973. In 1980, the party formed a one party minority government. Later during the 1980s, the party took place in two different three-party governments. The last time the Conservative Party joined the government was between 2001–2005, in Bondevik's Second Cabinet. The party reached a record in the 1981 election when it received 31.7% of the vote share. The vote share has since then declined and stabilised on a level of 14.1–22.2%.

Recent party leaders: Kaci Kullmann Five (1991–1994), Jan Petersen (1994–2004), Erna Solberg (2004–). Recent election results: 2001: 21.2% (38/165), 2005: 14.1% (23/169), 2009: 17.2% (30/169).

Labour Party, *Det Norske Arbeiderparti*

The Norwegian Labour Party was founded in 1887 and was from the beginning strongly associated with trade unions. From 1945 to 1961 the party enjoyed an absolute majority in the *Storting*. Later on, in 1971 the party formed a minority government. High on the agenda was negotiating a Norwegian entry into the EEC. The party resigned as a result of the parliamentary rejection of that policy. The Labour Party joined the socialist government coalition during the 1980s and then kept its dominance during that decade. All in all since the 1970s, the Labour Party had the leadership of the national government in the following years: 1971–1972, 1973–1981, 1986–1989, 1990–1997, 2000–2001 and 2005 to this present day. The Labour Party leader with the most years as a Prime Minister is Gro Harlem Brundtland with a total of 11 years (1981, 1986–1989, 1990–1996).

Recent Party Leaders: Gro Harlem Brundtland (1981–1992), Thorbjørn Jagland (1992–2002), Jens Stoltensberg (2002–). Recent election results: 2001: 24.3% (43/165), 2005: 32.7% (61/169), 2009: 35.4% (64/169).

Liberal Party, *Venstre*

The Liberal Party was founded in 1880. It joined the other Norwegian nonsocialist parties in the 1963 and 1965–1971 government coalitions. Due to the EEC question, the party was divided into two political factions. The Liberal Party fell out of the *Storting* in 1985 but returned in the 1993 election. In 1997, the party formed a coalition government together with the Centre Party and the Christian People's Party. The party ended up under the threshold for levelling seats in the elections 2001 and 2009, which gave the party only two seats in the parliament.

Recent Party Leaders: Odd Einar Dørum (1992–1996), Lars Sponheim (1996–2010), Trine Skei Grande (2010–). Recent election results: 2001: 3.9% (2/165), 2005: 5.9% (10/169), 2009: 3.9% (2/169).

Progress Party, *Fremskrittspartiet*

The Progress Party was founded as late as 1973, but under the name 'Anders Lange's Party for Substantial Reduction in Taxes, Duties, and Governmental Interference'. The party received 5% of the vote share in the 1973 election. That gave the party the amount of 4 seats in the parliament. The party leader, Anders

Lange, died only one year after the election, which led the party into a series of internal strife, resulting in a loss of their four seats in the 1977 election, only to return in the 1981 election. The biggest problem for the Progress Party is their difficulty with negotiation with the other parties in the *Storting*. Still, the party has received enormous gains in the elections since 1993. The party is today the second biggest in Norway.

Recent party leaders: Carl I. Hagen (1978–2006), Siv Jensen (2006–). Recent election results: 2001: 14.6% (26/165), 2005: 22.1% (38/169), 2009: 22.9% (41/169).

Socialist Left Party, *Sosialistisk Venstreparti*

In 1963 the Socialist People's Party was founded by a group of anti-NATO activists. The party had success in its policy of preventing Norway from entering the EEC and it was strengthened by its cooperation with other anti-NATO groups such as the Communist Party and factions from the Labour Party. These different groups formed the Socialist Electoral League – an organisation that took 11.2% of the vote in the 1973 election. In 1975 the Socialist Electoral League converted into the Socialist Left Party. The Socialist Left Party has received between 12.5 and 4.2% of the votes during the time after 1973. The party became a member of the Red-green Coalition in 2009.

Recent party leaders: Erik Solheim (1987–1997), Kristin Halvorsen (1997–2012), Audun Lysbakken (2012–). Recent election results: 2001: 12.5% (23/165), 2005: 8.8% (15/169), 2009: 6.2% (11/169).

Red Party, *Rød*

Founded in 2007 due to the merger of the Red Electoral Alliance and Workers' Communist Party. The party could be described as a left-wing political party that tries to get rid of the communist label.

Recent party leaders: Torstein Dahle (2007–2010), Turid Thomassen (2010–2012), Bjørnar Moxnes (2012–). Recent election results: 2009: 1.3% (0/169).

Green Party, *Miljøpartiet de Grønne*

A small party, formed in 1988 by the merger of a number of environmental election lists. The Green Party has never managed to enter the parliament. Still, it is represented in a couple of big cities such as Oslo, Bergen, Trondheim and Stavanger, among others.

Recent Party Leader: N/A. Recent election results: 2001: 0.2% (0/165), 2005: 0.1% (0/169), 2009: 0.3% (0/169).

SWEDEN

The Left Party, *Sveriges Kommunistiska Parti* (–1992)/*Vänsterpartiet*

The descendant of the Left Socialist Party of 1917. From 1921 to 1967, it had the name Swedish Communist Party, having joined the Third International in 1919. The Communists experienced repeated schisms and averaged only some 3% of the vote in the 1930s and 4.5% in the Post-World War II period. In 1998 The Left Party reached a record when it received 12 % of the vote in the parliamentary election. This was in much a result of Social Democratic austerity programs and continuing worries about the EU. On the whole, the party could be defined in terms of being a radical democratic and feminist party with a strong environmentalist plank.

Recent party leaders: Lars Werner (1975–1993), Gudrun Schyman (1993–2003), Ulla Hoffman (2003–2004), Lars Ohly (2004–2012), Jonas Sjöstedt (2012–). Recent election results: 2002: 8.3% (30/349), 2006: 5.8% (22/349), 2010: 5.6% (19/349).

The Social Democratic Party, *Socialdemokraterna*

The Social Democratic Party came into being in 1889 with Hjalmar Branting as party leader. In the early twentieth century, the Social Democratic Party collaborated with the liberals. After 1914 the party was polling over a third of the vote, and from 1932 to 1993 its vote share did not fall below 40 %. From 1940–1968, the party gained the majority of the votes cast. After 1968, it experienced fluctuating fortunes, losing office to non socialist coalitions between 1976 and 1982 and again in 1991, and winning the elections of 1985, 1988, 1994 and 1998. In the 2006 election they were defeated by the centre-right Alliance for Sweden coalition.

Recent party leaders: Ingvar Carlsson (1986–1996), Göran Persson (1996–2007), Mona Sahlin (2007–2011), Håkan Juholt (2011–2012), Stefan Löfven (2012–). Recent election results: 2002: 39.9% (144/349), 2006: 34.9% (130/349), 2010: 30.7% (112/349).

The Centre Party, *Centerpartiet*

A modern successor to the Agrarian Party. The party began life in 1913, chiefly to represent small farmers. To protect agricultural interests, they came to an understanding with the Social Democrats during the Depression (1933). Later they took part in two 'Red-Green coalitions' with the Social Democratic Party (1936–1939 and 1951–1957), both times as the junior partner, but both times with control of the Ministry of Agriculture. In the Post-World War II period the Centre Party has provided a Prime Minister (Thorbjörn Fälldin), three non socialist coalitions (Fälldin I: 1976–1978, Fälldin II: 1979–1981, Fälldin III: 1981–1982). The party participated in the Conservative-led coalition government of 1991–94 and the Alliance for Sweden coalition government (2006–).

Recent party leaders: Olof Johansson (1987–1998), Lennart Daléus (1998–2001), Maud Olofsson (2001–2011), Annie Lööf (2011–). Recent election results: 2002: 6.1% (22/349), 2006: 7.8% (29/349), 2010: 6.5% (23/349).

The Liberal People's Party, *Folkpartiet*

A party that began life as a parliamentary caucus in 1985. It created a national party organisation in 1902. From 1948 to 1956 the party revived to become the strongest on the non socialist side with almost a quarter of the total vote. Since 1956 it has ranged from a low of 4.7% in 1998 to a high of 14.2% in 1985. The party took its place in all three of Fälldin's governments (*see* the above description of the Centre Party). From 1978 to 1979 The Liberal People's Party formed a minority government with their then leader, Ola Ullsten, as Prime Minister. As a result of that, they were the only party continuously in office between 1976–1982. The party also participated in the Conservative-led coalition government of 1991–1994 and the Alliance for Sweden coalition government (2006–).

Recent party leaders: Bengt Westerberg (1983–1995), Maria Leissner (1995–1997), Lars Leijonborg (1997–2007), Jan Björklund (2007–). Recent election results: 2002: 6.1% (22/349), 2006: 7.8% (29/349), 2010: 6.5% (23/349).

The Conservative Party, *Högerpartiet (–1969)/Moderaterna*

A party that in the beginning of this century represented the powerful in Swedish society: higher civil servants, industrialists, and large landowners. The Conservative Party began as a parliamentary caucus and created a nationwide organisation in 1904. During the Post-World War II period, the Conservative Party has had a chequered career – ranging from 11.5% of the vote in 1970 to a high of 30 % in 2010. The party served in the Centre-led coalition government of 1976–1978 and 1979–1981. From 1991 to 1994 The Conservative Party formed a four-party minority government with their then leader, Carl Bildt, as Prime Minister. The Conservative Party participate as the biggest party in the four-party Alliance for Sweden coalition government (2006–) and their leader, Fredrik Reinfeldt, serves as Prime Minister.

Recent party leaders: Carl Bildt (1986–1999), Bo Lundgren (1999–2003) (Fredrik Reinfeldt 2003–). Recent election results: 2002: 15.2% (55/349), 2006: 26.2% (97/349), 2010: 30 % (107/349).

The Christian Democratic Party, *Kristen Demokratisk Samling* (–1987)/ *Kristdemokratiska Samhällspartiet* (1987–1995)/*Kristdemokraterna*

The party was founded in 1964 but did not poll high enough until 1991 when it was elected with 7.1% of the votes. The party suffered severely from internal divisions over whether Sweden should join the European Union. The Christian Democratic Party held three portfolios in both the 1991 Bildt government and the Alliance for Sweden coalition government (2006–). It received its highest results in 1998 by obtaining 11.8% of the vote.

Recent party leaders: Alf Svensson (1973–2004), Göran Hägglund (2004–). Recent election results: 2002: 9.9% (33/349), 2006: 6.6 (24/349), 2010: 5.6% (19/349).

The Green Environmental Party, *Miljöpartiet de gröna*

Founded in 1981, the party briefly entered the Swedish *Riksdag* in 1988 with 5.5% of the vote and a total of 20 seats. The Green Party was the first new party in 70 years to achieve representation in the parliament. The success was a direct result of concerns over acid rain, seal death, the Chernobyl disaster, and other environmental threats. After failing to clear the 4% barrier in 1991, it returned to parliament in 1994 with 5% of the vote. The party is characteristic of a party leader system consisting of two *språkrör* that share the mandate of leadership in a maximum of eight years.

Recent party leaders: Matz Hammarström and Lotta Nilsson Hedström (2000–2002), Peter Eriksson and Maria Wetterstrand (2002–2011), Gustav Fridolin and Åsa Romson (2011–). Recent election results: 2002: 4.6% (17/349), 2006: 5.2% (19/349), 2010: 7.3% (25/349).

The Sweden Democrats, *Sverigedemokraterna*

The party was founded in 1988 and is best described as a nationalist/xenophobic or populist far-right party. The Sweden Democrats stood outside the parliament until 2010 when they received a total vote share of 5.7%. Until then they had an overall vote in an election below the parliament threshold with a high of 2.9% in 2006.

Recent party leaders: Anders Klarström (1992–1995), Mikael Jansson (1995–2005), Jimmie Åkesson (2005–). Recent election results: 2002: 1.4% (0/349), 2006: 2.9% (0/349), 2010: 5.7% (20/349).

References

Aardal, B. (2003) *Velgere i villrede... En studie av stortingsvalget 2001*, Oslo: N.W. Damm and Søn.
— (ed.) (2007) *Norske velgere: En studie av stortingsvalget 2005*, Oslo: Damm.
— (ed.) (2011) *Det politiske landskap: En studie av stortingsvalget 2009*, Oslo: Damm.
Aardal, B., Krogstad, A. and Narud, H. M. (2004) *I valgkampens hete – Strategisk kommunikasjon og politisk usikkerhet*, Oslo: Universitetsforlaget.
Aardal, B. and Listhaug, O. (1986) *Economic Factors and Voting Behavior in Norway 1965–1985*, Working Paper No. 4, Oslo: Institute for Social Research.
Aardal, B. and Oscarsson, H. (2000) *The Myth of Increasing Personalization of Politics: Party leader effects on party choice in Sweden and Norway 1979–1998*, 2000 Annual Meeting of the American Political Science Association, Washington DC.
Aardal, B. and Valen, H. (1995) *Konflikt og opinion*, Oslo: NKS-forlaget.
Aars, K. and Wessels, B. (2005) 'Electoral Turnout', in J. Thomassen (ed.) *The European Voter: A comparatives study of modern democracies*, Oxford: Oxford University Press.
Alford, R. R. (1963) *Party and Society: The Anglo-American democracies*, Westport, Conn: Greenwood.
Allardt, E. (ed.) (1981) *Nordic Democracy*, Copenhagen: Det Danske Selskab.
Almond, G. A. and Verba, S. (1963) *The Civic Culture: Political attitudes in five nations*, Boston: Little, Brown.
Amnå, E. (2006) 'Playing with fire? Swedish mobilization for participatory democracy', *Journal of European Public Policy*, 13(4): 587–606.
Amnå, E., Ekman, T. and Almgren, E. (2007) 'The end of a distinct model of democracy? Country-diverse orientations among young adult Scandinavians', *Scandinavian Political Studies*, 30(1): 61–86.
Anckar, D. (1992) 'Finland: Dualism and consensual rule', in E. Damgaard (ed.) *Parliamentary change in the Nordic countries*, Oslo: Scandinavian University Press.
Andersen, J. (2007) 'Vælgerne, politikerne og den demkratiske kultur', in J. Andersen, O. Borre, J. Goul Andersen, K. M. Hansen and H. J. Nielsen (eds) *Det nye politiske landskab: Folketingsvalget 2005 i perspektiv*, Århus: Academica.
Andersen, J. and Borre, O. (2003) 'Personfaktorer' in J. Goul Andersen and J. Andersen (eds) *Politisk Forandring: værdipolitik og nye skillelinjer ved Folketingsvalget 2001*, Århus: Systime Academic.
Andersen, J., Borre, O., Goul Andersen, J. and Nielsen, H. J. (1999) *Vælgere med Omtanke – en analyse af folketingsvalget 1998*, Aarhus: Systime.

Anderson, C. J. (1995) 'Party Systems and the Dynamics of Government Support'. *European Journal of Political Research*, 27: 93–118.

— (2000) 'Economic Voting and Political Context: A Comparative Perspective'. *Electoral Studies*, 19: 151–70.

— (2011) *Electoral Supply, Median Voters, and Feelings of Representation in Democracies*, in R. J. Dalton and C. J. Anderson (eds) *Citizens, Context, and Choice: How context shapes citizens' electoral choices*, Oxford: Oxford University Press.

Anderson, C. J. and Guillory, C. (1997) 'Political institutions and satisfaction with democracy: a cross-national analysis of consensus and majoritarian systems', *American Political Science Review* 91 (March): 66–81.

André, A., Wauters, B. and Pilet, J.-B. (2012) 'It's not only about lists: explaining preference voting in Belgium', *Journal of Elections, Public Opinion and Parties*, 22(3): 293–313.

Arter, D. (1984) *The Nordic Parliaments: A comparative analysis*, Princeton: Princeton University Press.

— (1999) *Scandinavian Politics Today*, Manchester: Manchester University Press.

— (2008) *Scandinavian Politics Today*, 2nd ed. rev, Manchester: Manchester University Press.

— (2009) 'From a contingent party system to party system convergence? Mapping party system change in postwar Finland', *Scandinavian Political Studies*, 32(2): 221–39.

Austen-Smith, D. and Banks, J. S. (1988) 'Elections, coalitions and legislative outcomes', *American Political Science Review*, 82: 405–22.

Aylott, N. (2011) 'Parties and Party Systems in the North', in T. Bergman and K. Strøm (eds) *The Madisonian Turn: Political parties and parliamentary democracy in Nordic Europe*, Ann Arbor: University of Michigan Press

Bartels, L. M. (2010) 'The Study of Electoral Behavior', in J. E. Leighley (ed.) *The Oxford Handbook of American Elections and Political Behavior*, Oxford: Oxford University Press.

Bartle, J. and Crewe, I. (2002) 'The Impact of Party Leaders in Britain: Strong Assumptions, Weak Evidence', in A. King (ed.) *Leaders' Personalities and the Outcomes of Democratic Elections*, Oxford: Oxford University Press.

Bean, C. and Mughan, A. (1989) 'Leadership effects in parliamentary elections in Australia and Britain', *American Political Studies*, 83: 1165–79.

Bengtsson, Å. (2004) 'Economic voting: the effect of political context, volatility, and turnout on voters' assignment of responsibility', *European Journal of Political Research*, 43: 749–67.

— (2007) *Politiskt deltagande*, Lund: Studentlitteratur.

— (2012) 'Väljarnas val av kandidat: rörlighet och motiv', in S. Borg (ed.) *Muutosvaalit 2011*, Helsinki: Oikeusministeriö.

Bengtsson, Å. and Christensen, H. S. (2012) 'Medborgarnas förväntningar på politiskt beslutsfattande', in S. Borg (ed.) *Muutosvaalit 2012*, Helsinki: Oikeusministeriö.

Bengtsson, Å. and Grönlund, K. (2005) 'Ehdokasvalinta', in H. Paloheimo (ed.) *Vaalit ja demokratia Suomessa*, Helsinki: WSOY.

Bengtsson, Å. and Mattila, M. (2009) 'Direct democracy and its critics: support for direct democracy and 'stealth' democracy in Finland', *West European Politics*, 32(5): 1031–48.

Berelson, B. R., Lazarsfeld, P. F. and McPhee, W. N. (1954) *Voting: A study of opinion formation in a presidential campaign*, Chicago: University of Chicago Press.

Berglund, F. (2004) *Partiidentifikasjon og politisk endring*, Oslo: Unipax.

Berglund, S. and Lindström, U. (1978) *The Scandinavian Party Systems: A comparative study*, Lund: Studentlitteratur.

Bergman, T and Strøm, K (2011) *The Madisonian Turn: Political parties and parliamentary democracy in Nordic Europe*, Ann Arbor: University of Michigan Press.

Bergman, T. (2000) 'Sweden: When minority cabinets are the rule and majority coalitions the exceptions', in W. C. Müller and K. Strøm, K. (eds) *Coalition Governments in Western Europe*, Oxford: Oxford University Press, pp.192–230.

Bhatti, Y. and Hansen, K. M. (2012a) 'Leaving the nest and the social act of voting: revisiting the relationship between age and turnout among first-time voters', *Journal of Elections, Public Opinion and Parties*, 22(4): 380–406.

— (2012b) 'Retiring from voting: turnout among senior voters', *Journal of Elections, Public Opinion and Parties*, 22(4), 479–500.

Bhatti, Y., Hansen, K. M. and Wass, H. (2012) 'The relationship between age and turnout: a roller-coaster ride', *Electoral Studies*, 31(3): 588–93.

Bille, L. (2008) 'Denmark', *European Journal of Political Research*, 47: 952–61.

Bille, L., Elklit, J. and Jakobsen, M. V. (1992) 'Denmark: The 1990 Campaign', in S. Bowler and D. Farell (eds) *Electoral Strategies and Political Marketing*, London: Macmillan, pp. 63–81.

Bizer, G. Y., Tormala, Z. L., Rucker, D. D. and Petty, R. E. (2006) 'Memory-based versus on-line processing: Implications for attitude strength', *Journal of Experimental Social Psychology*, 42(5): 646–53.

Blais, A. (2000) *To Vote or Not to Vote: The merits and limits of rational choice theory*, Pittsburgh: University of Pittsburgh Press.

Blais, A., Gidengil, E., Nadeau, R. and Nevitte, N. (2001) 'Measuring party idenfication: Britain, Canada and the United States', *Political Behavior*, 23(1): 5–22.

Bobbio, N. (1987) *The Future of Democracy: A defence of the rules of the game*, Oxford: Polity Press.

— (1996) *Left and Right: The significance of a political distinction*, Cambridge: Polity Press.

Booth, J. and Seligson, M. (2009) *The Legitimacy Puzzle in Latin America: Political support and democracy in eight nations,* New York: Cambridge University Press.

Borg, S. (2009) 'Nuorten poliittinen osallistuminen', in S. Borg and H. Paloheimo (eds) *Vaalit yleisödemokratiassa. Eduskuntavaalitutkimus 2007,* Tampere: Tampere University Press.

— (2012) (eds) *Muutosvaalit 2011,* Helsinki: Oikeusministeriön julkaisuja, OMSO 16/2012.

Borg, S. and Moring, T. (2005) 'Vaalikampanja', in H. Paloheimo (ed.) *Vaalit ja demokratiassa Suomessa,* Helsinki: WSOY.

Borg, S. and Paloheimo, H. (2009) 'Johdanto', in S. Borg and H. Paloheimo (eds) *Vaalit yleisödemokratiassa: Eduskuntavaalitutkimus 2007,* Tampere: Tampere University Press.

Borre, O. (1995) 'Old and new politics in Denmark', *Scandinavian Political Studies,* 18(3): 187–205.

— (1997) 'Economic voting in Danish electoral surveys 1987–94', *Scandinavian Political Studies* 20: 347–65.

— (1980) 'Electoral instability in four Nordic countries, 1950–1977', *Comparative Political Studies,* 13(2): 141–71.

— (2003a) 'To konfliktdimensioner', in J. G. Andersen and O. Borre (eds) *Politisk forandring:* Værdipolitik og nye skillelinjer ved folketingsvalget 2001, Århus: Systime, pp. 171–86.

— (2003b) 'Træk af den danske vælgeradfærd 1971–2001', in A. W. Hansen, H. Krag, S. Larsen, P. Lykke and J. C. Manniche (eds) *Topforskning ved Aarhus Universitet – en jubilæumsantologi,* Århus: Århus Universitetsforlag, pp. 169–92.

Borre, O. and Goul Andersen, J. (1997) *Voting and Political Attitudes in Denmark,* Aarhus: Aarhus University Press.

Bowler, S. and Farrell, D. (1993) 'Legislator shirking and voter monitoring: impacts of European Parliament electoral systems upon legislator–voter relationships', *Journal of Common Market Studies,* 31: 45–69.

Brettschneider, F. and Gabriel, O. W. (2002) 'The Nonpersonalization of Voting Behavior in Germany', in A. King (ed.) *Leaders' Personalitites and the Outcomes of Democratic Elections,* Oxford: Oxford University Press.

Brody, R. A. (1978) 'The Puzzle of Political Participation in America', in A. King (ed.) *The New American Political System,* Washington DC: American Enterprise Institute.

Butler, D. and Stokes, D. E. (1969, 1974) *Political Change in Britain: The evolution of electoral choice,* London: Macmillan.

Cain, B. E., Dalton, R. and Scarrow, S. E. (2003) *Democracy Transformed? Expanding political opportunities in advanced industrialised democracies,* Oxford: Oxford University Press.

Campbell, A. (1966) 'Surge and decline', in A. Campbell, P. E. Converse, D. E. Stokes and W. E. Miller (eds) *Elections and the Political Order,* New York: Wiley.

Campbell, A., Converse, P. E., Miller, W. E. and Stokes, D. E. (1960) *The American Voter,* New York: Wiley.

Campbell, A. and Valen, H. (1961) 'Party identification in Norway and the United States', *Public Opinion Quarterly*, 25: 245–68.

Castles, F. G. and Sainsbury, D. (1986) 'Scandinavia: The politics of stability', in R. C. Macridis (ed.) *Modern Political Systems: Europe*, Engelwood Cliffs: Prentice Hall, pp. 251–94.

Colomer, J. (2008) *Economic Crisis Favors Incumbent Governments,* http://jcolomer.blogspot.com/2008_10_13_archive.html.

Craig, S. C., Kane, J. G. and Gainous, J. (2005) 'Issue-related learning in a gubernatorial campaign: A panel study', *Political Communication*, 22(4): 483–503.

CSES Module 3: The Comparative Study of Electoral Systems (www.cses.org)

CSES Module 3: Second advance release [dataset]. March 31, v.

Curtice, J. and Holmberg, S. (2005) 'Party leaders and party choice', in J. Thomassen (ed.) *The European Voter*, Oxford: Oxford University Press.

Curtice, J. and Phillips Shively, W. (2009) 'Who Represents Us Best? One Member or Many?' in H.-D. Klingemann (ed.) *The Comparative Study of Electoral Systems*, Oxford: Oxford University Press.

Dahl, R. (1966) *Political Opposition in Western Democracies,* New Haven: Yale University Press.

Dahlberg, S. (2009a) *Voters' Perceptions of Party Politics: A Multilevel Approach,* University of Gothenburg.

— (2009b) 'Political parties and perceptual agreement: the influence of party related factors on voters' perceptions in proportional electoral systems', *Electoral Studies* 1(7): 270–278.

— (2010) 'Premiär för TV-reklam', in H. Oscarsson and S. Holmberg (eds) *Väljarbeteende i Europaval,* Gothenburg: The Department of Political Science, Gothenburg University, pp. 191–201.

Dahlberg, S. and Holmberg, S. (2011) *Understanding Satisfaction with the Way Democracy Works: Democracy versus bureaucracy,* Gothenburg: University of Gothenburg.

Dahlberg, S. and Oscarsson, H. (2006) *En europeisk partirymd?* in H. Oscarsson and S. Holmberg (eds) *Europaval,* Göteborgs: Göteborgs universitet: Statsvetenskapliga institutionen.

Dalton, R. J. (1984) 'Cognitive mobilization and partisan dealignment in advanced industrial democracies', *The Journal of Politics*, 46(1): 264–284.

— (1999) 'Political Support in Advanced Industrial Democracies', in P. Norris (ed.) *Critical Citizens: Global Support for Democratic Governance,* Oxford: Oxford University Press.

— (2004) *Democratic Challenges, Democratic Choices: The erosion of political support,* Oxford: Oxford University Press.

— (2007) *The Good Citizen: How a younger generation is reshaping American politics,* Washington: CQ, Press.

—   (2008) 'The quantity and the quality of party systems: party system po-
         larisation, its measurement, and its consequences', *Comparative Politi-
         cal Studies*, 41(7): 899–920.

—   (2013) *The Apartisan American: Dealignment and changing electoral
         politics*, Thousand Oaks: CQ Press.

Dalton, R. J, McAllister, I. and Wattenberg, M. P. (2000) 'The Consequences of
         Partisan Dealignment' in R. J. Dalton and M. P. Wattenberg (eds) *Parties
         Without Partisans: Political change in advanced industrial democracies*,
         Oxford: Oxford Political Studies.

Dalton, R. J. and Wattenberg, M. P. (1984) 'Cognitive mobilization and partisan
         dealignment in advanced industrial democracies', *Journal of Politics* 46:
         264–84.

—   (2000a) *Democratic Challenges, Democratic Choices: The erosion of
         political support*. Oxford: Oxford University Press.

—   (2000b) (eds) *Parties without Partisans: Political change in advanced
         industrial democracies*, Oxford: Oxford Political Studies.

Dalton, R. J. and Weldon, S. (2007) 'Partisanship and party system institutional-
         ization', *Party Politics*, 13(2): 179–96.

Damgaard, E. (1974) 'Stability and change in the Danish party system over half a
         century', *Scandinavian Political Studies*, 9(A9): 103–25.

—   (1992) *Parliamentary Change in the Nordic Countries*, Oslo: Scandina-
         vian University Press.

—   (2000) 'Denmark: The life and death of government coalitions', in W. C.
         Müller and K. Strøm (eds) *Coalition Governments in Western Europe*,
         Oxford: Oxford University Press.

Danielsson, J. and Gylfi, Z. (2009) *The Collapse of a Country*: Available online at:
         http://www.riskresearch.org/files/e.pdf.

Delhey, J. and Newton, K. (2005) 'Predicting cross-national levels of social trust:
         global pattern or Nordic exceptionalism', *European Sociological Review*
         21(4): 311–27.

Demokratiutredningen (2000) *En uthållig demokrati!: politik för folkstyrelse på
         2000 – talet: Demokratiutredningens betänkande*, SOU 2000: 1. Stock-
         holm: Fritzes offentliga publikationer.

Denters, B., Gabriel, O. and Torcal, M. (2007) 'Norms of Good Citizenship', in J.
         van Deth, J. R. Montero and A. Westholm (eds) *Citizenship and Involve-
         ment among the Populations of European Democracies: A comparative
         analysis*, London: Routledge.

Dorussen, H. and Palmer, H. D. (2002a) 'The Context of Economic Voting: An
         introduction', in H. Dorussen and M. Taylor (eds) *Economic Voting*, New
         York: Routledge, pp. 1–14.

Dorussen, H. and Taylor, M. (eds) (2002b) *Economic Voting*, London: Routledge.

Downs, A. (1957) *An Economic Theory of Democracy*, New York: Harper and Row.

Downs, W. M. and Riutta, S. (2005) 'Out with "rainbow government" and in with
         "Iraqgate": the Finnish general election of 2003', *Government and Op-
         position*, 40(3): 424–41.

Dutch, R. and Stevenson, R. T. (2008) *The Economic Vote: How political and economic institutions condition election results,* New York: Cambridge University Press.

Easton, D. (1965) *A Systems Analysis of Politcal Life,* New York: Wiley.

Ekengren, A. M. and Oscarsson, H. (2009) 'Parties' Perception of Voter Rationality', Unpublished Paper, NOPSA 2008.

Elder, N., Thomas Alastair, H. and Arter, D. (eds) (1988) *The Consensual Democracies? The government and politics of the Scandinavian states,* Oxford: Basil Blackwell.

Elklit, J. (1986) 'Det klassiske danske partisystem bliver til', in J. Elklit and O. Tonsgaard (eds) *Valg og Vælgeradfærd,* Århus: Politica.

— (1993) 'Simpler than its reputation: the electoral system in Denmark since 1920', *Electoral Studies,* 12(1): 41–57.

— (2008a) 'Denmark: Simplicity Embedded in Complexity (or is it the Other Way Around?)' in M. Gallagher and P. Mitchells (eds) *The Politics of Electoral Systems,* Oxford: Oxford University Press.

— (2008b) 'Valgkredsreformen 2006 og folketingsvalget 2007: En første evaluering', in K. Kosiara-Pedersen and P. Kurrild-Klitgaard (eds) *Partier og Partisystemer i Forandring,* Odense: Syddansk Universitetsforlag.

— (2011) 'Preferential Voting in Denmark: How, Why, and to What Effect?' Paper presented at the ECPR General Conference, Reykjavik, Iceland, August 24–27, 2011(Panel: Electoral Systems and the Personal Vote)and at APSA Annual Meeting, Seattle, Wash., USA, September 1–4, 2011 (Division 34, Panel: The Determinants of Candidate Choice in Preferential Voting Systems).

Elklit, J., Møller, B., Svensson, P. and Togeby, L. (2005) *Gensyn med sofavælgerne: valgdeltagelse i Danmark,* Århus: Aarhus Universitetsforlag.

Epstein, L. D. (1967) *Political Parties in Western Democracies,* New York: Praeger.

Esaiasson, P. (2000a) 'How Members of Parliament Define Their Task', in P. Esaiasson and K. Heidar (ed.) *Beyond Westminster and Congress: The Nordic experience,* Cleveland: Ohio State University Press.

Esaiasson, P. and Heidar, K. (ed.) (2000b) *Beyond Westminster and Congress: The Nordic experience,* Kent: Ohio State University Press.

Esping-Andersen, G. (1990) *The Three Worlds of Welfare Capitalism,* Cambridge: Polity Press.

— (1991) *The Three Worlds of Welfare Capitalism,* Princeton: Princeton University Press.

Farrell, D. M. (2001) *Electoral Systems: A comparative introduction,* London: Palgrave.

— (2006) 'Political Parties in a Changing Campaign Environment', in R. Katz and W. Crotty (eds) *A Handbook of Party Politics,* London: Sage, pp.122–33.

Farrell, D. M. and McAllister, I. (2006) 'Voter satisfaction and electoral systems: does preferential voting in candidate-centred systems make a difference?' *European Journal of Political Research,* 45(5): 725–49.

Fiorina, M. P. (1981) *Retrospective Voting in American National Elections*, New Haven: Yale University Press.

Foss, P. (1990) 'Norway lost its 1989 parliamentary election', *Political Quarterly*, 61(1): 225–28.

Fournier, P., Nadeau, R., Blais, A., Gidengil, E. and Nevitte, N. (2001) 'Validation of time-of -voting-decision recall', *Public Opinion Quarterly*, 65(1):95–107.

— (2004) 'Time-of-voting decision and susceptibility to campaign effects', *Electoral Studies*, 23(4): 661–81.

Franklin, M. N. (2004) *Voter Turnout and the Dynamics of Electoral Competition in Established Democracies Since 1945*, New York: Cambridge University Press.

Franklin M. N and van der Eijk, C. (1996) *Choosing Europe? The European Electorate and National Politics in the Face of Union*, Ann Arbor: University of Michigan Press.

Freedman, P., Franz, M., Mair, P. and Goldstein, K. (2004) 'Campaign advertising and democratic citizenship', *American Journal of Political Science*, 48(4): 723–41.

Fuchs, D., Guidorossi, G. and Svensson, P. (1995) 'Support for the Democratic System', in H.-D. Klingemann and D. Fuchs (eds) *Citizens and the State*, Oxford: Oxford University Press.

Fuchs, D. and Klingemann, H.-D. (1995) 'Citizens and the State: A changing relationship', in H.-D. Klingemann and D. Fuchs (eds) *Citizens and the State*, Oxford: Oxford University Press.

Gallagher, M., Laver, M. and Mair, P. (2001) *Representative Government in Modern Europe*, New York: McGraw-Hill.

— (2006) *Representative Government in Modern Europe: Institutions, parties and governments*, New York: McGraw Hill.

Gallego, A. (2010) 'Understanding unequal turnout: education and voting in comparative perspective', *Electoral Studies*, 29(2): 239–24.

Gerring, J. (2007) *Case Study Research, Principles and practices*, New York: Cambridge.

Gibson, R. K. and Rommele, A. (2009) 'Measuring the professionalization of political campaigning', *Party Politics*, 15(3): 265–93.

Gilljam, M. and Holmberg, S. (eds) (1990) *Rött, blått, grönt. En bok om 1988 års riksdagsval,* Stockholm: Bonniers.

Gilljam, M. and Oscarsson, H. (1996) 'Mapping the Nordic party space', *Scandinavian Political Studies* 19(1): 25–43.

Goul Andersen, J. (2010) *"It's the Economy, Stupid!" -Eller "Crisis? What Crisis?",* Institutt for statskundskap, Universitetet i Aarhus.

— (2013) 'Den økonomiske udvikling op til 2011 – valget' in R. Stubager, K. M. Hansen and J. Goul Andersen (eds) *Krisevalg-Økonomien og folketingsvalget 2011,* København: DJØF-Forlag, pp. 45–60.

Goul Andersen, J., Andersen, J., Borre, O., Hansen, K. M. and H. J. Nielsen (eds) (2007) *Det nye politiske landskab. Folketingsvalget 2005 i perspektiv,* Aarhus: Academica.

Goul Andersen, J. and Borre, O. (eds) (2003) *Politisk forandring-værdipolitik og nye skillelinjer ved folketingsvalget 2001,* Aarhus: Systime.

Goul Andersen, J. and Hansen, K. M. (2013) 'Vælgernes krisebevidsthed' in R. Stubager, K. M. Hansen and J. Goul Andersen (eds) *Krisevalg – Økonomien og folketingsvalget 2011,* København: DJØF-Forlag, pp. 137–162.

Goul Andersen, J. and Hoff, J. (2001) *Democracy and Citizenship in Scandinavia,* New York: Palgrave.

Granberg, D. and Holmberg, S. (1988) *The Political System Matters: Social psychology and voting behavior in Sweden and the United States,* Cambridge: Cambridge University Press.

Graubard, S. R (ed.) (1986) *Norden: The passion for equality,* Oslo: Norwegian University Press.

Grendstad, G. (2003) 'Reconsidering Nordic party space', *Scandinavian Political Studies,* 26(3): 193–217.

Greve, B. (2007) 'What characterises the Nordic welfare state model', *Journal of Social Sciences,* 3(2): 43–51.

Grofman, B. and Lijphart, A. (eds) (2002) *The Evolution of Electoral and Party Systems in the Nordic Countries,* New York: Agathon Press.

Grönlund, K. (2009) 'Poliittinen tietämys', in S. Borg and H. Paloheimo (eds) *Vaalit yleisödemokratiassa. Eduskuntavaalitutkimus 2007,* Tampere: Tampere University Press.

Grönlund, K. and Westinen, J. (2012) 'Puoluevalinta' in S. Borg (ed.) *Muutosvaalit 2011,* Helsinki: Ministry of Justice, pp. 156–190.

Habermas, J. (1975) *Legitimation Crisis,* Boston: Beacon Press.

Hansen, K. M. (2008) *Hvordan påvirker valgkampen vælgerne,* in K. Kosiara-Pedersen and P. Kurrild-Klitgaard (eds) Odense: Syddansk Universitetsforlag): 149–62.

— (2009a) *Statsministerposten koster ca. to mandater årligt.* Aktuel graf nr. 4. Center for Valg og Partier. Aktuel Graf Serien. www.cvap.polsci.ku.dk.

— (2009b) 'Changing patterns of information effects on party choice in a multiparty system', *International Journal of Public Opinion Research,* 21(4): 525–46.

Hansen, K. M. and Bech, M. (2007) 'De sociotropiske vælgere: Ønsket om stigende beskæftigelse betyder mere end hvem der bliver statsminister og vælgerne kan ikke købes med lønstigninger', *Politica,* 39(1): 67–86.

Hansen, K. M. and Goul Andersen, J. (2013) 'En samlet model for partivalg' in Stubager, R., K. M. Hansen and J. Goul Andersen (eds) *Krisevalg – Økonomien og folketingsvalget 2011,* København: DJØF-Forlag, pp. 189–212.

Hansen, K. M. and Hoff, J. (2013) 'Gør den kommunale kampagne en forskel?', in U. Kjær and J. Elklit (eds) *KV09 – Analyser af Kommunalvalget 2009,* Odense: Syddansk Universitet.

Hansen, K. M. and Pedersen, R. T. (2008) 'Negative campaigning in a multiparty system', *Scandinavian Political Studies* 31(4): 408–27.

Hansen, K. M. and Stubager, R. (2013) 'Økonomisk stemmeadfærd in R. Stubager, R., K. M. Hansen and J. Goul Andersen (eds) *Krisevalg-Økonomien og folketingsvalget 2011*, København: DJØF-Forlag, pp. 115–136.

Harðarson, Ó. T. (1995) *Parties and Voters in Iceland*, Reykjavík: Social Science Research Institute University Press.

— (2002) 'The Icelandic Electoral System 1844–1999' in B. Grofman and A. Lijphart (eds) *The Evolution of Electoral and Party Systems in the Nordic Countries*, New York: Agathon Press, pp. 101–66.

Harðarson, Ó. T. and Kristinsson, G. H. (2008) 'The parliamentary election in Iceland, May 2007', *Electoral Studies*, 27: 373–377.

— (2009) 'Iceland', *European Journal of Political Research*, 48: 980–85.

— (2010a) 'The parliamentary election in Iceland, April 2009', *Electoral Studies* 29: 523–26.

— (2010b) 'Iceland', *European Journal of Political Research* 49: 1009–16.

Harrop, M. and Miller, W. L. (1987) *Elections and Voters*, London: Macmillan.

Heath A., Jowell, R. and Curtice, J. (1985) *How Britain Votes*, London: Pergamon.

Heidar, K. M. and Berntzen, E. (2003) *Vesteuropeisk politikk. Partier, regjeringsmakt, styreform*, 2nd edition, Oslo: Universitetsforlag

Helgason, T. (2006) 'Greining á úthlutun þingsæta eftir alþingiskosningarnar 12. maí 2007. Unnið fyrir landskjörstjórn sumarið 2008. Lítillega endurbætt í apríl 2010'.

Helgason, T. (2008) 'Greining á úthlutun þingsæta eftir alþingiskosningarnar 10. maí 2003. Unnið fyrir landskjörstjórn 2006. Lítillega endurbætt í apríl 2010'.

Hernes, H. (1988) 'Scandinavian citizenship', *Acta Sociologica*, 31(3): 199–215.

Holli, A. M. and Wass, H. (2009) 'Sukupuoli ja äänestäminen', in S. Borg and H. Paloheimo (eds) *Vaalit yleisödemokratiassa. Eduskuntavaalitutkimus 2007*, Tampere: Tampere University Press.

Holmberg, S. (1994) 'Party Identification Compared Across the Atlantic', in K. Jennings and T. E. Mann (eds) *Elections at Home and Abroad: Essays in honor of Warren E. Miller*, Ann Arbor: University of Michigan Press, pp. 93–121.

— (2003) 'Are political parties necessary?' *Electoral Studies*, Elsevier, 22(2): 287–299.

— (2007) 'Partisanship reconsidered' in R. Dalton and H.-D. Klingemann (eds) *The Oxford Handbook of Political Behavior*, Oxford: Oxford University Press.

— (2009) 'Candidate Recognition in Different Electoral Systems', in H.-D. Klingemann (ed.) *The Comparative Study of Electoral Systems*, Oxford: Oxford University Press.

Holmberg, S. and Gilljam, M. (1987) *Väljare och val i Sverige*, Stockholm: Bonniers.

Holmberg, S. and Möller, T. (1999) *Premiär för personal*, Stockholm: Statens offentliga utredningar.

Holmberg, S. and Oscarsson, H. (2004) *Väljare. Svenskt väljarbeteende under 50 år.* [*Voters: Fifty years of voting behaviour in Sweden*], Stockholm: Norstedts.

— (2007) *Swedish Voting Behavior,* Göteborgs universitet: Statsvetenskapliga institutionen.

— (2011) 'Party Leader Effects on the Vote' in K. Aarts, A. Blais and H. Schmitt (eds) *Political Leaders and Democratic Elections*, Oxford: Oxford University Press.

— (2013) *Nya svenska väljare,* Stockholm: Norstedts Juridik.

Idea (2002) *Voter Turnout since 1945: A Global Report,* Stockholm: International IDEA.

Indridason, I. (2005) 'A theory of coalitions and clientelism: coalition politics in Iceland 1945–2000', *European Journal of Political Research* 44(3): 439–64.

Inglehart, R. F. (1990) *Culture Shift in Advanced Industrial Society,* Princeton: Princeton University Press.

Inglehart, R. F. and Welzel, C. (2005) 'Liberalism, postmaterialism and the growth of freedom', *International Review of Sociology* 15(1): 81–108.

Iyengar, S. and Simon, A. (1993) 'News coverage of the Gulf Crisis and public-opinion – a study of agenda-setting, priming, and framing', *Communication Research* 20(3): 365–83.

Jenssen, A. T., Pesonen, P. and Gilljam, M. (eds) (1998) *To Join or Not to Join,* Oslo: Scandinavian University Press.

Johnston, R., Blais, A., Brady, H. E. and Crête, J. (1992) *Letting the People Decide: Dynamics of a Candian election,* Stanford: Stanford University Press.

Kaase, M. and Newton, K. (1995) *Beliefs in Government,* Oxford: Oxford University Press.

Karlsen, R. and Narud, H. M. (2004) 'Organisering av valgkampen – "tradisjonell" eller "moderne"' in B. Aardal, A. Krogstad and H. M. Narud (eds) *I valgkampens hete,* Oslo: Universitetsforlaget,pp. 112–37.

Karvonen, L. (2004) 'Preferential voting: incidence and effects', *International Political Science Review* 25(2): 203–26.

Karvonen, L. (2010) *The Personalization of Politics: A study of parliamentary democracies,* Colchester: ECPR Press.

Karvonen, L. and Söderlund, P. (2008) 'Candidate-Centeredness and Volatility', Paper presented at the XV NOPSA Conference in Tromsø, 2008.

Kautto, M., Heikkilä, M., Hvinden, B., Marklund, S. and Ploug, N. (eds) (1999) *Nordic Social Policy: Changing welfare states,* London: Routledge.

— (eds) (2001) *Nordic Social Policy: Changing welfare states,* London: Routledge.

Key, V. O. J. (1966) *The Responsible Electorate,* New York: Vintage.

King, A. (ed.) (2002) *Leaders' Personalities and the Outcomes of Democratic Elections,* Oxford: Oxford University Press.

Kirchheimer, O. (1966) 'The Transformation of West European Party Systems' in J. La Palombara and M. Weiner (eds) *Political Parties and Political Development*, Princeton: Princeton University Press.

Klingemann, H. -D. (1999) 'Mapping political support in the 1990s: A global analysis' in P. Norris (ed.) *Critical Citizens: Global Support for Democratic Governance*, Oxford: Oxford University Press.

Klingemann, H.-D. and Fuchs, D. (eds) (1995) *Citizens and the State*, Oxford: Oxford University Press.

Knutsen, O. (2001) 'Social class, sector employment, and gender as party cleavages in the Scandinavian countries: a comparative longitudinal study, 1970–95', *Scandinavian Political Studies* 24(4): 311–50.

——— (2006) *Class Voting in Western Europe: A comparative longitudinal study*, Lanham, MD: Lexington Books.

Koch, H. and Ross, A. (eds) (1949) *Nordisk Demokrati*, Oslo: Halvorsen og Larsen Forlag.

Korpi, W. (1981) *Den demokratiska klassekampen. Svensk politik i jämförande perspektiv*, Stockholm: Tiden.

Kosiara-Pedersen, K. (2008) 'The 2007 Danish general election: generating a fragile majority', *West European Politics* 31(5): 1040–48.

Kristinsson, G. H. (2001) 'The Icelandic Progressive Party: Trawling for the Town Vote' in D. Arter (ed.) *From Farm Yard to City Square? The electoral adaption of the Nordic Agrarian parties*, Aldershot: Ashgate: 132–61.

Kumlin, S. (2003) 'Finns det någon ansvarig?' in M. Gilljam and J. Hermansson (eds) *Demokratiens mekanismer*, Malmö: Liber.

Kvist, J. and Greve, B. (2011) 'Has the Nordic welfare model been transformed', *Social Policy and Administration* 45: 146–60.

Laakso, M. and Taagepera, R. (1979) '"Effective" number of parties: a measure with application to west Europe', *Comparative Political Studies* 12(1): 3–27.

Lane, J.-E. (1991) 'The Swedish model', Special issue of *West European Politics* 14(3): 1–7.

Lane, J.-E. and Maeland, R. (2004) 'Towards an analysis of voting power in parliament: an exploration into coalition-making in Nordic parliaments', *Acta Politica* 42(4): 355–79.

Lane, J.-E., Martikainen, T., Svensson, P., Vogt, G. and Valen, H. (1993) 'Scandinavian exceptionalism reconsidered', *Journal of Theoretical Politics* 5(2): 195–230.

Lau, R. R. and Redlawsk, D. P. (2001) 'Advantages and disadvantages of cognitive heuristics in political decision making', *American Journal of Political Science* 45(4): 951–71.

Laver, M. and Shepsle, K. (1990) 'Coalitions and cabinet government', *American Political Science Review* 84: 873–90.

Lazarsfeld, P. F., Berelson, B. R. and Gaudet, H. (1944) *The People's Choice: How the voter makes up his mind in a presidential campaign*, New York: Columbia University Press.

Leroy, P. and Siune, K. (1994) 'The Role of television in European elections: the cases of Belgium and Denmark', *European Journal of Communication* 9(1): 47–69.

Lewin, L. (1991) *Self-Interest and Public Interest in Western Politics,* New York: Oxford University Press.

Lewis-Beck, M. (1986) 'Comparative economic voting: Britain, France, Germany, Italy', *American Journal of Political Science* 30: 315–46.

—   (1988) *Economics and Elections: The major Western democracies,* Ann Arbor: The University of Michigan Press.

—   (1991) 'Introduction' in H. Norpoth, M. Lewis-Beck and J.-D. Lafay (eds) *Economics and Politics: The calculus of support,* Ann Arbor: University of Michigan Press.

Lewis-Beck, M. and Paldam, M. (2000) 'Economic voting: an introduction', *Electoral Studies* 19: 113–21.

Lijphart, A. (1997) 'Unequal participation: democracy's unresolved dilemma'. *American Political Science Review* 91(1): 1–14.

Lindvall, J. and Rothstein, B. (2006) 'The fall of the strong state', *Scandinavian Political Studies* 29(1): 47–63.

Lipset, S. M. and S. Rokkan (1967a). 'Cleavage Structures, Party Systems, and Voter Alignments: An Introduction', in S. M. Lipset and S. Rokkan (eds) *Party Systems and Voter Alignments: Cross-national perspectives,* New York, NY: The Free Press, pp. 1–64.

—   (1967b) *Party systems and voter alignments: Cross-national perspectives,* New York: The Free Press.

Listhaug, O. (1988) *Citizens, Parties and Norwegian Electoral Politics 1957– 1985: An empirical study,* Trondheim: Trondheim University.

—   (1989) *Citizens, Parties and Norwegian Electoral Politics 1957–1985,* Trondheim: Tapir.

—   (2005) 'Retrospective Voting', in J. Thomassen (ed.) *The European Voter: A comparative study of modern democracies,* Oxford: Oxford University Press.

—   (2007) *Oil Wealth Dissatisfaction and Political Trust in Norway: A resource curse?* in Ø. Østerud (ed.) *Norway in Transition,* London: Routledge.

Listhaug, O., Aardal, B. and Opheim Ellis, I. (2009) 'Institutional Variation and Political Support: An Analysis of CSES Data from 29 Countries' in H. -D. Klingemann (ed.) *The Comparative Study of Electoral Systems,* Oxford: Oxford University Press.

Listhaug, O. and Narud, H. M. (2011) 'The Changing Macro Context of Norwegian Voters: From Centre-Periphery Cleavages to Oil Wealth', in M. Rosema, B. Denters and K. Aarts (eds) *How Democracy Works: Political Representation and Policy Congruence in Modern Societies,* Amsterdam: Amsterdam University Press/Pallas Publications.

Listhaug, O. and Wiberg, M. (1995) 'Confidence in Political and Private Institutions', in H.-D. Klingemann and D. Fuchs (eds) *Citizens and the State,* Oxford: Oxford University Press.

Lodge, M., McGraw, K. M. and Stroh, P. (1989) 'An impression-driven model of candidate evaluation', APSA, *American Political Science Review:* 399–419.

Lodge, M., Steenbergen, M. R. and Brau, S. (1995) 'The responsive voter: campaign information and the dynamics of candidate evaluation', *American Political Science Review*, 89(2): 309–26.

Madsen, H. (1980) 'Electoral outcomes and macro-economic policies: the Scandinavian cases' in I. P. Whitely (ed.) *Models of Political Economy*, London: Sage.

Mair, P. (2006) 'Ruling the void: the hollowing of western democracies', *New Left Review* 42: 25–51.

Manin, B. (1997) *The Principles of Representative Government*, Cambridge: Cambridge University Press.

Marklund, S. and Nordlund, A. (1999) 'Economic Problems, Welfare Convergence and Political Instability', in M. Kautto (ed.) *Nordic Social Policy*, London: Routledge.

Martikainen, T. and Wass, H. (2002) *Äänettömät yhtiömiehet. Osallistuminen vuosien 1987 ja 1999 eduskuntavaalieihin Vaalit. 2002: 1*, Helsinki: Tilastokeskus.

Martinsson, J. (2009) *Economic Voting and Issue Ownership: An integrative approach*, Gothenburg: Department of Political Science.

Mattila, M. and Raunio, T. (2002) 'Government formation in the Nordic countries: the electoral connection', *Scandinavian Political Studies* 25(3): 259–80.

Mattila, M. and Sundberg, J. (2012) 'Vaalirahoitus ja vaalirahakohu, in S. Borg (ed.) *Muutosvaalit 2012*, Helsinki: Oikeusministeriö.

McAllister, I. (2002) 'Calculating or Capricious? The new politics of late deciding voters' in R. Schmitt-Beck and D. M. Farell (eds) *Do Political Campaigns Matter?*, London: Routledge, pp. 22–40.

— (2007) 'The Personalization of Politics', in R. Dalton and H. -D. Klingemann (eds) *The Oxford Handbook of Political Behavior*, Oxford: Oxford University Press.

Milbrath, L. W. (1965) *Political Participation*, Chicago: Rand McNally.

Mill, J. S. (1843/2002) *A System of Logic*, Honolulu: University Press of the Pacific.

Miller, W. E. and Shanks, J. M. (1996) *The New American Voter*, Cambridge: Harvard University Press.

Moring, T. (2006) 'Political Advertising on Television in the Nordic and Baltic States' in L. L. Kaid and C. Holtz-Bacha (eds) *The Sage Handbook of Political Advertising*, London: Sage.

Moring, T. and Mykkänen, J. (2007) 'Vaalikampanja' in S. Borg and H. Paloheimo (eds) *Vaalit yleisödemokratiassa*, Tampere: Tampere University Press.

— (2012) 'Vaalikampanjat ja viestinnällistyminen' in S.Borg (ed.) *Muutosvaalit 2012*, Helsinki: Oikeusministeriö.

Mueller, D. C. (2003) *Public Choice III*, Cambridge: Cambridge University Press.

Müller, W. C. and Strøm, K. (eds) (1999) *Policy, Office or Votes?*, Cambridge: Cambridge University Press.

Nannestad, P. and Paldam, M. (1997) 'The grievance asymmetry revisited: a micro study of economic voting in Denmark', *European Journal of Political Economy* 13: 81–99.

Narud, H. M. (1996) 'Electoral competition and coalition bargaining in multi-party systems', *Journal of Theoretical Politics* 8: 499–525.

— (1996) 'Party policies and government accountability: a comparison between the Netherlands and Norway', *Party Politics* 2: 479–507.

— (2003) 'Hvem skal styre landet? Velgernes syn på regjering-salternativene ved valget i 2001' in B. Aardal (ed.) *Velgere i villrede. En studie av stortingsvalget i 2001,* Oslo: NKS-forlaget: pp. 187–208.

— (2011) 'Et regjeringsvalg i skyggen av finanskrisen' in B. Aardal (ed.) *Det politiske landskap. En studie av stortingsvalget i 2009,* Oslo: Cappelen-Damm.

Narud, H. M. and Irwin, G. A. (1994) 'Must the breaker pay? Cabinet crises and electoral trade-offs', *Acta Politica* 29: 265–84.

Narud, H. M., Pedersen, M. and Valen, H. (eds) (2002) *Party Sovereignty and Citizen Control: Selecting candidates for parliamentary elections in Denmark, Finland, Iceland and Norway,* Odense: Odense University Press.

Narud, H. M. and Strøm, K. (2000) 'Norway: A Fragile Coalitional Order' in W. C. Müller and K. Strøm (eds) *Coalition Governments in Western Europe,* Oxford: Oxford University Press.

Narud, H. M. and Valen, H. (1996) 'Decline of electoral turnout: the case of Norway', *European Journal of Political Research* 29: 235–256.

— (2007) *Demokrati og ansvar. Politisk representasjon i et flerpartisystem,* Oslo: Damm and Søn AS.

— (2008) 'Coalition Membership and Electoral Performance in Western Europe' in K. Strøm, W. C. Müller and T. Bergmann (eds) *Cabinets and Coalition Bargaining: The democratic life cycle in Western Europe,* Oxford: Oxford University Press, pp. 369–402.

Nevitte, N., Blais, A., Gidengil, E. and Nadeau, R. (2009) 'Socioeconomic Status and Nonvoting: A Cross-national Comparative Analysis' in H.-D. Klingemann (ed.) *The Comparative Study of Electoral Systems,* Oxford: Oxford University Press.

Niemi, R. G., Craig, S. C. and Mattei, F. (1991) 'Measuring internal political efficacy in the 1988 national election study', *American Political Science Review* 85: 1407–13.

Nieuwbeerta, P. (1995) *The Democratic Class Struggle in Twenty Countries 1945–1990,* Amsterdam: Thesis Publishers.

Norris, P. (ed.) (1999) *Critical Citizens: Global support for democratic government,* Oxford: Oxford University Press.

Norris, P., Curtice, J., Sanders, D., Scammell, M. and Semetko, H. A. (1999) *On Message: Communicating the campaign,* London: SAGE Publications.

NOU (2004) *Penger teller, men stemmer avgjør. Om partifinansiering, åpenhet og partipolitisk fjernsynsreklame,* Oslo: Forvaltningstjeneste Informasjons-forvaltning.

Nousiainen, J. (2000) 'Finland: The Consolidation of Parliamentary Governnance' in W. C. Müller and K. Strøm (eds) *Coalition Governments in Western Europe*, Oxford: Oxford University Press, pp. 264–99.

Nousiainen, J. (2000) 'From Semi-Presidentialism to Parliamentary Government: Political and Constitutional Development in Finland', in L. Karvonen and K. Ståhlberg (eds) *Festschrift for Dag Anckar on his 60th Birthday on February 12, 2000,* Åbo: Åbo Akademi University Press.

Nygård, M. (2006) 'Welfare-ideological change in Scandinavia: a comparative analysis of partisan welfare-policy positions in four Nordic countries 1970–2003', *Scandinavian Political Studies* 29 (4): 356–85.

Offe, C. (1972) *Strukturprobleme des kapitalistischen Staates,* Frankfurt: Suhrkamp.

Onnudóttir, E. H. and Harðarson, O. T. (2011) 'Policy performance and satisfaction with democracy', *www.stjornmalogstjornsysla*, 7(2): 417–35.

Oscarsson, H. (1998) *Den svenska partirymden. Väljarnas uppfattningar av konfliktstrukturen i partisystemet 1956–1996* [*The Swedish Party Space. Voters perceptions of the conflict structure in the party system 1956–1996*] Gothenburg: University of Gothenburg: Department of Political Science.

— (2007) 'A matter of fact? Knowledge effects on the vote in Swedish general elections 1985–2002', *Scandinavian Political Studies* 29(3): 301–22.

— (2008) *Media and Quality of Government: A Research Overview,* Quality of Governance Working Paper Series 12 Gothenburg: University of Gothenburg.

— (2010) 'Valanalys til Nationalencyklopedins årsbok'.

Oscarsson, H. and Holmberg, S. (2008a) *Alliansseger. Redogörelse för 2006 års valundersökning i samarbete mellan Statsvetenskapliga institutionen vid Göteborgs universitet och Statistiska centralbyrån,* Allmänna valen 2006, del 4. University of Gothenburg: The Department of Political Science.

— (2008b) *Regeringsskifte. Väljarna och valet 2006,* Stockholm: Norstedts Juridik.

— (2011) *Swedish Voting Behavior*, Report 2011: 4 of the Swedish National Election Studies Program, Gothenburg: University of Gothenburg: Department of Political Science.

— (2011) *Åttapartivalet 2010. Redogörelse för 2010 års valundersökning i samarbete mellan Statsvetenskapliga institutionen vid Göteborgs univeristet och Statistiska centralbyrån,* Stockholm: SCB.

— (2013) *Nya svenska väljare.* Stockholm: Norstedts Juridik.

Oskarson, M. (1994) *Klassröstning i Sverige – rationalitet, lojalitet eller bara slendrian,* Stockholm: Nerenius and Santérus Förlag.

— (2005) 'Social Structure and Party Choice' in J. Thomassen (ed.) *The European Voter: A comparative study of modern democracies,* Oxford: Oxford University Press.

Pacek, A. and Radcliff, B. (1995) 'Economic voting and the welfare state: a cross-national analysis', *The Journal of Politics*, 57(1): 44–61.

Paldam, M. (1981) 'A preliminary survey of the theories and findings on vote and popularity functions', *European Journal of Political Research*, 9: 181–200.

Palmer, H. D. and Whitten, G. D. (2002) 'Economics, Politics, and the Cost of Ruling in Advanced Industrial Societies: How much does context matter? in H. Dorussen and M. Taylor (eds)*Economic Voting*, London: Routledge.

Paloheimo, H. (2003) 'The rising power of the Prime Minister in Finland', *Scandinavian Political Studies* 26 (3): 219–44.

— (2005) *Vaalit ja demokratia Suomessa*, Helsinki: WSOY.

Paloheimo, H. and Sundberg, J. (2005) 'Puoluevalinnan perusteet' in H. Paloheimo (ed.) *Vaalit ja demokratia Suomessa*, Helsinki: WSOY.

Papageorgiou, A. (2010) 'Simulation analysis of the effect of party identification on Finnish parties optimal positions', *Scandinavian Political Studies* 33(3): 224–47.

Pedersen, M. N. (1979) 'The dynamics of European party systems: changing patterns of electoral volatility', *European Journal of Political Research* 7(1): 1–26.

Persson, M. and Oscarsson, H. (2010) *Unga väljare i Sverige 1956–2006* Fokus 10, En analys av ungas inflytande, Stockholm: Ungdomsstyrelsen.

Pesonen, P., Sänkiaho, R. and Borg, S. (1993) *Vaalikansan äänivalta. Tutkimus eduskuntavaaleista ja valitsijakunnasta Suomen poliittisessa järjestelmässä*, Helsinki: WSOY.

Pesonen, P., Todal Jensen, A., Gilljam, M., Tamnes, R. and Moses, J. (1998) 'The Three Nations of Northern Europe' in A. Todal Jensen, P. Pesonen and M. Gilljam (eds) *To Join or Not to Join: Three Nordic referendums on membership in the European Union*, Oslo: Scandinavian University Press.

Petersson, O. (2005) *Nordisk politik*, Stockholm: Norstedts Juridik.

Petersson, O., Djerf-Pierre, M., Holmberg, S., Strömbäck, J. and Weibull, L. (2006) *Media and Elections in Sweden: Report from the Democratic Audit of Sweden*, Stockholm: SNS Förlag.

Petersson, O. and Valen, H. (1979) 'Political cleavages in Sweden and Norway', *Scandinavian Political Studies* 2(4): 313–31.

Pierre, J. and Peters, G. (2000) *Governance, Politics and the State*, Hong Kong: Macmillan.

Pierson, P. (ed.) (2001) *The New Welfare State*, Oxford: Oxford University Press.

Poguntke, T. and Webb, P. (2005) *The Presidentialization of Politics in Democratic Societies*, Oxford: Oxford University Press.

Popkin, S. L. (1991) *The Reasoning Voter: Communication and persuasion in presidential elections*, Chicago: University of Chicago Press.

Powell, G. B. and Whitten, G. D. (1993) 'A cross national analysis of economic voting: taking account of the political context', *American Journal of Political Science*, 37: 391–414.

Price, V. and Zaller, J. R. (1993) 'Who gets the news? Alternative measures of news reception and their implications for research', *Public Opinion Quarterly*, 57: 133–64.

Putnam, R. (2000) *Bowling alone: The collapse and revival of American community*, New York: Simon and Schuster.

Raunio, T. (2005) 'Finland: One hundred years of quietude', in M. Gallagher and P. Mitchells (eds) *The Politics of Electoral Systems*, Oxford: Oxford University Press, pp. 471–93.

Reunanen, E. and Suhonen, P. (2009) 'Kansanedustajat ideologisella kartalla', in S. Borg and H. Paloheimo (eds) *Vaalit yleisödemokratiassa*, Tampere: Tampere University Press.

Rokkan, S. (1987) *Stat, nasjon, klasse*, Oslo: Universitetsforlaget.

Rose, R. and Mackie, T. (1983) 'Incumbency in Government: Asset or liability', in H. Daalder and P. Mair (eds) *Western European Party Systems: Continuity and Change*, London: Sage.

Rose, R. and McAllister, I. (1986) *Voters begin to choose: From closed class to open elections in Britain*, London: Sage Publications.

Rosema, M., Bas, D. and Kees, A. (2011) *How Democracy Works: Political representation and policy congruence in modern societies*, Amsterdam Amsterdam University Press.

Rosenstone, S. J. and Hansen, J. M. (1993) *Mobilization, Participation, and Democracy in America*, New York: Macmillan.

Rothstein, B. and Stolle, D. (2003) 'Social Capital, Impartiality and the Welfare State: An institutional approach' in M. Hooghe and D. Stolle (eds) *Generating Social Capital: Civil society and institutions in comparative perspective*, New York: Palgrave.

Rustow, D. (1956) 'Scandinavia: Working multiparty systems' in S. Neumann (ed.) *Modern Political Parties*, Chicago: University of Chicago Press.

Saari, D. G. (1990) 'The Borda dictionary', *Social Choice and Welfare* 7: 279–317.

Sainsbury, D. (1987) 'Class voting and left voting in Scandinavia', *European Journal of Political Research* 15: 507–26.

Schattschneider, E. E. (1942) *Party Government*, New York: Farrar and Rinehart.

Schmitt, H. and Holmberg, S. (1995) 'Political Parties in Decline?' in H.-D. Klingeman and D. Fuchs (eds) *Citizens and the State*, Oxford: Oxford University Press, pp. 95–133.

Schmitt-Beck, R. (2007) 'New Modes of Campaigning' in R. J. Dalton and H.-D. Klingemann (eds) *The Oxford Handbook of Political Behavior*, pp. 744–64.

Schneider, F. (1984) 'Public attitudes towards economic conditions and their impact on government behavior', *Political Behavior* 6: 211–27.

Sciarini, P. and Kriesi, H. (2003) 'Opinion stability and change during an electoral campaign: results from the 1999 Swiss Election Panel study', *International Journal of Public Opinion Research* 15(4): 431–53.

Selle, P. and Østerud, Ø. (2006) 'The eroding of representative democracy in Norway', *Journal of European Public Policy* 13: 551–68.

Singer, M. M. (2010) 'Economic Voting and Welfare Programmes: Evidence from the American States', *European Journal of Political Research*, 50: 479–503.

Siune, K. (1987) 'The political role of mass media in Scandinavia', *Legislative Studies Quarterly* 12(3): 395–414.

— (1994) 'Political Advertising in Denmark' in L. L. Kaid and C. Holtz-Bacha (eds) *Political Advertising in Western Democracies: Parties and candidates on Television,* Beverly Hills: Sage.

Sniderman, P. M., Brody, R. A. and Tetlock, P. E. (1991) *Reasoning and Choice: Explorations in political psychology,* Cambridge: Cambridge University Press.

Statistics Denmark (2012) *Folketingsvalget den 15. September 2011 – Danmark, Færøerne, Grønland,* Statistik, D. Copenhagen: Danmarks Statistik.

Stolle, D., Hooghe, M. and Micheletti, M. (2005) 'Politics in the supermarket. political consumerism as a form of political participation', *International Political Science Review* 26: 245–69.

Strandberg, K. (2006) *Parties, Candidates and Citizens On-Line: Studies of politics on the internet,* Åbo: Åbo Akademi University Press.

Strömbäck, J. (2009) 'Selective professionalisation of political campaigning: a test of the party-centred theory of professionalised campaigning in the context of the 2006 Swedish election', *Political Studies* 57(1): 95–116.

Strøm, K. (1990) 'A behavioral theory of competitive political parties', *American Journal of Political Science* 34(2): 565–98.

Strøm, K. and Svåsand, L. (eds) (1997) *Challenges to Political Parties: The case of Norway,* Ann Arbor: The University of Michigan Press.

Stubager, R. (2003) 'Ændrede skillelinjer siden 1960›erne?', *Politica* 35(4): 377–90.

— (2008) 'Education effects on authoritarian-libertarian values: a question of socialization', *British Journal of Sociology* 59(2): 327–50.

— (2010) 'The development of the education cleavage: Denmark as a critical case', *West European Politics* 33(3): 505–33.

Stubager, R., Hansen, K. M. and Goul Andersen, J. (2013) *Krisevalg: Økonomien og Folketingsvalget 2011,* Copenhagen: DJØF-forlag.

Sundberg, J. (1999) 'The enduring Scandinavian party system', *Scandinavian Political Studies* 22(2): 221–41.

Sundberg, J. and Högnabba, S. (1992) 'Finland: The 1991 Campaign' in S. Bowler and D. Farell (eds) *Electoral Strategies and Political Marketing,* London: Macmilan, pp. 82–99.

Särlvik, B. (1970) *Electoral Behavior in the Swedish Multiparty System,* Gothenburg: Göteborgs universitet, Statsvetenskapliga institutionen.

Söderlund, P. (2008) 'Retrospective voting and electoral volatility: A Nordic perspective', *Scandinavian Political Studies,* 31(2): 217–40.

Taylor-Gooby, P. (2004) *New Risks, New Welfare: The transformation of the European welfare state,* Oxford: Oxford University Press.

Teixeria, R. A. (1987) *Why Americans Don't Vote: Turnout decline in the United States 1960–1984,* New York: Greenwood Press.

Teorell, J., Charron, N., Samanni, M., Holmberg, S. and Rothstein, B. (2009) *The Quality of Government Dataset,* 17 June 2009, from http://www.qog.pol.gu.se.

Thomassen, J. (1976) 'Party Identification as a Cross-national Concept: Its Meaning in the Netherlands' in I. Budge, I. Crewe and D. Farlie (eds) *Party Identification and Beyond*, New York: Wiley.

—— (2005) 'Introduction' in J. Thomassen (ed.) *The European Voter: A comparative study of modern democracies*, Oxford: Oxford University Press.

Thomsen, S. R. and Elklit, J. (2007) 'Hvad betyder de personlige stemmer for partiernes tilslutning' in J. Goul Andersen, J. Andersen, O. Borre and K. M. Hansen (eds) *Det nye politiske landskab. Folketingsvalget 2005 i perspektiv*, Århus: Academica.

Tingsten, H. (1966) *Från idéer till idyll: den lyckliga demokratien*, Stockholm: Norstedt.

Togeby, L. (2007) 'The context of priming', *Scandinavian Political Studies* 30(3): 345–76.

Togeby, L., Goul Andersen, J., Christiansen, P. M., Jørgensen, T. B. and Vallgårda, S. (2003) *Magt og demokrati i Danmark. Hovedresultater fra Magtudredningen*, Århus: Aarhus Universitetsforlag.

Valen, H., Aardal, B. and von Otter, C. (1990) *Endring og kontinuitet. Stortingsvalget 1989*, Oslo: Statistisk Sentralbyrå.

Valen, H. and Katz, D. (1964) *Political Parties in Norway*, Oslo: Universitetsforlaget.

Valmyndigheten (5 of October 2010) From www.val.se/val/val2010/slutresultat/R/rike/personroster.html.

Van der Brug, W., van der Eijk, C. and Franklin, M. N. (2007) *The Economy and the Vote: Economic conditions and elections in fifteen countries*, Cambridge: Cambridge University Press.

Van Schuur, H. W. and Post, W. (1990) *MUDFOLD User's Manual: A Program for Multiple Unidimensional Unfolding*, Groningen: ProGamma.

Wass, H. (2007) 'The effects of age, generation and period on turnout in Finland 1975–2003', *Electoral Studies* 26(3): 648–59.

—— (2008) 'Generations and turnout: the generational effect in electoral participation in Finland', *Acta Politica* 35.

Wass, H. and Borg, S. (2012) '*Äänestysaktiivisuus*' in S. Borg (ed.) *Muutosvaalit 2012*, Helsinki: Oiekusministeriö.

Wattenberg, M. P. (2000) 'The Decline of Party Mobilization' in R. J. Dalton, and M. P. Wattenberg (eds) *Parties Without Partisans: Political Change in Advanced Industrial Democracies*, Oxford: Oxford University Press.

Weil, F. D. (1989) 'The sources and structure of legitimation in western democracies: a consolidated model tested with time-series data in six countries since World War II', *American Sociological Review* 54, 5: 682–706.

Wolfinger, R. E. and Rosenstone, S. J. (1980) *Who votes?*, New Haven: Yale University Press.

Zaller, J. R. (1992) *The Nature and Origins of Mass Opinion*, Cambridge: Cambridge University Press.

Zukin, C., Keeter, S., Andolina, M., Jenkins, K. and Delli Carpini, M. X. (2006) *A New Engagement? Political participation, civic life, and the changing American citizen*, Oxford: Oxford University Press.

Østerud, Ø., Engelstad, F. and Selle, P. (2003) *Makten og demokratiet. En sluttbok fra Makt-og demokratiutredningen*, Oslo: Gyldendal Akademiske.

Index

www.ingramcontent.com/pod-product-compliance
Lightning Source LLC
Chambersburg PA
CBHW072100020426
42334CB00017B/1576